Documentation

ALSO BY ROBERT HAUPTMAN

Journal of Information Ethics, editor (1991–present)

Ethics and Librarianship (2002)

EDITED BY RICHARD N. STICHLER
AND ROBERT HAUPTMAN

Ethics, Information and Technology: Readings (1998)

FROM MCFARLAND

DOCUMENTATION

*A History and Critique of Attribution,
Commentary, Glosses, Marginalia, Notes,
Bibliographies, Works-Cited Lists, and
Citation Indexing and Analysis*

ROBERT HAUPTMAN
Foreword by David Henige

McFarland & Company, Inc., Publishers
Jefferson, North Carolina, and London

LIBRARY OF CONGRESS CATALOGUING-IN-PUBLICATION DATA

Hauptman, Robert, 1941–
    Documentation : a history and critique of attribution, commentary, glosses, marginalia, notes, bibliographies, works-cited lists, and citation indexing and analysis / Robert Hauptman ; foreword by David Henige.
    p.   cm.
    Includes bibliographical references and index.

    ISBN 978-0-7864-3333-9
    softcover : 50# alkaline paper

    1. Bibliographical citations — History. 2. Marginalia — History.
3. Bibliography — History. 4. Plagiarism — History. I. Title.
PN171.F56H38   2008
808'.027 — dc22   2008007099

British Library cataloguing data are available

©2008 Robert Hauptman. All rights reserved

No part of this book may be reproduced or transmitted in any form or by any means, electronic or mechanical, including photocopying or recording, or by any information storage and retrieval system, without permission in writing from the publisher.

On the cover: Photographic collage by Trudi Gershenov (with elements of an annotated draft of James Joyce's *Finnegans Wake* and Galileo's drawings entitled "Phases of the Moon")

Manufactured in the United States of America

McFarland & Company, Inc., Publishers
  Box 611, Jefferson, North Carolina 28640
    www.mcfarlandpub.com

To Don Hauptman
with thanks for your ongoing help

Acknowledgments

I would like to thank various reference, special collections, and interlibrary loan librarians at St. Cloud State University, the University of Minnesota, Rutgers, St. Michael's College, the University of Vermont, and the Colchester (VT) Public Library who helped me locate materials; Kerry Magruder of the History of Science Collection at the University of Oklahoma for information and images; Reed Lowrie of the Cabot Science Library at Harvard, Karen A. Bucky of the Clark Art Institute, and Charlotte Tancin and Gavin Bridson of the Hunt Institute for Botanical Documentation at Carnegie Mellon University, who provided some apposite material that I would have missed; Keith Ewing for suggestions; Elizabeth Buchanan for marginalia; Chris Matthew Sciabarra and Michael Bugeja for information; Matthew Edney for a generous comment on maps; and Steve Scully for thoughtful discussions and inspiration. I am also grateful to the representatives of collections who granted permission to reprint illustrations. Thank you!

Contents

Acknowledgments vii
Foreword by David Henige 1
Preface 5

1. Purpose 7
2. Development 14
3. Commentary 35
4. Marginalia 71
5. Footnotes 112
6. Illustration 128
7. The Major Systems 148
8. Errors 168
9. Misconduct 179
10. Citation Indexing and Analysis 189
11. Conclusion 200

Notes 205
Bibliography 209
Index 223

Foreword
by David Henige

A surprisingly large segment of the world of scholarship routinely depends on assertion, sometimes repeated assertion, to form its conclusions. By *assertion* I mean statements that are made without supporting evidence or argument; presumably their authors hope that these assertions will go unchallenged, and much more often than not, they are right in this assumption, which is in a sense a self-fulfilling prophecy. One reason for this is what appears to be a natural inclination to believe rather than doubt. Another, hardly unrelated, is the fact that, as Robert Hauptman points out, few scholars bother to consider explicitly issues of documentation in their own work, appearing to be largely uninterested in ruminating about matters that can only cause trouble.

Hauptman treats *documentation* in its broadest possible connotation, ranging from simple acknowledgments to predecessors through normal generic citing practices attributing ideas to attributions of words — quoting — requiring detailed and accurate citations. Hauptman traces the incidence of citation — or more often non-citation — from ancient Mesopotamia to the present, noting how ancient authors seldom found it necessary to support their works by references to authorities, other than autopsy (eyewitness), and how no one seemed to mind for a long time. This lapse of course makes it easy for skeptics to query almost every statement in these accounts with little fear of refutation, although perhaps with not much better chances of agreement by those who prefer to believe, if only from predisposition.

Like many others, Hauptman laments the triumph of the endnote or no-note over the footnote, and the portmanteau note over the unambiguous one. All these expedients have been initiated by publishers and printers anxious to work on the cheap regardless of the costs to efficient communication. Still, while Hauptman regrets the prevailing paucity of documentation, he also is at pains to notice unfavorably the not uncommon footnote apparatus clearly designed to intimidate readers, although more likely to succeed only in boring them. Here reference and/or commentary outweigh the text proper to the point that readers find themselves at first unable and then unwilling to digest it. While documentation must be present, it is best confined to cases — but all of them — where it is necessary to establish an argument's *bona fides*. While this practice will inevitably vary depending on audience, it can too easily be breached in the observance.

Hauptman is duly attentive to the less obvious forms of documentation such as marginalia, illustrations, even word placement, on the grounds that each of these can contribute to tracking down that most elusive will o' the wisp — authorial meaning. There is a useful and minatory treatment of the vanishing bibliography, sometimes to a Web site, more often to oblivion. Again, this is a publisher's expedient to save money, even if it forces serious readers to dredge through page after page of notes looking for the full citation.

Adventitious and plain obstructive journal abbreviations rightly draw Hauptman's fire. For instance — my example rather than his — would "Arch." stand for Archeology, Archaeology, Archéologie, Archaeological, Archeological, Archives, Archival, Archaeometry, Archeometry, or Archief? Or maybe even something else? No doubt this is an extreme example, but how about "Bibl."? And how many "ands" and "ofs" are lurking unnoticed in such abbreviations, lying in wait to ambush unwary searchers? In all these things — large and small — it is the readers' needs that must be served and not the authors' — and certainly not the publishers'.

In his canvass of the several disciplinary citation styles and practices, Hauptman shows all too clearly, if possibly inadvertently, C. P. Snow's Two Cultures at work. Although there are innumerable citation styles, usually varying little in presentation, one can see an almost palpable effort in the sciences (and an extraordinary one in law) to fashion citations in such ways as to make them very much *entre nous*, disinviting any outsiders from the disciplinary high tables by discouraging, if not actually interdicting, their efforts to track citation spoors to their points of origin. Coincidentally or not, the non-humanities also do a pretty good job of failing to provide page numbers, even for quoted matter.

Hauptman briefly presents a number of cautionary tales of the unpleasant consequences of poor and/or disingenuous documentation practices. He could have increased the examples manyfold. Several tools of the electronic variety make it easier to track plagiarism, to find details lacking in the original citation, to consult full-text PDF versions without leaving one's office chair. But does this matter if today's academy really doesn't care very much whether this occurs—unless forced to by occasional eruptions of bad publicity?

It would be insanely quixotic to expect that a widely consistent, economical, and universal citation system will ever be developed, but perhaps all hope should not be abandoned. Compromises and concessions would be required, of course (is publisher information necessary? how many multiple authors should be cited before "et al." is used?), but if all pertinent—and no impertinent—data appeared in every citation, it might be the case that more efficient investigation would result, and error would not be allowed a stubbornly comfortable incumbency for as long and as often as now seems to be the case.

The need to understand both the history of citational practices and the importance of providing full and accurate citations whenever necessary has never been more important, now that Web sites and other elusive sources have been added to the mix. Since these often alphanumeric addresses have almost no intuitive aspects to them, even a simple and single typographical error can prohibit access permanently.

As Hauptman observes, both initial and ultimate responsibility to "get things right" rest with authors. But authors are sometimes indifferent to this or are simply not aware of the ramifications. Thus publishers and editors and readers have a stake—virtually a moral obligation—to ferret errors out and report them. If the catalog becomes a litany and the litany a threnody, well, that's a shame. But the real shame is that the need to make these points explicitly and at length has become so pressing.

I have to confess to being a bit biased myself in all these matters for the best of reasons. I have spent over thirty years as a journal editor engaging in extensive copy-editing involving, as often as not, questions of proper documentation. That said, I believe that *Documentation* needs to find a home not only in every library, but in the collections of scholars and especially of graduate students in all fields, who desperately need to learn the lessons taught here, but who are likely to find that they are not taught in the typical classroom. Not only will this save editors work but it will enhance the chances of authors' arguments being accepted because they are appropriately and accurately documented. In a world where gatekeeping seems almost a dying principle, nothing less should be tolerated. *Documentation* should serve as a natural point of departure for all those intent on raising the bar of effective colloquy in all disciplines.

David Henige is Bibliographer of African Studies at the University of Wisconsin–Madison

Preface

With some notable exceptions, few scholars have interested themselves in the various forms of documentation that researchers use. A limited number of germane articles have appeared in the literature of different disciplines; these are supplemented by a handful of monographs that deal with specific forms of documentation, the footnote, for example, which Anthony Grafton has dissected so scrupulously, but there is no overview of this important subject, one that offers both an historical perspective as well as critical remarks on the diverse systems used for acknowledgment, attribution, explanation or commentary, and protection against accusations of plagiary. *Documentation* fills this lacuna by bringing together the available literature and the perspectives of an author, editor, and academic who, for almost half a century, has worked in the humanities and the social sciences, and has employed or taught not only the Modern Language Association (MLA) style from its inception to its current avatar and the many recensions of the format preferred by the American Psychological Association (APA), but other eccentric systems as well including Turabian, Manheimer, and perverse and insistent variations that italicize or bold or decapitalize in profuse, illogical confusion.

This is a scholarly study of all forms of documentation used in the Western world — from ancient thinkers and Biblical commentators to the medieval gloss and the current systems utilized today in the humanities and social and hard sciences. The following chapters deal with the historical development; usage; specific problems with Chicago, APA, MLA, and other styles; misuse and abuse; inadvertent error; and purposeful deception.

The works that I have used to exemplify various forms of documentation were chosen based on chronology and pertinency. Tangential considerations including the author's nationality, linguistic and political affiliations, academic discipline, gender, and reputation were not taken into account.

1
Purpose

Oral historians, interpreters, critics, authors, auteurs, and scholars have documented, in the broadest sense of the term, since humans began to refer back to past events, codified ethical or religious doctrine, or promulgated diverse points of view. Documentation, through some form of allusion or citation, serves six sometimes mutually exclusive purposes: acknowledgment, attribution, tracing, validation, protection against accusations of misconduct, and tangential substantive commentary.[1] In many instances, especially in contemporary scholarship and particularly in the hard sciences, a reference is merely a citation to an earlier source or influence. But in the humanities, and especially in the past generally, footnotes additionally tendered corrections, potent narrative confirmation or exegesis of or excursus from the primary text. Anthony Grafton points out that footnotes, especially those produced on the European continent, may carry a secondary or tertiary meaning comprehensible only to those versed in the arcana of the specialized discipline. (Layered footnotes can extend through as many as four levels, i.e., notes to notes to notes to notes, and a number of works consist exclusively of notes without any text) (*Footnote*, passim). Pierre Bayle uses his notes to present anti-religious comments that he feared might harm him if included in the text. Gibbon offers a parallel account in his footnotes. And Linda Greenhouse observes that Supreme Court justices do something similar: They "...revealed their real feelings in the footnotes" (A1). According to Norman Kaplan, for scientists, citing is merely a societal means of protecting the rights of one's intellectual forebears (qtd. in Cronin, *Citation* 9). And Thomas McFarland iconoclastically insists that it is untrue that readers require citations so that they can consult sources and it is equally false that annotation connects a text with its cultural milieu (172, 173).

Acknowledgment

An author, whether reciting or declaiming as scops and griots do, or articulating in written form, often chooses to acknowledge those who have come before: the anonymous or known poet or playwright, previous oral historians, the creator of a hypothesis or theory, a commentator, indeed anyone whose work helped or influenced the person now offering an interpretation, creation, explanation, or formal theory to a new audience. Acknowledgment is often tendered because the person really is grateful and wishes to offer thanks for the idea or stimulus that has helped bring about the new recitation or work. Occasionally, one acknowledges a predecessor in order to indicate the earlier perspective was limited or incorrect; thus the acknowledgment acts as a foil for the new interpretation or point of view. Some of humanity's classic tales or myths, what Jung referred to as archetypes, stories concerning the gods (of ancient Greece) or Coyote, the Native American trickster, have been retold with variations many times by successive generations. Faust appears in Marlowe, then in Goethe, and once again in Thomas Mann's modern version. The Don Juan account turns up in Byron's English poem and Pushkin's Russian work (considered by some to be an analogue to *The Divine Comedy* in Italy or *Hamlet* in England, i.e., the Russian national masterpiece). The Greek Eumenides (the Furies) turn up in a modern T. S. Eliot play. The earlier avatar may be formally acknowledged in a preface, the text, and perhaps in a subsequent bibliographic listing, but in some sophisticated contexts the acknowledgment is implicit, and anyone familiar with the discipline or work will immediately recognize that the new author is signaling assistance from a predecessor. This is especially complex in scholarly endeavors and rather dangerous because one could be accused of plagiary; it is usually, though not always, clearer in literary composition, where themes recur; but it is always blatantly obvious to the knowledgeable in classical music when a composer quotes someone else. When Shostakovich includes more than a mere snippet of *Wellington's Victory* in one of his symphonies, he is not trying to fool anyone. This type of quotation also functions as its own acknowledgment, for by doing this Shostakovich indicates that he is grateful to Beethoven for providing a composition that works well within this new context (and this is the case whether Shostakovich respects this particular work or happens to consider it a tedious warhorse). The same may be said for a particular (and outmoded) style: When Philip Glass offers his audience hours of repetitive fugal variations, which often sound as if Bach could have composed them 300 years ago, Glass is telling us that he likes Bach (and other Baroque composers), that he prefers this style to contemporary possibilities, and that he is grateful to those who have preceded him. All of this is contained in the acknowledgment that is implicit in the style, structure, and substance of his compositions that form the backdrop to Godfrey Reggio's *Qatsi* Trilogy, for example.

Contemporary authors of monographic and periodical studies often acknowledge specific people who or organizations that have helped in some way. These remarks appear in a preface or specialized section in a book, or at the head of an article — sometimes as a unique footnote — as the first endnote, or as a separate brief section at the conclusion of the article. (When papers are presented orally, the speaker may articulate his or her thanks to those who aided in some way.) The most extreme form of acknowledgment is the dedication. Books are frequently dedicated to a mentor, colleague, or loved one, but even articles are occasionally offered in dedication to a respected peer, relative, or friend. These notations take various prepositional forms including *to* or *for* or *because of* or *without whom*. Acknowledgments can be succinct or extremely involved. They can fulfill a mandate from a granting agency or be truly heartfelt and necessary for the author's integrity. Here is a detailed example that concludes a multi-authored article in the journal *Sex Roles*:

> The authors thank the students and staff of the participating schools and Richard Fabes and Stephanie Shepard for their assistance. Funding for this project was provided by a grant from the Office of the Research Council, the American Psychological Association, and the John Templeton Foundation to Gustavo Carlo; grants from the Institute of Ethnic Studies and the Family Research Policy Initiative to Maria de Guzman; a minority fellowship grant from the National Science Foundation to Lenna Ontai, and a Conselho Nacional de Desenvolvimento Cientifico e Tecnologico grant (350383/95-2) to Silvia H. Koller [de Guzman et al. 224].

Occasionally, such sections can go on at great length. The acknowledgments in Jamling Tenzing Norgay's *Touching My Father's Soul* cover three pages, and there are instances in which an author thanks many hundreds of individuals and organizations. Dan Pinck points out that in her biography of Nancy Reagan, Kitty Kelley individually acknowledges the help of 795 people (103); she obviously makes a habit of this because in *The Royals*, she allocates seven of 13 pages of author sources to dense lists of names. (There are also cases in which a scientific work is authored by many hundreds of collaborators, and each of these might have a handful of acknowledgments to tender. If this were allowed, the acknowledgees could run into the thousands and merely naming them would take up more room than the article.)

Attribution

Scholars, inventors, and creators do not work in a vacuum. Even the finest minds, those who have made humankind's greatest discoveries or contributions, are indebted to others. Pythagoras, Euclid, Galileo, Darwin, Edison, Einstein, Watson, Crick, Gibbon, James, Skinner, Dante, Shakespeare, and Joyce all triumphed because of the work of their less original, less perceptive, less imaginative predecessors whose influence helped to shape their discoveries or works. Even for these god-like people some form of attribution may be required. For mere mortals it is the very essence of scholarly and creative endeavor. Attribution in a preface, within the text, or in some form of bibliographic citation indicates to the reader that there is a source for whatever is being articulated at a given point. When a source is not indicated, it is fair to assume that this is fully and completely original work, although two exceptions exist. First, in literary materials, an author may fail to mention an influence, but as the novel or play or poem is read and analyzed, others are struck by similarities and analogues, and discuss these in reviews, critical articles, or monographs. Shakespeare did not scrupulously communicate his readings to his audiences, but we know that he did not create an imaginary history of England in his history plays. He learned about Richard, John, the Henrys, and the War of the Roses by studying earlier accounts including Hollingshead's *Chronicles*. In this context, even a total failure to attribute would not appear to be improper. Shakespeare was not stealing ideas or events; he was using, restructuring, and imagining generally accessible information. And this leads to the second exception: when one rearticulates what is called common knowledge, it is unnecessary to attribute. But this concept is very tricky indeed. What is common knowledge to an adult is arcana to a child; what is obvious to a Daoist is obscure to a Hindu; what is a given for a Samoan is incomprehensible to a Belgian; and what is the very life blood of a scholar who has worked for decades on chemical bonding, mineral exploration, familial dysfunction, or Eudora Welty's fiction is esoteric to everyone else. What this means is that when Edmund Wilson analyzes civil war literature or Erich Auerbach writes about mimetic theory, he does not have to expend a great deal of effort on documenting his sources, because he is the source. But when the inexpert do the same thing, they must indicate their influences. This is a human politeness and scholarly obligation. Attribution protects and legitimates.

Tracing

Acknowledgment may be made anywhere within a work and in any fashion: by thanking anonymously, by naming specific people, or by noting a precise work in passing, but it is merely an informal indication that some help has been rendered; it is a way of offering thanks. Attribution is different: Here, by citing a specific work in a formal fashion, the author is telling readers that he or she is indebted to a predecessor for a precise idea or articulation. It is a scholarly obligation, but even creative authors (poets, novelists, playwrights) are expected to note ideational or inspirational sources. When they fail to do this, they are often accused of plagiary. But attribution requires no defense. It is the physical and ethical foundation upon which virtually all scholarly and many creative works rest. And yet it does serve a secondary and most important purpose. By scrupulously noting the precise source for data, information, ideas, or articulations, an author provides a reader with the means of tracing material back to the original source so that he or she can verify what has been said or follow up on the previous author's sources. This does not merely provide a system of checks and balances — especially since very few readers actually return to the earlier documents, even in legal analyses, where documentation in the form of interminable and lengthy footnotes leading to precedents, analogues, opinions, and other material, is carried to an intolerable, sometimes parodic, extreme. Rather, the possibility of tracing a source via an attribution legitimates the scholarly process while it simultaneously makes it easily possible to verify whatever it is that an author claims based on a predecessor.

Validation

Thinkers and scholars in earlier civilizations (e.g., Greece, Rome, Renaissance Italy) cited predecessors for various reasons, but especially to validate their own work, i.e., to persuade and prove by presenting evidentiary sources. Grafton is more precise: "A hundred years ago, most historians would have made a simple distinction: the text persuades, the notes prove" (15). By indicating that a respected mathematician, astronomer, historian, or philosopher held that such and such was the case, the author had a foundational basis for his or her reconceptualization or new idea, and since it agreed to some extent with the earlier thinker's work, how could a reader fail to give at least partial credence to what was now tendered? Even the most original minds (Descartes, Kant, Einstein, Planck) returned to their forebears for grounding, although sometimes only to reject what was offered. In scientific work this is especially important because it is impossible to repeat every natural observation, every taxonomic analysis, every chemical experiment; one must trust and build upon the past. Thus, Brahe built upon Ptolemy (who had fudged his data), and Kepler used Brahe's observations as a basis for his theoretical conclusions. For contemporary scholars, validation is equally important, but additional demanding necessities often obtrude so that this is but one legitimate reason for scrupulously documenting sources and influences.

Protection

In the past, there were a limited number of philosophers, theologians, scientists, and other thinkers who published the results of their research. Some of these often well-known people may have inadvertently or purposely deceived readers, but misconduct was not a pressing problem. Indeed, most practicing scientists deny that it is a problem today, but they are deceiving themselves. It is certainly true that only a minuscule percentage of scholarly periodicals and monographs contain fraudulent material, but a small percentage of an enormous body of work is nevertheless meaningful, and incorrect data sometimes has extremely detrimental results, as it did in the Breuning case, where medicine was dispensed to disturbed people based on Breuning's ostensible research findings, which turned out to be fabricated. Some people may have been irrevocably harmed. By carefully and accurately documenting all source material in some form (notes and/or a concluding bibliographical listing), contemporary authors protect against accusations of misconduct including fraud, fabrication, data distortion, or plagiarism. One of the most frequently cited defenses in misconduct cases is that the person was working quickly and lost track of what was happening and thus failed to record accurately, misplaced data or citations, believed that he or she had written something because quotation marks were elided, and so on.[2] These all boil down to the same thing: inefficient, disorganized, or careless work habits. Naturally, some perpetrators purposely, distort, manufacture, or steal. In these cases, careful documenting practices are merely a cover for dishonesty,[3] but for everyone else, accurate documentation is the best defense against a disgruntled peer's accusations or suit.

Commentary

Citing precedential authors in order to validate was undoubtedly the first application of documentation, but this was followed closely by the intercalation of commentary. Scholars respond to their own work in progress by offering tangential remarks within the text; separately, somewhere on the text's page including the margin; or in a note located elsewhere in the complete document. Today, such notes are usually placed at the end of a book and less frequently at the conclusion of individual chapters. The precise physical form that these remarks take depends on the chronological period in which the author lived as well as the scholarly conventions operative at the time. When more than one possibility exists, different people choose different methods. Astonishingly, this is true even today, when publishers' financial constraints control layout and disciplinary conventions have become so rigidified that the misuse of a colon or period is considered a breach of scholarly etiquette. Nevertheless, variation is possible. In Ernst Robert Curtius's famous study, *European Literature and the Latin Middle Ages,* the 400 pages of text are followed by almost 200 pages containing 25 separate excursuses. And an author who insistently cares about graphic design or one whose name carries some weight, Jacques Derrida, for example, may demand parallel texts, foot- rather than endnotes, or more extreme solutions (to problems that may only exist in the author's imagination) such as alterations in type size or alternating fonts. In contemporary scholarship, tangentially noted comments are less important in physics, chemistry, or biology than they are in the social sciences; in the humanities, they may be the raison d'être for the work; and in legal scholarship, they sometimes appear to supplant the primary text. Documentation lends itself to commentary.

2
Development

Antiquity

The earliest form of documentation occurred when a person reciting orally or composing in some written form referred back to a predecessor either because he or she wished to acknowledge a debt or, what is more likely, because the person wanted to lend credence to whatever point was being made by citing a historical precedent or source. This would have occurred in religious, secular, literary, or scientific contexts in Sumeria, Babylonia, Egypt, Greece, China, and other early civilizations. Anonymous authors of Egyptian medical papyri or original and renowned thinkers such as Herodotus or Aristotle could enhance the validity of their work by indicating that a previous author or the gods also held that such and such was the case. These comments would have been made directly within the recitation or text rather than in some ancillary or tangential manner such as remarks tendered after the discussion or in marginalia or parallel commentary. As the knowledge base of an individual civilization increased, acknowledgment undoubtedly began to play a bigger role. Many scholars take great pleasure in indicating their sources and thereby thanking those who have come before. Thus, acknowledgment and precedent were the primary stimuli for early documenters.

A second though not entirely parallel track chronologically was the need to comment on religious and philosophical texts. Early versions of such commentary can be found in specific Egyptian, Mesopotamian, and Buddhist traditions. The *Talmud* (500 BC–AD 500) consists of the Mishna (four volumes of rules) clarified by the Gemara (63 volumes of commentary). Rashi (Rabbi Solomon ben Isaac) (1040–1105) wrote what is still considered the most important commentary on the Torah or Pentateuch. Shortly thereafter, Aquinas (1225–1274) oriented his theological writings in terms of Aristotle's philosophical perspective, despite the obvious fact that Aristotle had lived hundreds of years prior to the birth of Christianity. As secular historical, literary, and scientific texts became more sophisticated and wide-ranging, a need for commentary developed here as well. These comments might be brief (the type of succinct clarifying remark one now finds in an endnote in any scholarly discipline's papers) or extremely comprehensive so that someone might write an entire monograph to comment on or vociferously rebut an original thinker's controversial work, Stanley Milgram's *Obedience to Authority* or Edward O. Wilson's *Sociobiology*, for example. Both secular and religious thinkers in the distant past were just as opinionated, just as stubborn, and just as defensive as their contemporary analogues are. Indeed, though contemporary academic commentary and rebuttal is of extreme importance both to the career of the scholar and to those who may benefit, for example, from valid genetic or pharmaceutical discoveries, the very lives of those writing in ancient Egypt or China may have been in peril, depending on their point of view. As a form of documentation, commentary is as important as acknowledgment and precedent.

Scholarship followed diverse paths in different societies, and the emphasis placed upon documentation differed depending on whether the society valued originality or repetition, whether the thinkers of the past were merely respected or were apotheosized, and whether religious dogma, tracts, and commentary were esteemed exclusively or, in more limited cases, literary creations or scientific hypothesizing were promulgated. Additionally, it is easy to forget that many parallel scholarly traditions coexisted and sometimes for many hundreds of years. But the ancient Egyptians, Chinese, Greeks, Persians, Romans, Arabs, Byzantines, Ottomans, early and medieval Christians, and Renaissance and Enlightenment Europeans all had diverse and often controlling agendas. It is difficult to disagree with one's peers, and so it sometimes took hundreds of years to progress beyond an accepted and theistically defended belief, terracentrism, for example. Giving credit here to Ptolemy was probably superfluous. Everyone knew that he was responsible for the articulation of what is obvious to a five year old. Only when a new idea came along was it necessary to credit the thinker, and so Copernicus was mentioned when one discussed the new heliocentric theory (in the West; it seems natural that ancient Africans or Inuits also thought that the sun revolved around the earth).

Even more important is the general certainty that different thinkers are diversely motivated. Some wish to thank or validate, but some may prefer to imply that they stand alone. Unless they are truly stealing an idea (plagiarizing), failing to acknowledge, thank, or attribute has never been a scholarly crime. On the other hand, citing a predecessor has always helped to validate historical fact as well as new and original speculation. Even the greatest of thinkers acknowledge those who have come before. (Newton insisted that he succeeded because he stood on the shoulders of giants.) It is very unusual to find attributions in the earliest extant documents; this is especially so because of the nature of these texts: prayers, religious tracts, myths, poems, rules, laws, accounts, judicial hearings, and letters do not necessitate reference to past events or influences. But historical accounts do, and one may very infrequently stumble upon a reference even in Sumerian texts, the earliest of which go back to 2400 BC: "...the *ishakku* of Umma, the plunderer of fields and farms ... said: 'The boundary ditch of Ningirsu, (and) the boundary ditch of Nansha are mine...'" (Kramer 39). This is very different than the typical literary or religious reference in which the author indicates that some mythical or imagined entity may have said something. Here the *ishakku* presumably did say this in order to claim the land, and he is given credit for his precise articulation. Although the Bible is replete with ahistorical attributions—"...and god said to Joshua the son of Nun, Moses' minister, thus: '...now arise...'" (my translation)—one searches in vain for attributions in coeval documents. For example, there are none in *Le Papyrus Médical Chester Beatty* (Jonckheere). This, however, is to be expected, because *Chester Beatty* consists exclusively of pharmaceutical formulas. But neither *The Papyrus Ebers* (1553–1550 BC) (Ebbell) nor *A Medical Book from Crocodilopolis* (Reymond) contain any attributions, despite the narrative nature of these important early medical texts. The anonymous authors simply assimilated their predecessors' contributions, and in a sense, claimed these works as their own. To mitigate what appears to be a harsh assessment, I would also note that those few literate people who could read these documents may have had a different understanding of attribution; it is not improbable that they were already familiar with a corpus of medical material and made the attributions mentally. What is much more startling is that some modern scholars purposely (and at times with good reason) eliminate attributions. In a review of James Risen's *State of War*, James Bamford observes that it "...has interesting and important new details, [but] it also has almost no named sources..." (B6).

When very early references are contrasted with Xenophon's (434?–355 BC) method some 2000 years later, one stands in awe, for example, of the Sumerian recorder. In the *Anabasis,* Xenophon cites no one, although he refers frequently to Xenophon! Even Herodotus (484?–425 BC), in book I, where he recounts the life and exploits of Cyrus and his peers, *inter alios,* is deficient; it is as if the father of history created much of this *ab ovo* because attributions occur infrequently. In book II, he offers an overview of Egypt, and here he is more generous with sources, basing his often inaccurate account on personal experience and discussions with informants. Sometimes, even in book I, he resorts to the general attribution so popular with early recorders: "Some say," "they say," "so the story runs," (5) "say the Persians" (5). But he can also be quite precise: "He is mentioned in the iambic verses of Archilochus of Parus..." (17) or "Thus far I know the truth, for the Delphians told me" (23). At times, he insists that he simply knows: "So much I can say of them of my own certain knowledge" (179). At others, he indicates that he does not: "I myself have not seen it, but I tell what is told by the Chaldeans" (229). In book II, Herodotus travels to discover and confirm: "...I heard also other things at Memphis ... and I visited Thebes too and Heliopolis for this very purpose, because I desired to know if the people of those places would tell me the same tale..."(277). And very precisely, "He [a recorder in Sais], I thought, jested with me when he said that he had exact knowledge; but this was his story..." (305). And here is a multi-layered attribution: "This is enough to say concerning the story told by Etearchus the Ammonian; except that he said that the Nasamonians returned — as the men of Cyrene told me..." (313). When Herodotus shifts to royal lineages, he offers this general comment: "Thus far all I have said is the outcome of my own sight and judgment and inquiry. Henceforth I will record Egyptian chronicles, according to that which I have heard..." (385). There are many other instances of attribution in book II. Rosalind Thomas points out that "Thucydides [ca. 460–ca. 400] cited contemporary documents only in Book V..." and made minimal use of inscriptions elsewhere (90). And she notes that "[h]istorical decrees were often cited in the fourth-century [Athenian] assembly to provide examples from the past..." (84).

History, even in earliest antiquity, would seem to demand verifying attributions, but other disciplines may not. Hippocrates (ca. 460–360 BC) produced a large body of medical material, and in at least some of these tomes, e.g., *Epidemics,* books 2 and 4–7, he offers cases including the names of the patients, observations, cures, and ideas, but no sources. (For Galen, who is quite different, see below.) Aristotle (384–322 BC), on the other hand, working in diverse areas, cites predecessors in order to either counter or strengthen an argument. In his *Historia Animalium,* he only infrequently cites others. For example, he observes that snakes "are so described by the Egyptians" (91) or "Herodotus is mistaken when he writes that the Ethiopians emit black semen" (235), but more precisely, "Such are the accounts given by Syennesis and Diogenes. Here is Polybus's account: 'There are four pairs of blood vessels'" (169). He continues to quote in this manner for a long paragraph, and then concludes, "These passages give a pretty fair idea of what other writers have said" (173). In the *Meteorologica,* Aristotle is much more generous with his referrals, and this is extremely ironic because H. D. P. Lee, the translator, claims that his conclusions are generally incorrect; perhaps that is why he felt it necessary to cite others so often. He does offer general attributions (the

Egyptians, ancient meteorologists), but in this work he names many specific Greek thinkers including Homer, Aesop, Anaximenes, Empedocles, Hippocrates, and Plato. Sometimes he appears to be doing a literature review: "First let us examine the views of others on these subjects. 1. Anaxagoras and Democritus say that comets are a conjunction of planets..." (39).

Almost 500 years later, Plutarch (ca. 46–ca. 120), in "Pericles," employs a similar hierarchy of validations depending both on what information is accessible to him and exactly what he is emphasizing. It is very important to keep in mind that first, Aristotle bases a great deal of what he writes on observation, whereas Plutarch is recounting historical fact, and second, despite this, much of what Plutarch says is completely unattributed, but when he wishes to call upon past authority, in the most general terms, he will merely mention an anonymous source: "Caesar asked, we are told" (3) or "a story is told that once on a time" (15) or again "One of these, as they say" (21). Here, there is no real source, just something someone may have heard or read or said. More precisely, he can also cite specific authors: "The poet Ion, however, says that Pericles..." (13). This is especially useful because Ion disagrees with the general point of view previously noted. And when truly interested in confirming a point, Plutarch not only cites a major authority, he quotes him directly: "Thucydides describes the administration of Pericles as rather aristocratic,—'in name a democracy...'" (25). It is extremely improbable that Plutarch cited the exact source for this in his original composition, but it is impossible to know with certitude, because the original scrolls are no longer extant. (Even the scrolls discovered at Pompeii, had they included Plutarch—which they could not because he wrote the *Lives* shortly after the eruption that preserved this material — would not have solved this problem, since there is no way to know whether a specific (copied) artifact represents exactly what the author originally wrote, and a citation might very well have been elided by a later scribe or copyist.) What we do know is that the carefully edited Greek text included in the Loeb Classical Library (the edition I consulted) does not contain an exact source, but Bernadotte Perrin, the translator for its interlinear English version, provides just what one might expect in a scholarly edition: a footnote that reads, "In the encomium on Pericles, ii, 65, 9" (25). Another example occurs further on when Plutarch observes that "the art of speaking, is, to use Plato's words, 'an enchantment of the soul'" (49, 51). And these two sources illustrate an extremely useful anomaly, one that helps to confirm that authors are unreliable and that scribes and copyists alter or emend: In the Loeb Library Greek text, Thucydides's words are placed within quotation marks, but Plato's are not. In the English version, both quotations are set off by appropriate diacritical marks. Finally, Plutarch includes a limited number of examples of quite precise citation: "Cratinus, in his 'Cheirons,' says: 'Faction and Saturn...'" (9). But this occurs most infrequently. Citation, in its many forms, helps to validate an author's contentions.

In *The Jewish War,* Josephus (?30–100) draws upon his participation in the conflict as a soldier and observer, but it is impossible for him to have known all that he puts into the seven books that comprise this epic work. He begins by noting that other historians have written what for him are unacceptable, distorted accounts (3), so he was unequivocally aware of other source material. Additionally, external evidence seems to indicate that he used the *Commentaries* of both Vespasian and Titus for pertinent data and information (xxi). Nevertheless, Josephus does not further acknowledge nor attribute though these many hundreds of pages are replete with explicit details. The translator, H. St. J. Thackeray, notes that "[t]he *War* contains no allusions to authorities such as are interspersed throughout [Josephus's] ... *Antiquities.* The historian in this earlier work is silent as to his sources..." (xix). This is an astonishing development given the long history and tradition of acknowledgment and attribution that precedes *The Jewish War.* Josephus's well-respected predecessors (Herodotus or Aristotle, for example) offer a paradigm that one would have thought he would choose to emulate especially in order to validate at least some of his remarks. Apparently, he preferred standing alone, implying that for this work he was the all-knowing and judicious recorder of what occurred, since his peers were mere apologists in their accounts, presented in order to laud the conquering Romans (3).

Josephus admittedly is an extreme case, but it appears that Roman authors generally are loathe to indicate their sources. Lucretius, a philosopher, Pliny, a naturalist, and Tacitus, a historian, often abjure attribution. In *On the Nature of the Universe,* Lucretius (97?–54 BC) draws upon earlier scholars' work in his discussions of physics, biology, meteorology, and other subjects, but recognizes them in less than a dozen instances, at times disparagingly: "To say, as Heraclitus does, that everything is fire ... seems utterly crazy" (47). He also mentions Homer, Anaxagoras, and Democritus. In books 20–23 of his enormous *Natural History* (collected in ten interlinear volumes), Pliny (23–79) discusses botanical applications, especially in medicine. The plants are so numerous and the detail so precise that it is obvious that he derived much of this from other sources; botanical pharmacology is not something one studies from scratch. W. H. S. Jones, the translator, observes that Pliny listened to texts read out loud and transcribed the information (xviii). And yet, one scours these pages for attributions with infrequent success. Now and again, someone such as Cato is cited, but this occurs infrequently; indeed, Pliny does not even mention Dioscorides's influential *Materia Medica* at all (xix). The index to this volume of Pliny's work contains an assortment of names, but for a 500 page tome, it is unusually abbreviated. It is therefore truly astonishing that Jones alludes to "Pliny's pride in acknowledging the sources from which he derived his information..." (xix). Tacitus (ca. 55–ca. 120) recites history, and here sources are particularly meaningful. Nevertheless, he fails to credit his predecessors or coevals: In the first three books of *The Histories*, with the exception of a handful of generalities, e.g., "according to report" (27) or "according to ancient tradition" (163), I find no cited sources at all. Galen (ca. 130–ca. 200) is different, but he also happens to be Greek. Some 500 years after Hippocrates, this extraordinary scholar codified medical knowledge in a diverse array of publications. In *On the Usefulness of the Parts of the Body*, he is extremely generous in his attributions. He mentions, questions, quotes, and gives credit to Homer, Plato, Aristotle, Hippocrates, Anaxagoras, Herophilus of Chalcedon, Epicurus, Asclepiades, Aesculapius, Erasistratus, Praxagoras, and Philotimus. He directly quotes various authors, at times at some length. He says that Hippocrates observes, "The nails neither to project beyond, nor to fall short of, the finger tips" (74). And here is Plato, for whom the precise source is cited within the text: "...I shall give in the very words of the author who has best described them: Plato says in *Timaeus*: 'Flesh is a protection from the burning heat of the sun...'" (85). This continues for many more lines. A final example indicates Galen's most unusual attitude toward his predecessors: "'But,' says he, 'Not all the instruments of the senses extend to the encephalon.' Aristotle! What a thing for you to say!" (391). On the other hand, Grafton insists that Roman legal scholars were punctilious in their attributions (*Footnote* 29–30).

The Middle Ages

For centuries, historians and critics have insisted that the demise of the Roman empire and its extraordinary array of great scholars (Cato, Cicero, Caesar, Livy, Seneca, Vitruvius, ad infinitum) led to a barren period devoid of creativity and scholarship, a loss of contact with the knowledge of the past, and a descent into barbarism. There is some truth to this, especially when a contrast is drawn between classical antiquity or the Renaissance and this period. But I have always claimed that the dark ages were much brighter than they superficially appear. Apparently, some historians are beginning to agree. It was, after all, during these years that the *Hildebrandslied* and *Beowulf* were composed and later recorded and monastic scribes created treasures such as *The Book of Durrow, The Lindisfarne Gospels,* and *The Book of Kells*. Many learned men continued to ply their craft despite the general descent into illiterate, superstitious confusion. Scholars documented, though not very generously. Most of these often prolific authors were clergymen, and their works deal with theology. Augustine (354–430), Boethius (475?–525?), Gregory the Great (540–604), the Venerable Bede (673–735), and Anselm of Canterbury (1033–1109), in at least some of their works, do not cite nor mention sources; even scripture is sometimes unattributed. When they infrequently do mention predecessors, the attributions are succinct.

From the earliest instances of acknowledgment, attribution, and commentary in Sumer, and Egypt until the 13th century, the means, style, and extent of assigning credit remained fairly consistent. When general learning began to revive in the early middle ages, it often remained theological in nature. Aquinas (1225?–1274), returns to classical sources, especially Aristotle, whom he venerated, and scrupulously apportions credit. His *Summa Theologiae* (60 volumes in the Blackfriars interlinear edition) is one of the great works of medieval scholarship. Aquinas discusses in some detail innumerable concepts ranging from angels and pleasure to justice and the Resurrection. He continually refers to predecessors and their specific works within his text. Aquinas draws upon a diversity of sources including Aristotle, Cicero, Ambrose, Augustine, Jerome, Gregory, and scripture, and cites them in various ways. For example, "Quia secundum Philosophum in I *Post. Una scientia est quae est unius generis subjecti*[2]" (I, 12). Thomas Gilby translates this, "...according to Aristotle, *a science has unity by treating of one class of subject-matter*[2]" (I, 13). The superscript numeral following both texts leads to the editorial note: "[2]*Posterior Analytics* I, 28. 87a38" (I, 12). It is crucial to observe that the title of Aristotle's work is an integral part of the original Latin text, whereas it is elided in the translation. At times, Aquinas does not indicate the source within the Latin text, but when he does the translator often expunges it. Herewith follows a single sentence that exemplifies Aquinas's bifurcate method: "Sicut enim dicit Apostolus *ad Hebr. Lex vetus figura est novae legis,*[4] et ipsa nova lex, ut Dionysius dicit, est *figura futurae gloriae*[5]" (I, 38). ("For, as St Paul says, *The Old Law is the figure of the New,*[4] and the New Law itself, as Dionysius says, is the figure of the glory to come[5]" (I, 39). The superscript four leads to the editorial note "[4]*Hebrews*, 7, 19" and the five to "[5]*De Ecclesiastica Hierarchia* v, 2. PG 3 501." Within the text, Aquinas cites a work in only one of the two cases; Gilby expunges the source in his translation.

The Renaissance

In *On the Revolutions of the Heavenly Spheres* (*On the Revolutions*), Copernicus (1473–1543) offers his radical heliocentric theory to a world just emerging from the middle ages. That these were regressive times is clearly shown by the fact that Galileo (1564–1642), who was forced to recant his belief that the earth moved, was born 21 years after Copernicus died. Amazingly, Copernicus had less trouble, perhaps because he liberally and generously cites his predecessors including Homer, Hesiod, Aristotle, Plato, Euclid, Plutarch, Cicero, Ptolemy, Virgil, Callippus, Ibn Rushd, Regiomontanus, and Ptolemy, whose terracentric theory was accepted for more than a millennium. He adduces sources with great frequency: "And in fact first I found in Cicero that Hicetus supposed the earth to move. Later I also discovered in Plutarch that certain others were of this opinion. I have decided to set his words down here, so that they may be available to everybody: 'Some think that the earth remains at rest. But Philolaus the Pythagorean believes that, like the sun and moon, it revolves around the fire in an oblique circle. Heraclides of Pontus and Ecphantus the Pythagorean make the earth move...'" (4–5). Copernicus simultaneously adduces classical predecessors to affirm (document) his case, and undercuts the originality of his own contribution. Apparently his strategy worked: He is given credit for changing the way humans view the universe. His citations can be as precise as those of a contemporary scholar: "In the *Laws*, Book VII, he [Plato] thinks that it should be cultivated..." (7) and in the *Elements* "in accordance with Euclid, Book II, Problem 1..." (27).

Chuck Zerby, in *The Devil's Details,* an eccentric history of footnotes, declares that the first footnote is (f), the sixth note in a lettered sequence that begins in the margin and then continues at the bottom of the first page of "Job" in The Holie Bible (The Bishops' Bible), published in 1568; (f) is followed by (g), the second footnote, one presumes. Zerby goes on at great imaginary length concerning the print shop and the process that resulted in what for him is an earth-shattering event (34 and passim).

Boethius (475?–525?) was a Roman Christian whose *Consolation of Philosophy* has consoled and influenced readers for 1500 years. He occasionally mentions other authors, either directly or obliquely, but what is important in this context is I. T.'s 1609 English translation. This is an early example of a printed book that includes "...Marginall Notes, explaining the obscurest places" (17). The modern edited version that appeared in 1963 shifts the marginal remarks to the bottom of the page and numbers them, but retains their Renaissance orthography. Of course, these were not originally footnotes, but they were qualitatively different than the remarks found in the margins of manuscripts, some of which were afterthoughts. Here the more precise attributions, explanations, and comments appended to Boethius's text by I. T. are an integral part of the 1609 publication. Many pages are devoid of footnotes, but others are replete with a plethora of I. T.'s helpful and always succinct remarks; e.g., the second page is adorned with 20 notes. Boethius provides a cryptic reference: "Thou has heard in the Poet's Fables how the Gyants..." (81), and I. T. expands the attribution: "Ovid. lib 2. Metamor. E. Macrobius. Lib 1. Sat-

2. Development

The first footnote (*The Bishops' Bible*, 1568). School of Theology Library, Boston University.

urna 1" (81). This, naturally, does not conform with contemporary conventions, the punctuation is inconsistent, and one must know something about classical literature to understand exactly what is being conveyed, but the data to trace the reference back to two sources are exact and complete. Indeed, even current Modern Language Association style allows citation to acts and scenes or chapter and verse either in addition to or rather than a page number for certain genres and texts. "Peripateticall" in Boethius leads to the noted explanation: "Eleaticis of Elea, the City where Aristotle studied" (29). And when Boethius complains, "...for these be they, with the fruitless thornes of affections[20] doe kill the fruitful crop of reason..." (28), I. T. editorializes: "[20]This is the common fault of Poets, to feede and nourish passion against reason" (28).

In *The Prince,* Machiavelli (1469–1527) rolls through history but does not offer any attributions except in the occasional case of a literary quotation from Virgil or Petrarch. In the 1640 English translation, published in a 1905 recension, five of *The Prince*'s 26 chapters conclude with short indented paragraphs set in smaller type. These are editorial comments (animadversions) provided by the translator, Edward Dacres. He apportions credit in two ways: Either he indicates a source within the text: "'...and setteth up over it the basest of men.' Daniel. 4. 17" (289). Or he attributes marginally. The text reads: "...the answer of Charles the fifth ... *Fides rerum promissarum...*" (324); the source is printed in the margin thus:

> *Gulielmus*
> *Xenocarus* in
> vit. Car.
> Quinti [324].

This is a clear and fairly complete citation, lacking only a precise page number. The 1640 translation contains innumerable marginal descriptors (similar to running heads) which merely summarize the page's content; they are fairly typical in books of the period, and are of very little significance in the history of documentation.

The Enlightenment to the Present

In 1665, the first issue of what is often considered the first scholarly journal appeared. The *Philosophical Transactions* of the Royal Society of London presented new scientific discoveries in an amazingly modern way. Even in this earliest number, Walter Pope, the author of an extract of a letter, cites Achatio Kappenjagger, within the test, as the precise source for the data on mercury production that he presents (25). Just three years later, in the 33rd number, the anonymous author of "An Account of the Invention of Grinding Optick" leads the reader from the text to an indented note in a smaller typeface via an asterisk (632). This is very close to the beginnings of footnoting. (This article also includes a tipped-in illustration.) Coincidentally, it was also in 1665 that *Le Journal des Scavans* commenced publication. In the first number, one finds a brief critique of *Dissertatio de Praecedentia Regum Galliae* ... in which the anonymous reviewer also uses an asterisk, which precedes the notated textual sentence,

(25)

Thofe Mine coft the *Emperour* heretofore 70000. or 80000. *Florens* yearly, and yielded lefs *Mercury* than at prefent, al hough it cofts him but 28000. *Florens* now. You may fee what his Imperial Majefty gets by t 1e following account, of what *Mercury* the Mines of *Idria* have prcduced thefe laft three years.

1661. *l.*	1662. *l.*
Ordinary *Mercury* 198481	Ordinary *Mercury* 225066
Virgin *Mercury* 6194	Virgin *Mercury* 9612
204675	

  1663.   *l.*
Ordinary *Mercury* 244119
Virgin *Mercury*   11862
              255981

There are alwaies at work 280 perfons, according to the relation I received from a very civil perfon, who informed me alfo of all the other particulars above mentio 1ed, whofe name is *Achatio Kappenjagger;* his Office, *Contra-forivano per fua Maeftà Cefarea in Idria del Mercurio*.

To give fome ligl t to this Narrative, take this Diagramme: *F.* is the water, *C. B.* a veffel, into which it runs. *DG. EH. FI.* are ftreams perpetually iffuing from that veffel; *D. E. F.* three fives, the diftance of whofe wires at bottom leffen proportionably. *G.* the place, wherein the Earth, that pafs'd through the five *D.* is retained; from whence 'tis taken by the fecond man; and what paffes through the five *E.* is retained in *H.* and fo of the reft. *K. L. M.* waft water, which is fo much impregnated with *Mercury*, that it cureth Itches and fordid Ulcers. See Fig. 1.

I will trefpafs a little more upon you, in defcribing the contrivance of blowing the Fire in the *Brafsworks* of *Tivoli* neer *Rome* (it being new to me) where the Water blows the Fire, not by moving the Bellows, (which is common) but by affording the Wind. See Fig. II. Where *A.* is the
          D   River

Early in-text source (*Philosophical Transactions*, 1665). University of Minnesota

*Mais pour ne pas exceder les bornes qu'ons'est prescriptes dans ce Journal, on se contentera de remarquer que Mathaeus Paris ... [6]

to lead the reader to an italicized footnote:

*Math. Paris edit. Lond. p.430. Regnum Regnorum, Sciliccet Gallia. Obiit Dominarom saecularium Domina Blanchia Francorum Regis Mater. Ib. p.859. Dominus Rex Francorum, qui terrestrium, Rex Regum est. Ib. p. 900 [6].

(632)

held to the fire, burned Gloves and Garments at the diſtance of about hree foot from the Fire.

Which were the particulars, the *R. Society* obſerved in theſe Glaſſes, and gave order to be Regiſtred in their Books; encouraging the *Inventor* to proceed in this Work with all poſſible care and diligence, for enabling himſelf to inſtruct others in the way of Grinding theſe *Glaſſes* with facility.

The *Inventor* having declared his reſolution to do ſo, added theſe Particulers. *Firſt*, That the Lord Biſhop of *Salisbury*, *Seth Ward* (who was then abſent from the Meeting of the *Society*) had been by, when the *deeper* of his two Concaves turned a piece of Wood into flame in the ſpace of *ten* ſeconds of time; and the *ſhallower*, in *five* ſeconds at moſt, in the ſeaſon of *Autumn*, about 9 of the Clock in the Morning, the Weather gloomy*. *Secondly*, That the deeper Concave, when held to a lucid Body, would caſt a Light ſtrong enougl to read by at a conſiderable diſtance. *Thirdly*, That expoſing the ſame to a Northern Window, on wiich the Sun ſhined not at all, or very little, he had perceived, that it would warm ones hand ſenſibly, b collecting the warm'd Air in th᾿ day-tim , which t would not do after Sun-ſet.

*Thu the ſaid judicio Prelate at another Meeting of the Royal Society, atteſted to be true.

Asterisk leads to indented note (*Philosophical Transactions*, 1668). University of Minnesota.

This is not only an early instance of a true footnote, but the author additionally uses *Ib.* (for the more recently applied ibid., an abbreviation for *ibidem*, meaning "in the same location") to indicate the previously cited source.

In the first issue of the *Giornale de Letterati d'Italia,* which appeared in 1710, the editor offers a long introduction ("Introduzione") in which he uses lettered footnotes to comment or cite: "...che copió (*a*)" (42) leads to its appropriate note: "(a)*Come le 83. 84. 85. dell'anno 1669*" (42). And "...con grandissima lode il *Giornal del Palazzo* (*b*)" does the same: "(b)*Juncher. p.* 12" (42). Other articles in this first number offer fuller lettered citations that include abbreviated author and title as well as page number. So, on the cusp of the eighteenth century, real footnotes, with their modern usages, begin to adorn scholarly publications in England, the Netherlands, and Italy.

Leopold von Ranke (1795–1886), the scholar whom Grafton honors as the first scientific historian (34) and to whom Zerby ascribes the decline of the footnote (90ff), was a prolific author whose *History of England Principally in the Seventeenth Century* rolls along for six interminably lengthy volumes.

6 LE JOURNAL

titre de cette dissertation suffit pour en faire connoistre le dessein. Il faut seulement observer, que M. Howel declare d'abord, que son dessein n'est que de rapporter ce que les Historiens, & les autres Auteurs de chaque nation ont dit sur ce sujet, sans pretendre rien decider de ces differends. Mais il y a plus d'addresse dans ce dessein qu'il ne semble. Car supposant que les Historiens de chaque nation ont donné l'avantage à leur Prince, il voudroit inferer de là, que les uns n'ont pas plus de droit que les autres à pretendre la presseance : & qu'ainsi estant reduits au droit commun, ils sont égaux entre eux.

 Toutesfois pour peu que l'auteur de ce livre se fust donné la peine de lire les histoires de sa nation, il eût reconnu que les Historiens mesme Anglois ont donné la presseance aux Rois de France sur ceux d'Angleterre. S'il estoit necessaire, on prouveroit cette verité par cent autoritez irreprochables. ★ Mais pour ne pas exceder les bornes qu'on s'est prescriptes dans ce Journal, on se contentera de remarquer que Mathæus Paris, un des plus celebres Historiens d'Angleterre, prefere le Royaume de France à tous les autres, & l'appelle le Royaume des Royaumes. Qu'il appelle aussi les Reines de
Fran-

---

* Math. Paris edit. Lond. p. 430. Regnum Regnorum, scilicet Gallia. Obiit Dominarum secularium Domina Blanchia Francorum Regis Mater. Ib. p. 859. Dominus Rex Francorum, qui terrestrium, Rex Regum est. Ib. p. 900.

Asterisk leads to footnote (*Le Journal des Sçavans*, 1665). University of Minnesota.

Forlì: divideasi in compilazioni, e non potea dirsi affatto inutile ne disprezzabile. Ma ritornò nel 1706. l'Autore del Gran Giornale, e prese a divulgare in Parma, benchè sol per 6. mesi, gli strepitosi suoi *Fasti*, lodandosi, stralodandosi, ma in effetto nulla riuscendo, se non in quelle pagine, che copiò (a) talvolta da' vecchj Giornali di Roma, fingendo altri nomi.

Ora ritornando a quell' Opere, di cui l'Italia si vanta; poichè nel Catalogo dell' Efemeridi letterarie vien riposto con grandissima lode il *Giornal del Palazzo* (b), ch'è una Raccolta delle de-

(a) *Come le* 83. 84. 85. *dell'anno* 1669.
(b) *Juncher. p.* 12.

decisioni de' primarj Tribunali di Francia, e' si converrà tanto più riporvi la serie delle *Decisioni della Rota Romana*, che si pubblicano insieme con le ragioni; e tanto più questa, quanto che ella fu l'esemplare di tutte l'altre somiglianti fatiche, essendo stata cominciata dal Farinaccio fin nel 1618. e quanto che ella fu sempre della facoltà Legale il maggior tesoro: poichè siccome la Giurisprudenza fu lo studio proprio e speziale di Roma antica, così può dirsi aver quella mantenuto nella moderna la primaria sua sede. Il Morosio nel suo dottissimo Polistore (a) fra'

(a) *Tom.* 1. p. 194.

Letters lead to footnotes (*Giornale de Letterati d'Italia*, 1710). University of Minnesota.

che eglino con poca avvedutezza ubbidendo, spezzarono nell'alzarla la lapida, ed il Prelato sdegnatosene, e sgridati aspramente coloro, ne commise poscia la cura *decimo Presbytero in ordine sedis suo nomine Agnellus, qui Andreas vocabatur*, il quale era fra tutti loro in riputazione di eccellente ingegnere: *erat autem illo tempore artificiorum omnium ingeniis plenus*. Ed in fatti ben corrispose alla espettazione il successo. Sotto la direzione di Agnello fur tratte di sotto l'acqua e il sasso quelle insigni reliquie, e pi degnamente nella sua Chiesa riposte. Il Rossi (a) nel riferir questo fatto si vissi quasi delle stesse parole di Agnelo, dicendo che l'Arcivescovo nel vedere quella lapida in pezzi, *ut irritabilis naturæ, vehementer commotus, acriter illis minitans, Andream Agnellum sacerdotem, in ordine sua decimum, præstantissima arte suamoque in omnibus rebus ingenio prætum illis præfecit*.

Da queste parole del Rossi, po bene considerate, in due notabili errori, avvertiti ancora da Cristofo San-

(a) *Rub. Hist. Rav. l.* 5. *p.* 238.

Sandio, (a) si lasciò indurre il per altro accuratissimo Vossio, dicendo che Agnello fu Arcivescovo di Ravenna e decimo in ordine a quella Sede. (b) *Ravennatis Ecclesiæ Archiepiscopus fuit, ordine in ea sede decimus*. Il primo errore si è, che Agnello lo Storico non fu mai Arcivescovo Ravennate, comechè paja accennarlo prima di lui Desiderio Spreti che scrisse latinamente verso il 1460. per testimonianza del medesimo Rossi, (c) e indirizzò a Jacopo-Antonio Marcello chiarissimo Letterato e Senator Veneziano, il quale in nome della sua Repubblica era allora al governo di quella Città, un piccolo Comentario *della grandezza, ruina e ristorazione di Ravenna*, diviso in tre libri, nel cui primo, giusta la versione che ne fece Tommaso Tommai, allega (d) la autorità di Agnello *Pontefice di Ravenna*, confondendolo tutti e due in tal maniera con l'Arcivescovo Agnello vivente nel VI. secolo. L'altro errore del Vossio si è, che se anche Agnello fosse stato Arcivesco-vo

(a) *Sand. Not. in Voss. de Hist. Lat. p.* 290.
(b) *Voss. de Hist. Lat. l.* 3. *c.* 4. *p.* 737.
(c) *Rub. l.* 7. *p.* 634.
(d) *Spret. l.* 1. *p.* 13.

Letters lead to bibliographically complex footnotes (*Giornale de Letterati d'Italia*, 1710). University of Minnesota.

The notes, which are surprisingly infrequent (and the appendix), attribute, clarify, or document in English, Dutch, German, French, Spanish, and Italian. Here is a typical example, from volume five, which attempts to prove a point: "William, moreover, indicated that the participation of Spain was the indispensable condition of any undertaking¹" (4–5). The numerical hint leads to the foot of the page: "¹Ronquillo, Jan. 25, 1689: 'Ponderando en sus pocas palabras, quanto importaria, que V. M. hiziese algo...'" (5) and so on. Ranke relates that the king attempted to convince Heinsius to accept a position permanently: no one should refuse to serve the state. The note reads: "Ende mien ick, dat een goed regent, jae selfs een particuliere ingeseten sigh niet magh ontrekken den dienst te doen, die in syn maght is, an den staet" (9). This is certainly strange, because it is not unequivocally clear who says this, although it does *appear* to be the king; and the physical location of the source, which *might* be a letter, is not given. This is very different indeed from a note which concludes, "This correspondence is in Sir Thomas Phillipps' Library at Cheltenham" (47) or another, which reads in its entirety: "See Rousset's communications in Louvois, t. iv. c. 8" (13). The 424 pages of text and notes contained in this fifth volume of the *History* are followed by a 100 page appendix of original documents. The appendix continues for 400 additional pages in the sixth volume; it is followed by a 90 page index to the entire set. There is no comprehensive bibliography.

Ranke, like his colleagues — who were interested in scientizing history by creating an objective discipline based on evidence presented in primary sources, especially official documents (letters, papers, despatches, declarations, *Journals of Lords, Journals of the Commons*, and here, occasionally, Macaulay's *History of England*) — burdened his works with vast quantities of original source material in the original languages. This, he thought, would provide incontrovertible proof that his history was factual, reliable, and valid. Historians still erroneously insist that it is possible to recount and interpret as objectively as a scientist ostensibly does in a laboratory. But even the exact history of a specific event recorded through the lens of a video camera and played back to an audience is fraught with potential problems: All of the peripheral action is missing, since the tape only presents what was framed in the viewfinder. And it is easily possible to distort the action either inadvertently (through chronological lapses) or purposely (through editorial fabrication). Nevertheless, Ranke's documentation, in non-analytical and sometimes consolidated notes (Zerby 92) as well as in appendices, does lend credence to his 54 volume oeuvre, something that may be sorely lacking in contemporary political or cultural history or journalism, where agendas and ideologies confuse whatever minimal documentation is offered to the reader or viewer.

On the Origin of Species (1859), like Copernicus's work, is a ground-breaking contribution to our understanding of our evolution and place in the great chain of being. On the first page, Darwin (1809–1882) mentions Wallace, who simultaneously came up with the same ideas. He continues to cite others, though infrequently and obscurely: "...in the view propounded by Andrew Knight..." (7); "The principle of selection I find distinctly given in an ancient Chinese encyclopedia..." (34); "In a letter to me, in 1839, Mr Herbert told me..." (251). There are no notes and no concluding bibliography of his sources. *Origin* is unequivocally an original contribution to scholarship, but Darwin did assimilate the ideas of others, and so this lacuna is most surprising and disconcerting given the contemporary importance of documenting one's sources, especially in this controversial case so that readers could confirm the other scholars' perspectives. This methodology stands in direct contradistinction to Darwin's work in *The Descent of Man*, published a decade and a half later. Here he uses consecutively numbered footnotes, which recommence with the number one at the head of each new chapter. In these notes, he attributes, clarifies, and supplements. The attributions are complete and easily allow the reader to trace the precise material back to an original source. The first note in chapter 12 combines all three of these functions: "¹Yarrell, 'Hist. of British Fishes,' vol. ii. 1836, pp. 417, 425, 436. Dr. Günther informs me that the spines in *R. Calvata* are peculiar to the female" (2). Most of the 58 notes in this 35 page chapter (and in the work generally) are succinct attributions. The two volume set concludes with a 49 page index but a comprehensive bibliography is lacking. In order to consider or evaluate Darwin's sources, readers must create their own bibliographical listing, a time consuming task, and one that has once again become a major tribulation for scholars, since in the late twentieth century publishers, including university presses, began to expunge bibliographies (see chapter 5 for a discussion of this barbaric practice).

Francis Bacon (1561–1626) was a prolific author whose works were collected in the mid–nineteenth century. The three editors of the complete edition and the two volume popular version which it spawned were dissatisfied with Bacon's self-sufficiency, which is manifested in a general lack of attributions in the original text, although Bacon infrequently mentions or lists classical authors: "But the elder of the Greek philosophers, Empedocles, Anaxagoras, Leucippus, Democritus, Parmenides, Heraclitus, Xenophanes, Philolaus, and the rest (I omit Pythagoras as a mystic), did not, so far as we know, open schools..." (103, of the *Novum Organum*). They over-edit: Their notes are both attributive and explanatory; surprisingly, notes to the important *Novum Organon* have apparently been replaced by a 65 page preface, which constitutes but a fraction of the ca. 200 pages of fore-matter they provide.

2. Development

An 1877 edition of the philosophical works of John Locke (1632–1704) provides two examples of skewed documentation practice. The first is endemic to scholars who specialize in making older texts comprehensible to readers whose linguistic and substantive knowledge of the western literary, historical, and scientific canon is ostensibly sorely lacking: It is a misguided overzealousness that induces, indeed, forces the editor to annotate, clarify, and explain the most obvious or insignificant fact, observation, or detail. Nabokov's translation of Pushkin's *Eugene Onegin* provides an extreme and bizarre example. To "Of Truth in general," a concise chapter found in *An Essay Concerning Human Understanding*, J. A. St. John, the editor, adumbrates a long and pedantic footnote in which he quotes Bacon (in English), Aristotle (in Greek), an anonymous author and Victor (in Latin), and Montaigne (in French). He additionally refers the reader to Hierocles. Precise citations for the sources are intercalated within the note (181–183). Had Locke wished to lead the reader along such a tangential path, I am certain that he was familiar with Bacon on truth and the ethical conjectures that Aristotle addresses to his son.

The second problem concerns the use of symbols in lieu of superscript numerals as keys to the notes. When a single asterisk is the only sign required on a given page, there is no confusion, but when the editor must use half a dozen conflicting and duplicative signs on page after page, it becomes annoying and confusing . This system is now, mercifully, abjured in favor of numbered notes, although all numerical systems are currently in disfavor and are often replaced by in-text documentation and a works-cited list or bibliography. In "Some Thoughts Concerning Reading and Study, for a Gentleman," St. John has five of these teratisms following each other on a single page (502).

In an 1896 article in the *Publications of the Modern Language Association of America* (*PMLA*), the official journal of the arbiter of documentation style in the humanities, Gustav Gruener provides a rash of footnotes (one or more on virtually each of its 38 pages). Some are purely bibliographic while others present lengthy comments. Here is an example (the numeration is consecutive but recommences with "1"on subsequent pages):

[1]Stopford Brooke, *Tennyson*, New York, 1894, pp. 346, 347 [252].

One hundred and twelve years ago, the arbiters were not especially fastidious or consistent, as one may observe in a second example:

[2]*The Sources of Le Morte Darthur* (London, 1891, III, 294) [253].

and a third:

[1]Robert Prölss, *Geschichte des Neuren Dramas*, VI, 329 [224].

Parentheses are added and cities and dates elided for no apparent reason. Otherwise these notes are certainly similar in style and content to those presented in *PMLA* up until the mid-1980s, when MLA switched to in-text documentation and a works-cited list.

In *The Protestant Ethic and the Spirit of Capitalism*, Max Weber (1864–1920) scrupulously documents his points and their confirming data, thus strongly implying that earlier thinkers or statistics confirm his hypothesis. This process validates literally (it is true because an earlier person discovered it) and by implication (this must be the case because the note necessarily leads one back to hard data that can be perused, analyzed, and confirmed). But documentation convinces by its mere presence, for very few people actually trace the lead backwards in order to view the original conception. And it is for this reason that Weber's insistence on a correlation between a specific religious orientation and the success of capitalism has gone unchallenged. It will undoubtedly come as a major shock to most readers that when Richard Hamilton did follow up on Weber's citations, he discovered that they do not indicate what Weber stated: the citations are deficient, misleading, or non-existent.

More recently, Francis Fukuyama (1952–) published *The End of History and the Last Man*. He is diligent in his attributions, all of which are gathered together at the conclusion of the work and individually accessible via superscript numbers. Many of his often lengthy notes offer supplemental information. Here is what two unadorned consecutive citations look like:

> 7. Joseph A. Schumpeter, *Imperialism and Social Classes* (New York: Meridian Books, 1955), p. 69.
> 8. Ibid., p.5 [381].

Fukuyama employs a system that is extremely similar to the one promulgated in the distant past by the MLA, including the now obsolete use of Latinisms to indicate repetitions. Apparently, some social scientists have not fully capitulated to necessity and therefore continue to use notes rather than in-text attribution. A comprehensive 11 page bibliography follows the 49 page note section. When a note is placed at the foot of a page, it has a physical as well as intellectual relation to the text. It demands immediate consultation; it draws the reader downward, if not upon encountering the superscript number at least before turning the page. When notes are gathered together at the end of a chapter or at the conclusion of a study, it is more difficult both physically and psychologically to consult them as one reads the text. This is a disservice to the reader. Endnotes have replaced footnotes, for the same reason that bibliographies are often expunged; it cuts down on publishers' costs.

A survey of current documentation practice in a small group of journals randomly chosen from different disciplines indicates the diversity of style and format that now obtains. There exists a reasonable consistency of purpose, style, and structure within specific disciplines, but what is more intriguing is that general documentation style is converging, even though some disciplines or editors still favor notes over in-text documentation and works-cited lists. Historians obviously continue to believe that the more documentation one adumbrates, the more convincing the argument will be. In a brief piece in *The Journal of Modern History*, the author, Till van Rahden, covers half of each page with footnotes. Some are purely bibliographic in nature and follow what basically amounts to MLA style,

> [14]Friedrich Wilhelm Graf, *Die Wiederkehr der Götter: Religion in der modernen Kultur* (Munich, 2004) ... [1026].

although MLA no longer advocates the use of footnotes, and it additionally requires the name of the publisher. The American Historical Society obviously does not. Van Rahden uses *ibid.* when appropriate. Much of the notational space is taken up by substantive comments. The notes roll out of her computer with such abandon that by the end of the article, there are 101 of them; this is documentation with a vengeance. Political scientists also use numbered notes but in *Terrorism and Political Violence,* they are appended at the conclusion of the articles. Here they are exclusively bibliographic in nature and *ibid.* makes frequent appearances. The format is similar to MLA — which, of course, now abjures citational notes:

> Bell, Beverly. *Walking on Fire: Haitian Women's Stories of Survival and Resistance.* Ithaca, NY: Cornell UP, 2001.
> Charles, Carolle. "Gender and Politics in Contemporary Haiti..." *Feminist Studies* 21.1 (1995): 135–64 [Both citations from Braziel 95].

MLA controls the bibliographic style in most monographs and journals published in the humanities and APA does the same, to a great extent, in the social sciences generally, but despite the shift away from notes on the part of these two hegemonic and influential organizations, some disciplines, including women's studies and bibliographic studies, continue to favor them. In the hard sciences, endnotes are the primary means by which documentation is provided. *Applied Optics,* which is probably representative of a high percentage of science journals, offers numbered endnotes of a purely bibliographic nature:

> 1. C. A. Klein, "Optical distortion coefficients of high-power laser windows," Opt.Eng. **29**, 343–350 (1990) [Wang 7450].

Well, every journal or every discipline or every group of related disciplines, spurred on no doubt by hubris, must of necessity come up with its own variation in format. Long ago, someone in the hard sciences decided that saving space was more important than clarity. Here, first names are always expunged in favor of initials (a feature foolishly adopted by APA), so that people with similar names are easily confused. And these precise observers and experimenters prefer abbreviated titles, so that even the initiated may have to ponder whether the unitalicized Opt.Eng. should be expanded to *Optical Engineering* (which seems probable) or *Optimal Engineering* or *Optometric Engineering* or *Optometry Engineers*. And this is an easy case. That is why the enormous multivolume *CASSI* (*Chemical Abstracts Service Source Index*) is a necessary adjunct for bibliographic work in the sciences, although occasionally, even CASSI lets one down. And the bolding of the volume number is a useful feature. What else could possibly be enumerated prior to pagination? This too is ubiquitous in the hard sciences. Finally, there is the infrequent citation of a monograph. Everything follows exactly as it would under MLA format except that instead of the city of publication (which history provides), science tenders just the publisher. (In the distant past, MLA required only the city, but current MLA practice demands both, except for books published prior to 1900.) This is all unnecessarily confusing, and it is why various software products will now create a correct citation for an author in one of 300 or so different formats, thereby eliminating one of the major pleasures of scholarly writing: the scrupulous construction of the work's bibliography. (See chapter 5.)

Finally, herewith follows an extraordinary and wonderful pair of examples. In 1952, the great medical iconoclast Thomas Szasz published a long article in *The Psychoanalytic Review*. He used parenthetical numeration followed by a page number, thus: "...he stated (39, p. 496)..." (117). At the conclusion of the essay, one finds a list of corresponding numbered bibliographic citations. Excluding some minor differences, both the monographic and journal listings are similar to current MLA practice. As is sometimes the case, the parenthetical numbers that act as keys to the list are given in non-numerical order in the text, so that the very first number in Szasz's piece is (8) (115). This system is still in use today in some publications. For someone trained in MLA, more recent APA, or general scientific practices, this is bizarre and extremely disconcerting. In 2004, fifty-two years after the piece described above appeared, Szasz published another article in the same journal. For this he used current APA practice, the author-date system, when he writes that Laing notes that someone "'...requires care and attention in a mental hospital.' (1960, p. 27)" (331). Laing and the date lead to the correct citation in an appended alphabetically arranged works-cited list, which, naturally, follows current APA practice. This is scrupulously laid out in excruciating detail in the APA manual. (See chapter 7 for an overview and critique of APA style.)

3
Commentary

The interpretation of auguries, haruspications, and especially oracular pronouncements (from various sybils) are logical predecessors to the early commentaries on both religious and secular texts that followed. In this context, the substantive content of the commentary is of little import. What matters is that a text demanded some ancillary remarks from either its author or an editor who placed them within the same physical entity: in the text, margin, foot- or endnote, appendix, or separate section or, in the case of a commentator's lengthy explanatory or exegetical study, in a separate volume, which exists only because of and in direct relation to the original text. A commentary is a series of remarks necessitated by the ambiguity, allusiveness, complexity, or controversial nature of the primary text. It is not a new and original work merely inspired by the earlier document. Scholars who interest themselves in documentation invariably prefer the substantive footnote over all other possibilities, and when they discuss the long, complex, and incisive remarks found at the bottom of the great annotators' pages, they usually tender panegyrics to their glory or eulogies to their fall and ultimate demise.

Along with passing references to predecessors, commentary was the major application of documentation for scholars of the past. Originally, brief peripheral comments may have been included parenthetically within the text, but as commentary increased in importance and thus in length, it was shifted to other physical locations. Sometimes, the often wide margins of a papyrus, parchment, manuscript, or book served for the original author or scribe or later for the document's owner as a convenient location for remarks. Occasionally, a manuscript may have been scraped or erased, and its text replaced, ironically, with a commentary on the eradicated work. Many of these palimpsests are extant, though an extensive study of their current texts in relation to what was originally offered may never have been undertaken.

Earlier scholars came up with two viable solutions to the need for extended space for comments on a specific text. The first was to divide the page into sections: The text was preceded, followed, paralleled, or surrounded by remarks directly related to what the original author tendered. In some instances, biblical exegesis, for example, the complexity of the situation led to extreme graphic diversity. The page came to resemble a confusing farrago. The text in bold (sometimes just one word, *b'reshis*) could be surrounded by different commentaries (Rabbi Shlomo Itzchaki, known as Rashi) and textual translations (Yiddish, Aramaic) in different alphabets (Hebrew, Rashi script), fonts, and point sizes. This system is still in use today for editions of both the Torah and the Talmud. (A complete edition of this latter work is contained in 72 folio-sized volumes and costs $3650.) These various texts, and not just biblical narrative, are pored over by scholars and students, as if they too were the word of god! Indeed, in religious narrative generally, commentary and allusion (and ultimately practical application) may become more important than the primary text despite its sacred nature. The second solution was to publish the commentary as a separate book, so that the author had to make reference to the specific text under discussion and perhaps even quote it in part, but for the complete text, the reader would be forced to refer to another physical volume, which might or might not be at hand.

Contemporary exegetical or hermeneutical practice favors this second possibility, so that American and European biblical scholars publish separate volumes of commentary. Naturally, in periodical articles and within autonomous texts, a foot- or endnoted reference to a previous work may lead to a brief or lengthy comment and, of course, a note may contain straight commentary without referring back to another study. In some disciplines, postmodern cultural studies, for example, scholars appear to measure the quality of their output by the length, detail, and esoteric nature of their tangentially noted remarks; at times, the notes might be longer than the text. Legal scholars are notorious for producing innumerable and lengthy notes so that a typical article in a law review can cover a hundred pages. (This stands in direct antithesis to even a ground-breaking paper published in *Science* or *Nature*, which may be multiply authored but will run just one or two pages.)

There is an interesting reason why legal scholarship ostensibly demands all of this tangential commentary whereas the hard sciences abjure it, and this warrants a brief excursus, because it will help to explain why certain forms of documentation are ample in some disciplines but frequently lacking in others. Empirical discovery is apodictic: If something is valid or true, it does not require anything other than its own proof, offered in the cited data; computations; statistical analysis; graphic displays; spectral charts; computer enhanced images of astronomical phenomena, cellular anomalies, and similar material;

or logical reasoning. The physical world is a given: It exists even if human beings do not observe, experiment, analyze, deduce, interpret, and draw sometimes valid conclusions concerning its nature.

The law, on the other hand, is a (frequently illogical, irrational, subversive, and harmful) construct. Its existence and validity is socially and culturally mandated. There is, naturally, a great deal of contiguity in the laws of culturally similar entities, sometimes because a conqueror, such as Rome, imposed its law on its victims. This is then passed down to future generations so that today diverse countries have similar systems. The United States, Canada, Australia, and New Zealand, for example, all base their laws on English Common Law. European continental law, when derived from the Napoleonic Code, is very different. But despite the major differences here, these two systems are extremely similar when contrasted, say, with the cultural practices (uncodified law) of the Ik or other similar autonomous peoples living in locations untouched by the practices of the world's more hegemonic cultures, including the ancient Egyptians and Incas or modern European and Asian empires. The law's extreme and antithetical diversity (even within a specific country where local ordinances, and state, provincial, and national law may all clash with each other) requires argumentative recourse through citation of statutes and precedents established through case law. Some of this demands additional commentary, and so legal scholars go on at excruciating length multiplying examples, all of this in an attempt on the part of the author to prove whatever he or she is arguing. As Chuck Zerby observes, in another context: "Thus he piled up footnotes to defend his arguments…" (10). But empirical proof is impossible, since the law is a mere construct and its relative variance allows for diametrically opposed conclusions. That is why it is legally necessary to teach intelligent design in some school districts but not in others. It might be noted that all inhabitants in all districts have blood circulating in their veins. When this blood is analyzed, there is an extraordinary number of contiguities and similarities even for those with hepatitis. Science requires data; the law sometimes obfuscates with verbosity.

Herewith follows an extreme example, but an example nonetheless. In 2004, Penelope Pether published "Inequitable Injunctions" in the *Stanford Law Review*. This 145 page article contains 595 footnotes, some of which, to be sure, are purely bibliographic. Others, however, are informational or exegetical: The 102nd suggests that readers see various sources and informs them, among other things,

> … that a prisoner was not entitled to free transcript unless he had filed a habeas action … [1457].

This note runs on for 26 lines in a minuscule typeface. The 240th is similar: In nineteen lines the author tells readers that

> While they are searchable on Westlaw, one needs the unofficial reporter cite to do a straightforward search by citation; the original cite to the official reporter does not recover the opinion. Both citations are effective on LEXIS if the opinion is published in the unofficial as well as the official reporter [1480].

There is lots more on unpublication and depublication. One of the irrational reasons that a law review article that approximates the length of a small monograph can contain almost 600 tedious notes is that the young (and inexperienced) student editors, presumably at the behest of their faculty advisors, insist that every remark be documented. Thus, authors are forced to increase their notes in submitted articles, doubling or tripling them, and thereby increasing the aggregate number of pages. This is a truly bizarre practice.

Examples of pure commentary can be found in antiquity, e.g., Chalcidius's (fl. 325 AD) remarks on Plato's *Timaeus* (which spawned B. W. Switalski's 1902 *Des Chalcidius Kommentar zu Plato's Timaeus*, a commentary — replete with innumerable lengthy footnotes — on a commentary) or Proclus's (411–485) *Commentary on the First Book of Euclid's Elements*, which in its 1970 recension additionally contains Glenn R. Morrow's detailed introduction as well as hundreds of bibliographic and explanatory footnotes. Naturally, supplementary interpretive commentaries increase as we move closer to the present.

It is worth spending a few moments with a typical page of the Talmud (500 BC–500 AD), which consists of the Mishnah (the primary text of oral law, in six volumes, called orders) and the Gemara (a commentary, in 63 volumes). The original recent recensions, the Vilna Shas (or edition), for example, are naturally written in Hebrew and Aramaic. But there are complete English language versions that include all of the peripheral material. In the Steinsaltz edition, one finds the following layout on the opening, folio-size page of the tractate known as "Bava Metzia" ("Middle Gate"). In the upper center is the brief Hebrew or Aramaic text of the Mishnah beginning with "Shinaim" ("two") and continuing for just 33 words (on other pages, this is followed by the appropriate portion of the Gemara). To its upper left is a translation and commentary in English (including the repetition of the appropriate Hebrew or Aramaic text). To the upper right is a literal translation. Both of these sections contain superscript numbers that link the various sections on the page. Below the literal translation is Rashi's commentary in Hebrew and printed in Rashi script, which is slightly different from the Hebrew alphabet. It should be noted that the Hebrew or Aramaic text is pointed, i.e., it contains vowels, which makes it much easier to read; Rashi's comments lack pointing. Below these texts, one finds explanatory notes and below this, Halakhah (Jewish law). To the right (or left) of everything, in the wide margin, one finds background material (and on subsequent pages, information about terminology, sages, concepts, realia, or language). A single large page containing seven separate, parallel, and interrelated sections in three languages and three alphabets is difficult to conceptualize and even more difficult to use. Reading requires constant shifting among the different sections supplemented by careful consideration and discussion. A study of the entire Talmud requires a lifetime commitment. This is documentation (sources, translation, commentary, and explanation) run amuck. It is extreme, but serves its purpose well, for a scholar pursuing all possible byways would have to keep half a dozen books open and constantly shift among them. The annotated Talmud brings everything necessary together on a single helpful page. (Analogues to the structure utilized in the Talmud do exist. The Pentateuch is treated in a similar fashion. And in Edward Coke's *First Part of the Institutes of the Laws of England* [1775] one finds a central French text in a narrow column; to its left, part is repeated followed by a comment; to its right is an English translation. Above is the continuation of a text from the preceding page. Below is commentary. To the left of all of this, in a secondary margin, are lettered attributions. Below everything are numbered notes and below this more commentary. To the left of everything, in the primary margin, are hand-written annotations. English and French; Roman, italic, and script; bold and plain text; and medium and diminutive typefaces in nine separate entities all vie with each other in a bizarrely confusing farrago.)

When the Talmud and other laws, rules, customs, and traditions do not provide an adequate answer to a specific question, an epistolary query may be referred to a great rabbi. The replies are called *responsa*; they stretch back to Biblical times, and they may act as precedents when the same problem arises in the future. Responsa are based in part on the Talmud and are thus commentaries on commentaries. Questions may sometimes appear petty to the uninitiated but they are extremely meaningful to those who pose them. Typical queries concern the permissibility of reading philosophy, the validity of Marrano marriage, the wearing of hats, and the consumption of sturgeon (Freehof, passim). An unusual dilemma concerned the permissibility, on the Sabbath, of opening a book that had images painted on the edges of its pages. These fore-edge illustrations are visible when the book is closed but disappear when the book is opened and the pages are fanned. Thus, opening and closing cause the image to disappear and reappear, and if this is considered work, it is not allowed on the Sabbath. (The conclusion is that it is acceptable, but one would be better off not using this book on the day that God rested) (Freehof 253–255).

Aquinas (1225?–1274) offers scrupulous and detailed exegetical analyses of Biblical texts. His *Commentary on Saint Paul's Epistle to the Ephesians* is a

TALMUD PAGE

Detailed explanations of these numbers are to be found in the following pages. Large circles indicate the various texts appearing on the Talmud page. Small circles with arrows indicate references to the texts.
1) Page number. 2) Page heading. 3) Talmud text. 4) Indication of the Mishnah and the Gemara. 5) Punctuation. 6) Parentheses and correction of the Talmud text. 7) Rashi's commentary. 8) Tosafot. 9) References in Rashi and in Tosafot. 10) Rabbenu Hananel. 11) *Ein Mishpat Ner Mitzvah.* 12) *Torah Or.* 13) *Masoret HaShas.* 14) *Haggahot HaBah.* 15) *Haggahot HaGra.* 16) *Gilyon HaShas.* 17) *Haggahot Rav B. Ronsburg.*

Opposite and above: The Talmud. Published by Random House.

3. Commentary

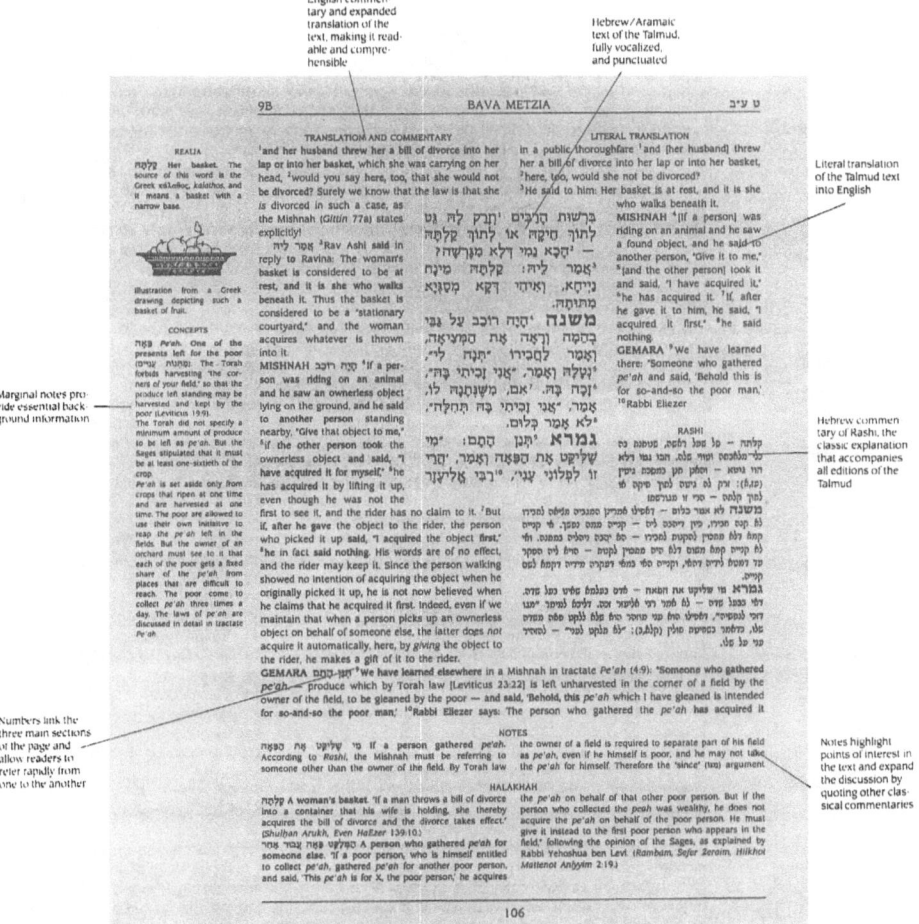

good example of how he operates. He cites a portion of the text in short numbered sections and then comments generally; this is followed by requotation of very short phrases which elicit additional specific remarks on each in turn, thus:

> 6b In which he hath graced us in his beloved Son.
> 7 In whom we have redemption through his blood, the remission of sins, according to the riches of his grace.

Now the Apostle writes of the fourth blessing (cf. 1:3), that of becoming pleasing [to God] through the gift of grace. Regarding this he does two things:

First, he touches on the giving of this blessing.
Secondly, he shows the manner and conditions of its bestowal (1:7).

> Hence, he first asserts: We are predestined unto the adoption of sons, for the praise of the glory of his grace — that grace, I say, **in which he hath graced us in his beloved Son.** In this respect it should be noted that to be loved by someone is identical to being pleasing to him [51].

And so on for four pages. There is a great deal of repetition of the original text as well as Aquinas's comments; he makes the same observations from various points of view and in various ways. (Aquinas's method is similar to that of the Jewish Biblical and Talmudic commentators who preceded and followed him; Rashi, for example.)

The 1978 edition of Coperenicus's (1473–1543) *Revolutions of the Heavenly Spheres* (*On the Revolutions)*, concludes with more than 100 pages of often lengthy and detailed remarks that sometimes contain complex numerical data. Edward Rosen, the editor, offers his comments in direct relation to specific articulations in Copernicus's text and leads the reader to the exact original statement by citing page and line numbers. Some commentaries are more precisely situated, as in Biblical or Talmudic studies, where they are geared to specific words, and in others the discussion is generalized to a larger textual message: a chapter or series of chapters, an entire study, or a specific idea or conceptualization derived from the original work.

Georgio Vasari (1511–1574) published two recensions of his acclaimed *Lives of the Artists,* one in 1550 and a much expanded version in 1568. He covers the biographies of the great Italian Renaissance artists in detail, so it is obvious that he had recourse to either oral or written source material, but there do not appear to be any attributions within the published work. This is not unusual even in more recent biographical sketches, so it is not surprising that Vasari should fail to document. What is stunningly interesting, though, is the 1976 six volume edition of *Le Vite de' Più Eccellenti Pittori Scultori e Architettori,* edited by Rosanna Bettarini and Paola Barocchi. Here each page is divided by a horizontal line, above which one finds the 1568 edition and below, in italics, the earlier recension. In some paragraphs, there are few or no changes; e.g., the opening of the Leonardo da Vinci essay is the same in both cases:

> Grandissima doni si veggono piovere dagli influssi celesti ne' corpi umani, molte volte naturalamente, e sopranaturali talvolta ... [IV, 15].
>
> *Grandissima doni si veggono piovere dagli influssi celesti ne' corpi umani, molte volte naturalamente, e sopranaturali talvolta ...* [IV, 15].

In other instances, the alterations commence with the very first words, as in Correggio's life:

> Io non voglio uscire del medesimo paese, dove le gran madre Natura ... [IV, 49].
>
> *Sforzasi bene spesso la benigna Natura infondere tanta grazia ne' nostri artefici con tanta divinità nel maneggiare de' colori ...* [IV, 49].

Here is the unusual case of an author documenting (commenting on his own work) through the parallel publication of his own emendations.

Abraham Cowley (1618–1667), like Alexander Pope and a handful of other littérateurs, includes sometimes extremely detailed exegetical endnotes with his poems. (Those appended to the *Pindarique Odes* are sometimes longer than the texts.) *Davideis* is a 163 page poem in rhyming iambic pentameter couplets. It describes the troubles of King David in allusive detail. Since the substantive content derives directly from the Bible, one might expect that Cowley's seventeenth century readers were intimately acquainted with the material, but apparently this was not the case for not only are the pages often adorned with marginal Biblical attributions, each of the four books that comprise this epic work concludes with page after page of notes in a diminutive typeface. These notes can be extremely detailed; even a simple geographical explanation is replete with every allusion to Nobe Cowley can locate. The text,

> 1 To *divine Nobe* directs then his flight ... [324]

leads to

> 1. A Town not far from *Jerusalem*, according to *S. Hieron.* in his *Commentary* upon *Isaiah*, by which it seems it was re-edified, after the destruction of it by *Saul* ... [351].

And so on for five additional allusive lines. More complex issues elicit extremely detailed remarks:

> 32 And true it was, soft *musick* did appease ... [253]

which brings forth a disquisition on the powerful effects of music:

> 32. That *Timotheus* by *Musick* enflamed and appeased *Alexander* to what degrees he pleased, that a *Musician* in *Denmark* by the same art enraged King *Ericius* [and so on for many more examples] ... is well known to all men conversant among Authors [274].

This thirty-second note then continues for 47 additional lines (in English, Greek, and Latin). Exegetical commentary included as an integral part of a literary work by its author is an unusual and peculiar ploy. It may be a meaningful explanation of something the author really believes to be esoteric or incomprehensible or an attempt to create a scholarly aura or humorous, witty, or sarcastic atmosphere. But all of these are merely unnecessary excuses for the creation of this type of annotation, which in the history of world literature occurs very rarely. With only a few exceptions, the quality and comprehensibility of literary works are not enhanced by an author's integrated notes.

Zerby contends that in *A General Dictionary, Historical and Critical,* Perre Bayle (1647–1706) first uses footnotes to their fullest potential (63–64). The *Dictionary* is an enormous, multi-volume work whose frequent, lengthy, detailed, and interminable notes are informative, digressive, and iconoclastic. In fact, E. A. Beller and M. duP. Lee, Jr., in their introduction to *Selections from Bayle's Dictionary,* contend that the notes (and cross references) were meant to confuse censors because Bayle often took an unacceptable, irreligious position. This, however, is a barely defensible argument. Any censor reading the text could easily drop down to the notes and continue his perusal. If a cross reference was also meant to lead him astray, there is no reason why he could not additionally follow along this ostensibly obfuscating path. In any case, even if all of this is true, it did not fully work, because complaints were brought against the *Dictionary* and Bayle did make at least some alterations in subsequent editions (Beller and Lee, passim). It is important to recall that publishing unacceptable points of view, anti-religious remarks, blasphemy, complaints against the state, and other horrors were often grounds for imprisonment or even death. *Mutatis mutandis,* William Slights makes the same point generally, viz., that controversial political asides could be disguised when snuck into marginal comments or that a political text could be defended if it were attributed to the right if misleading sources (*Managing* 107).

The early French editions and the English translations were published in folio so that the typesetter had ample room on these enormous pages both to use large fonts and to lay out the text, footnotes, and citations in a graphically pleasing if complex manner. Many of the entries are biographical accounts of well-known historical figures, although some insignificant people as well as movements and countries are also included. The text offers the main thread and the notes move off in various digressive and sometimes philosophical and skeptical directions. A fairly extensive text may lead to an equally extensive footnote, but there are many instances when a single textual sentence elicits sometimes brief or often very lengthy notes; then a return to the following textual sentence repeats the pattern. Here is a simple example from the entry on Hobbs (taken from a modern edition of selections that interpolates the bracketed notes into the body of the text).

> **Hobbes** (THOMAS), one of the greatest geniuses of the XVIIth century, was born at Malmesbury in England the fifth of April 1588.[A]
>
> [A][His mother, frighted with the reports that were current of the approach of the Spanish Armada, was delivered of him before her time....]
>
> He had made great progress in the languages,[B] when at fourteen years of age he was sent to Oxford, where he studied Aristotle's philosophy five years.

B[Before he went from Malmesbury school to Oxford, he translated Euripides's *Medea* into Latin verse....] [Bayle, *Selections* 125–126, all texts and notes].

Above and next three pages: The entry, James (or Jacques) Alting (Pierre Bayle, *A General Dictionary, Historical and Critical,* 1734). University of Minnesota.

ALT

rus. He took possession of this employment the 13th of January 1643, the same day that Samuel Des Marets was installed in the Professorship of Divinity, which had been held by the same Gomarus. In process of time his titles and employments were increased; he was admitted Doctor of Philosophy the 21st of October 1645, Preacher to the Academy in 1647, Doctor and Professor of Divinity in 1667. He went twice to Heidelberg, viz. in 1651 and 1662, where the Elector Palatine Charles Lewis expressed a great value for him, and often pressed him to accept of the Professorship of Divinity, but he begged to be excused. He soon fell out with Samuel Des Marets his Collegue, which indeed could hardly be avoided, since they differed as to the method of teaching, and in some points, as to their principles. Alting kept to the Scripture, without meddling with scholastic Divinity: he was in the career of glory, and hastened to go on in it; he wanted neither wit nor learning to maintain his opinions. The first Lectures which he read in his own house upon the Catechism drew such crowds of hearers to him, that for want of room in his own chamber, he was obliged to use the Hall of the Academy; most of the foreign Students were on his side. His Collegue was accustomed to the distinctions and method of the School-men; had been a long time in great esteem; published a great many books, and had a sprightly genius with a great deal of learning: the Students in Divinity of the country adhered to him, thinking that the surest way to church-preferments; for such only were admitted to serve the Parish-churches, as had studied according to his method. This was sufficient to occasion, and keep on foot, a misunderstanding between the two Professors, even though their temper had had no share in the quarrel. Alting had great difficulties to struggle with; the majority of votes, and the authority of age, were on his adversary's side, who besides had a battery capable to alarm the world, and revive the most venerable prejudices. This was to give out that Alting was an innovator, a man who plucked up the boundaries, which our fathers had so wisely placed on the confines of truth and falshood. He set up for a publick informer, and charged James Alting with thirty one erroneous propositions. The Curators of the Academy sent both the information and the answer to it, to the Divines of Leyden, without acquainting the parties, begging them to give their opinion upon the subject in debate. Their judgment is remarkable [B]. Alting was cleared from all heresy, but his imprudence was blamed in broaching new hypotheses; on the other hand Des Marets was found fault with for acting contrary to the laws of charity and modesty (a). The latter would not submit to that judgment, nor accept of the silence that was proposed: He was for having the cause examined by Assemblies, Schools and Synods, which the heads would not agree to, forbidding all writings either in favour, or against the judgment of the Divines of Leyden; and thus the work of Des-Marets, intitled, *Audi & alteram partem*, was suppressed. This quarrel made a great deal of noise, and might have been attended with bad consequences; especially when Des Marets was called to the University of Leyden (b); but he died at Groningen (c) before he could take possession of that employment. He made some sort of reconciliation on his death-bed, which shall be mentioned in the note [C]. Alting was obliged to complain that he had been imposed

(c) In May 1673.

(a) Cum Altingium ab omni haerefos notâ absolverent, in ipso dutem prudenti-am in proponendis suis inventis, in Marefio modestiam & charitatem requirerent. Vita Jacob. Alting.

(b) Et res miram habitura catastrophen, Marefio quanquam Jam ad Theologicae Professionem Lugdunum in Batauis vocato. Vita Jacob. Alting.

[B] *Their judgment is remarkable.*] I do not intend to declare myself in this dispute, for either side; all I have to say is, that on the like occasions one cannot help judging as the Divines of Leyden did. Those who invent new hypotheses, are but too apt to maintain them at the expence of the peace and tranquility both of the Church and Universities. They may be orthodox, but cannot be prudent; for it is a piece of imprudence and temerity to disturb the public without some great and urgent cause. Those who oppose a new method of teaching, shew commonly too much passion and violence? I am willing to grant, that sometimes they have no private views; but they run upon extremes, alarm the whole Church for trifles, and make the world fear a total depravation as to the confession of faith, when there is yet no attempt against it. They may therefore be zealous, but at the same time it must be owned, that their zeal is not accompanied with moderation, charity, or justice. Nay they are often as imprudent as their adversaries: they do not reflect, that a new method, if not minded, drops of itself; but, if opposed, degenerates into a party. The author of the new method may have relations in the Government, who will sustain him with all their efforts. Thus you will soon see the Civil and Canon Laws combined, and the factions of the Church and State matched together. What mischiefs may we not fear from such a conflict? How many evils would Religion, and likewise the State, avoid, were men contented only to oppose fundamental innovations?

[C] *He made some sort of reconciliation on his death-bed.*] A Clergyman of Groningen seeing that Mr. Des Marets was past all hopes of recovery, suggested a reconciliation between him and his collegue; and having his consent, he went to make the same proposals to Mr. Alting, who answered, that his silence in the midst of the clamours and books of his adversary witnessed for his peaceable temper; that he was always ready to accept of a peace upon reasonable terms; but that he demanded satisfaction for the injurious reports that had been spread abroad to the prejudice of his honour and reputation; and that he did not understand how any one could court his friendship while he believed him to be a man of such a character, as he had been represented to be. Upon this the mediator retired, without making any further proposals. Not long after it was given out in the city, that Mr. Alting had been so hard hearted as absolutely to refuse to be reconciled with his dying collegue; so true it is, that town-reports do not represent things as they are in themselves. The mediator, accompanied by another Clergyman, returned to Mr. Alting, and obtained from him a formulary of the satisfaction he desired. This formulary was no ways liked by Mr. Des Marets, and that, which Mr. Des Marets drew up, did not at all please Mr. Alting; there was more goings to and fro on this occasion than in the capitulation of a fortress. At last, the alteration which Mr. Alting made in the formulary of Mr. Des Marets having been accepted of, upon condition that Mr. Alting would approve of what Mr. Des Marets added to it, to make the conditions equal on both sides, the articles were signed; and this was all the reconciliation. Note, that the parties only retracted the personal injuries; as to the accusations in point of doctrine, the accuser referred them to the judgment of the Church (a).

(a) Taken from a Letter of James Alting in the fifth volume of his works.

250
ALTING.

gues dans la prémiere : mais il fut le seul Inspecteur général dans la seconde ; le Comte de Bentheim l'aiant fait venir pour informer contre le Socinianisme qui menaçoit le païs, & pour mettre un bon ordre dans les Eglises. Alting, à ce que dit son Eloge, n'étoit point un Théologien querelleux (*G*) : il ne s'amusoit point à la vetille des faux scrupules ; il n'aimoit point les nouveautez : il étoit zélateur de l'ancienne traditive, ennemi des subtilitez de l'Ecôle, & il ne vouloit puiser que dans l'Ecriture (*f*). Toutes les personnes de sa profession devroient régler leur domestique comme le sien étoit réglé (*H*). On n'en parloit que pour dire en général que tout y étoit dans l'ordre : il ne fournissoit point d'autre matiere aux conversations. Il s'étoit marié à Heidelberg, l'an 1614, & avoit eu sept enfans. Il y en a eu trois qui lui survêcurent, une fille & deux garçons. L'ainé a été Professeur en Droit à Deventer (*g*). L'Article suivant traite de l'autre.

(*f*) *Theologiam prehabat ne turbaretur solidam ac masculam, non ex canonis Scholasticorum, sed illarum ineptiarum non esset, sed ex sanctissimi Silvi & Scripturarum derivatam, ut gloria sint petitis unanimiter nojurti Palamonibus tradunt eam quam Toulingum scripturam aut & biblicum.* Vita Alting.

(*g*) *Tiré de la Vie de Jaques Alting, parmi celles des Professeurs de Groningue, imprimées infusis, l'an 1654.*

(*G*) *Il n'étoit point un Théologien querelleux.*] Raportons les propres termes de son Historien. *Alienus à jurgiis & virilitigiis Cuminisectorum ; ab iis distinctiunculis & ineptiis Sophistarum, quibus mysteria salutis potius implicantur quàm explicantur ; à scrupulositatibus Praecisistarum, qui nodum quaerunt in scirpo, colant culicem, camelum deglutientes* (11). La secte des Précisistes faisoit du bruit en Hollande, il y a 40 ans (12) plus ou moins : la voilà fort bien caractérisée ; on y coule le moucheron, on y engloutit le chameau ; on y ouvre la porte à des disputes qui ne servent qu'à l'armement des profanes & des libertins. Poursuivons : *ab omni denique novationes & novationes in Theologicis, quasi illud semper Tertulliani tenens, « primum quodque verissimum. »* Il n'y a point de doute que l'amour des nouveautez ne soit une peste, qui, après avoir mis en feu les Académies & les Synodes, ébranle & secoué les Etats, & les boulverse quelquefois : ainsi l'on ne sauroit trop louer les Professeurs, qui recommandent à leurs disciples de s'éloigner de cet esprit d'innovation. Il ne faut point le rebuter ; sous prétexte qu'en recommandant fortement l'observation de l'ancienne & commune traditive, il semble qu'on suppose le principe ou la voie de l'autorité, que l'on a rejettée quand on a eu à combattre l'Eglise Romaine ; il ne faut point, dis je, se décourager pour tout cela ; car si l'on attendoit à se servir d'une raison jusques à ce qu'elle fut à couvert de toute difficulté, on seroit trop long-tems sans rien faire.

(11) *Vita Jacobi Alting.*
(12) *On écrit ceci en 1698.*

(*H*) *Les Ministres devroient régler leur domestique comme le sien étoit réglé.*] On savoit seulement que personne ne savoit ce qui s'y passoit, hormis qu'on n'ignoroit pas que toutes choses y étoient dans la bienséance, & selon la crainte de Dieu. *Hinc in familia ejus omnia semper pacata, omnia ordinata, de qua hoc solùm sciretur, quòd à nemine sciretur quid in illâ fieret, nisi quod pie, composite, decenter, omnia fieri neminem lateret* (13). Cela est cent fois plus beau, que si le monde s'entretenoit de ce qui se dit, & de ce qui se passe chez un Ministre. On y a débité une telle nouvelle ce matin (14), dit l'un. On y disputailleroit au soir sur une telle réflexion de Nouvelliste, dira l'autre. Il peut s'excuser comme Adam, dit un troisiéme, & dire, la femme que tu m'as donnée me l'a fait faire. Quoi, dit un quatriéme, *vous n'avez après cette circonstance qu'en ce lieu-là ; je m'en défie. C'est un mauvais Bureau d'adresse, &c :* la Nympha loquax, qui y préside, ajoute & fait ajouter ce que bon lui semble aux relations. Je ne veux point de ses gloses, ni de ses commentaires sur le texte, quelque incertain qu'il puisse être. Il ne faut pas s'étonner qu'Alting ait été inconsolable, après la mort de son épouse, s'il est vrai, comme son Historien le débite, qu'il ait vécu avec elle près de trente ans, sans aucune plainte ni contestation. *Cum eâ per annos propè triginta sine vixâ, sine querelâ, conjunctissimè vixit* (15). Peu de gens se peuvent vanter d'une telle chose, & se plaindre d'ignorer si les effets de la reconciliation sont aussi doux dans le mariage, que dans la galanterie ;

Amantium ira amoris redintegratio est (16).

(13) *Vita Jacob Alting.*
(14) *Conferez aussi la Remarque (c) de l'Article de BRUTEAUS.*
(15) *Vita Jacob Altingii.*
(16) *Terent. And. Act. III, Sc. III, 23.*

ALTING (JAQUES) fils du précédent, a été Professeur en Théologie à Groningue. Il naquit à Heidelberg, le 27 de Septembre 1618, pendant la députation de son pere au Synode de Dordrecht. Toute son enfance fut un perpétuel changement de lieu (*A*). Il fit ses études à Groningue, avec beaucoup de succès ; &, comme sa grande passion étoit pour les langues Orientales, il s'en alla à Embden, l'an 1638, afin de profiter des lumieres du Rabin *Gumprecht Ben-Abraham*. Il alla en Angleterre, l'an 1640, s'y fit connoître aux plus grans hommes, y prêcha, & y fut reçu Prêtre de l'Eglise Anglicane par le docte Jean Prideaux, Evêque de Worcester. Il avoit résolu d'y passer toute sa vie ; mais il accepta la Profession en Hebreu que la mort de Gomarus rendit vacante à Groningue. Il y fut installé le 13 de Janvier 1643, le même jour que Samuel Des-Marets fut installé à la Profession en Théologie, que le même Gomarus avoit exercée. Les titres & les charges d'Alting augmentérent avec le tems : il fut

(*A*) *Toute son enfance fut un perpétuel changement de lieu.*] Car, à l'âge de deux ans, on l'envoia chez Chrétien Chytræus, Ministre de Bretten. L'année suivante, sa mere, nonobstant sa grossesse, fut obligée de se retirer à Heilbron, où elle le mena ; & delà, au bout d'un an, il falut se retirer à Schorndorf. *Sequente mox anno propter imminentem Heidelbergæ obsidionem, matre etiam comite, eâque tum gravida Haldbronnam, indeque exacto anno Schorndorfium missus est*

(1). Henri Alting, son pere, l'amena ensuite, avec toute sa famille, à Embden, par des chemins détournez. D'Embden, il se transporta à Leide, où il fut Précepteur des fils du Roi de Boheme. La peste l'obligea d'aller de Leide à Honslaerdijk ; enfin il passa de Honslaerdijk à Groningue, lors qu'il y fut apellé pour la Profession en Théologie, l'an 1627. Jaques Alting étoit alors âgé de neuf ans.

(1) *Vita Jacobi Altingii.*

ALTING.

fut reçu Docteur en Philosophie, le 21 d'Octobre 1645; Prédicateur Académique, l'an 1647, Docteur & Professeur en Théologie, l'an 1667. Il avoit fait deux voiages à Heidelberg, l'un en l'année 1651, l'autre en l'année 1662: & il avoit reçu mille témoignages d'estime de l'Electeur Palatin Charles Louïs, qui le sollicita plusieurs fois d'accepter là une Chaire de Théologie, de quoi il s'excusa honnêtement. Il se brouilla dans peu de tems avec son collegue Samuel Des-Marets; & il étoit difficile que cela n'avint, vû que leur méthode d'enseigner n'étoit pas la même, & que sur divers points ils n'avoient pas les mêmes principes. Alting s'attachoit à l'Ecriture, sans aucun mélange de Théologie Scholastique. Il entroit dans la carriere de la gloire: il se hâtoit de s'y avancer; il ne manquoit, ni d'esprit, ni d'érudition, pour soutenir ses sentimens. Les prémieres Leçons, qu'il fit chez lui sur le Catéchisme, attirerent tant d'Auditeurs, que, faute de place dans sa chambre, il falut qu'il se servît de l'Auditoire Académique. Il avoit pour lui la plûpart des Etudians étrangers. Son collegue étoit habitué à se servir des distinctions & de la méthode des Scholastiques: son nom faisoit du bruit depuis long tems, il publioit quantité de Livres, il avoit un grand feu d'esprit, beaucoup de savoir: les Proposans du païs s'attachoient à lui comme au chemin le plus sûr d'avoir une Eglise; car toutes les Paroisses étoient servies par des Ministres qui avoient étudié selon sa méthode. En voilà plus qu'il n'en faut pour allumer & pour entretenir la division, quand même le temperament ne le mettroit pas de la partie. Alting avoit à combatre des obstacles trés-puissans: la pluralité des voix & l'autorité de l'âge étoient du côté de son adversaire, qui d'ailleurs avoit pour lui une baterie capable de gendarmer tout le monde, & de réveiller les préjugés les plus vénérables; c'étoit de dire qu'Alting étoit un innovateur, un homme qui remuoit les bornes sacrées que nos peres avoient si sagement mises sur les confins de la vérité & du mensonge. Il devint accusateur public seulement sur XXXI Propositions erronées, qu'il imputoit à Jaques Alting. Les Curateurs de l'Académie envoiérent aux Théologiens de Leide l'Ecrit de l'accusateur, & la Réponse de l'accusé, sans en avertir les parties, & les prierent de prononcer là-dessus. On rendit un jugement digne de remarque (*B*): on trouva Alting exemt d'hérésie, on blâma seulement son imprudence à forger de nouvelles hypotheses; d'autre côté, on trouva que Des-Marets avoit manqué de modestie & de charité (*a*). Ce dernier n'aquiesça point à ce jugement, & n'accepta pas l'offre du silence: il voulut que la cause fut examinée par les Consistoires, par les Classes, & par les Synodes; mais les Supérieurs n'y voulurent pas consentir, & défendirent d'écrire ni pour ni contre le jugement des Théologiens de Leide: ainsi l'Ouvrage de Des-Marets, *Audi & alteram partem*, fut suprimé. Cette querelle fit un grand bruit, & eut pu avoir de fâcheuses suites, par la vocation de Des-Marets à l'Académie de Leide (*b*); mais il mourut à Groningue (*c*), avant que de prendre possession de cet emploi. Il se fit une maniere de reconciliation au lit de mort (*C*); j'en

(*B*) *On rendit à son sujet un jugement digne de remarque.*] Je ne prétens point prendre parti dans l'affaire particuliere dont il s'agit en cette rencontre; je me contente de dire, que dans le général, on ne sauroit s'empêcher, sur de pareilles contestations, de juger comme firent les Théologiens de Leide. Ceux qui avancent de nouvelles hypoteses, se piquent trop de les soutenir au préjudice de la paix, & de la tranquillité Ecclesiastique & Académique. Ils seront donc orthodoxes tant qu'il leur plaira; mais ils n'auront pas assez de prudence: il y aura de la témérité dans leur fait; car c'est être téméraire que de troubler le repos public sans une grande & urgente nécessité. Ceux qui s'opofent à une nouvelle méthode d'enseigner, témoignent trop de passion; je veux croire que quelquefois il n'y a rien de personnel qui conduise leurs démarches; mais ils outrent les choses, ils allarment toute l'Eglise pour des bagatelles, ils font craindre la dépravation totale de la Confession de Foi, lors qu'on n'y donne encore aucune atteinte. Ils feront donc zelez tant qu'il leur plaira: mais ils ne feront ni modérez, ni charitables, ni équitables. Ils feront même aussi imprudens que leurs adversaires; ils ne prennent pas garde, qu'une nouvelle méthode, dont on ne fait pas semblant de s'apercevoir, tombe d'elle-même, au lieu que si on la choque de droit front, elle dégénére en parti. Le nouveau méthodiste aura des parens dans la Régence, qui le soutiendront de tous leurs cliens; & ainsi, vous verrez bientôt la combinaison du Droit Civil & du Droit Canon, les factions d'Etat, & les factions d'Eglise, apariées ensemble. Que n'a-t-on point à craindre de ce conflict? Qu'on épargneroit de maux à la Religion & à l'Etat, si l'on se contentoit de s'oposer aux innovations fondamentales!

(*C*) *Il se fit entre lui & des Marets une maniere de reconciliation au lit de mort.*] Un Ministre de Groningue,

The *Dictionary* is impressive because of its substantive content (which repeated, supplemented, and enlarged on earlier encyclopedias' entries) but also because of the complex graphic layout of its enormous pages. For example, in the entry on James Alting in the English version in ten volumes entitled *A General Dictionary*, the first ca. 700 page volume of which appeared in 1734, the text consists of a substantial block of material, which leads to substantial lettered (majuscule) notes of a substantive nature in a reduced typeface. Both the text and the notes additionally lead to secondary lettered (minuscule) and numbered citational notes, respectively. It sounds confusing because it is. The original French text, in five ca. 1000 page volumes, precisely mirrors all of this except that James is called Jacques.

In *A Tale of a Tub*, Jonathan Swift (1667–1745) presents a structurally complex satire replete with lengthy sections that Swift ludicrously multiplies: an analytical table, apology, postscript, dedications, and preface as well as purposeful digressions (on critics, on madness, in praise of digressions), which Ernst Robert Curtius also employs. Swift's substantive notes, which adorn many of the *Tale's* pages, offer bits of useful information as in the following examples.

> The Egyptians worshipped a monkey, which animal is very fond of eating lice, styled here creatures that feed on human gore [425].
>
> I was told by an eminent divine, whom I consulted on this point, that these two barbarous words ["Bythus and Sigé"], with that of Acamoth and its qualities, as here set down, are quoted from Irenaeus. [And so on.] [507].

Swift pokes fun at all human foibles including his own construction and use of footnotes.

Historians who concern themselves with documentation apotheosize Bayle and Edward Gibbon (see below), whose footnotes are replete and overwhelming in their substantive generosity. But they should also admit Alexander Pope (1688–1744) (and Vladimir Nabokov — see below) into the footnoters' pantheon. Pope's poetic gifts were extraordinary; he could turn almost anything into witty and mellifluous rhymed couplets. He translated both *The Odyssey* and *The Iliad*, for which he additionally provided a running commentary in detailed footnotes. Indeed, a third to a half of the 1,000 pages that comprise *The Iliad* in the Twickenham edition of Pope's works are allocated to his referential (Eustathius, Spenser, Milton, Scaliger), critical, explanatory, definitional, and lexicographic notes, which at times quote Greek, Latin, and French texts. As is sometimes the case with poetry or drama (Shakespeare's plays, for example), the lines are numbered, and these numbers are used to connect the text to the notes. Here are two examples, culled from many hundreds of possibilities. The 285th line of the 16th book reads in its entirety:

Oh Great! *Pelasgic, Dodonaean Jove!*

This elicits almost two pages, in a typically minuscule typeface, of remarks on oracles in Homer by quoting a lengthy excerpt from Temple Stanyan's *Grecian History*, which begins,

> The *Oracles* were rank'd among the noblest and most religious kinds of Divination; the Design of them being to settle such an immediate way of Converse with their Gods ... [250].

and so on interminably. Book 18 concludes with 13 pages of "Observations on the Shield of *Achilles*." The apparatus is staggering and includes the notes (supplemented by modern intercalated bibliographical citations), three complex indices, and "textual notes to Pope's notes on the *Iliad*." I am aware that Pope wanted to provide readers with a valid, replete, poetic, and comprehensible edition of his translation and that twentieth century scholarship demands completeness. But this is typical overkill, and probably is less helpful than either Pope or the five twentieth century *Iliad* editors (including Maynard Mack and Robert Fagles) would like to believe. Naturally, the notes and ancillary materials are useful for those who wish to understand the nuances of Greek myth, Homeric composition, ancient and contemporary critical commentary, and Pope's perspective on the poem and its characters, but they are concomitantly distracting and annoying for those readers who prefer to follow the text in a committed and participatory fashion. They interrupt in precisely the same way that a narrator remarking on Othello's or Hamlet's monologues would, should he or she stop a performance in order to "help" the audience understand by offering summaries of 400 years of critical commentary. The dramatic and emotional impact of a tragedy does not necessarily depend on lexical or historical comprehension.

Pope also wrote poetry, and his *Dunciad* is an extremely complicated and difficult work not only because it alludes to many esoteric matters but also because it adduces and satirizes many of the poet's dull and offensive peers. All of this requires explanation and clarification. Indeed, someone immediately created a key to the original, primarily unadorned edition. Then Pope decided to offer his own annotated recension, and so he appended innumerable lengthy, detailed, and esoteric footnotes to the first version of the poem. (Some years later, he published an altered and expanded edition.) The *Dunciad* volume in the Twickenham edition is one of the most complex books ever published. The original 52 page poem is ensconced in a 550 page compilation replete with so many different prefaces, introductions, tables, lists, advertisements, letters, testimonies, and other paraphernalia that the incomplete table of contents must run on to a second page. The notes mirror Pope's work in the Homeric translations. They are extremely detailed and a line of text may elicit a page of commentary. For example, the title's asterisk leads to almost a page of orthographical musing (in a reduced typeface, naturally) including intercalated remarks offered by James Sutherland, this edition's modern editor. Line 104 (book I), "And all the Mighty Mad in Dennis rage..." (72) results first in a half-page note commencing, "This is by no means to be understood literally, as if Mr *D.* were really mad [and so on]..." (72). But then he again rants on in a second comment about an earlier version of the same line, and Sutherland has some other comments to add, so that this note fills more than two additional pages. This is annotation with a furious, unrelieved, and annoying vengeance. Line 240 (book I), "Can make a Cibber, Johnson, or Ozell..." (91), must lead to four separate footnotes explaining who these people are in ludicrous detail: of Johnson, Pope observes, "He may justly be called a Martyr to obesity..." (91).

Seconding P. W. Cosgrove, Zerby insists that Pope's footnotes in *The Dunciad* (which are much more extensive than Swift's) are not merely exegetical, explanatory, or argumentative; they are rather satiric barbs aimed at the footnote itself. Pope is satirizing scholarly apparatus and critical commentary: "...a careful reader finds footnotes are *The Dunciad's* obvious target" (54). Zerby adduces as proof the fact that the poem contains 358 (in actuality, 1014) lines but the notes run on for an astounding 7,000 (54). Even if this is partially true, i.e., even if Pope's avowed but covert purpose is to demean the footnote, the substantive content of the notes cannot be discounted. They are so numerous and extreme that they alter the tenor of the poem. Unlike the often superfluous comments with which authors occasionally burden their literary creations, these notes demand scrutiny even as they distract one from the work. They are an integral part of *The Dunciad* in the same way that Nabokov's notes to *Pale Fire* are an integral part of his novel. If one cares to fully understand and profit from *The Dunciad*, it is necessary to take its footnotes into account regardless of Pope's purported motives.

Edward Gibbon 's (1737–1794) footnotes in *The Decline and Fall of the Roman Empire* hold an honored place in the history of documentation. Grafton retells (*Footnote* 103) and Zerby repeats (79–80) the well-known story of how Gibbon did not care very much about the location of his bibliographic and excursive notes. After David Hume complained, upon the publication of the first volume, he relocated them from the back of the book to their rightful place at the bottom of the page, and there they offer a parallel but divergent history of Rome. "Someone once said," observes Zerby, "that notes ran along the bottom of Gibbon's pages like dogs yapping at the text..." (81). His annotations are attributive and serious but also witty and satiric. He aims his barbs at historical figures and those who (mis)record and (mis)interpret their actions. His armamentarium includes "grotesque detail, low humor, and references to bodily functions" (Palmeri 249). But the annotation adulators fail to remark that many of Gibbon's notes are merely functionally and tediously informative. The Milman, Guizot, and Smith edition of *The Decline* is contained in six large volumes, the third of which runs 714 pages and holds chapters 25–37. All but four of the thirty-first chapter's 88 pages are undergirded by 191 replete footnotes (which implies that *The Decline*'s complete text probably contains something on the order of 8,000 notes). As if this were not adequate, Milman provides lettered footnotes to Gibbon's texts and numbered notes. Here is how this works: The text tells us "…that by the mysterious force of spells and sacrifices, they could extract the lightning from the clouds…[77]." This leads to

> [77]Zosimus (l.v. [c.41] p. 355, 356) speaks of these ceremonies like a Greek unacquainted with the national superstition of Rome and Tuscany.
> …
> … Scire nefas homini.[a]

There is a lot more in this note but for our purposes this in turn leads to Milman, who thought it necessary to notationally inform readers that

> [a]On the curious question of the knowledge of conducting lightning possessed by the ancients, consult Eusébe Salverte, Des Scienecs Occultes, ch. xxiv. Paris, 1829.—M. [391].

After just a few thousand pages, this constant bombardment is bound to disenchant.

Zerby points out that a single footnote (on the Roman wall) in John Hodgson's mammoth *History of Northumberland*, published during the early years of the nineteenth century, is so long and detailed that it requires its own volume (1). Almost as unusual is the general physical layout of this work. Text and footnotes share pages equally, which implies that they are equally important and merit equal attention. Additionally, the notes may lead to appended historical documents, so that the page appears to be divided into three sometimes unequal parts (155).

Travelers, adventurers, explorers, and mountaineers have produced innumerable accounts of their journeys, and many of these, including Richard Byrd's *Alone*, Slavomir Rawicz's *Long Walk*, P. R. Reid's *Colditz* sagas, and Joe Simpson's *Touching the Void* are among the most powerful and enticing books ever written. They are a subset of the memoir and are based on real experiences and presumably reflect the truth. Their authors have much to tell and describe and they invariably do so in a straightforward narrative easily accessible to the general public. Documentation, which is an (often mandatory) adjunct of scholarly publication is only rarely found in profuse abandon in other genres. Memoirs, though they are often replete with new and original information, lack documentation because they are aimed at a non-scholarly

REDESDALE.—ELSDEN PARISH.—REDESWIRE AFFRAY. 155

conjecture is supported by the circumstance of the place being wholly exempt from tithes. It was the property of the earl of Carlisle, who sold it to the late Mr Simon Dodd, to whose grandsons, Mr Michael Dodd, of Cornhill, and Mr Simon Dodd, of Old Town and Bell Shield, it belongs at present. Its proprietors pay a sort of anomalous quit-rent of 6s. 8d. a year " to the representatives of the late Edward Noel, Esq. for part of the rectory of Corsenside." In 1821, it contained only one house and seven inhabitants.

THE REDESWIRE is the *neck* of land from which the water falls one way into the valley of the Rede, and the other into Scotland. The highway runs over it, and the prospect from it into the two kingdoms is extensive. It is remarkable for the blood which has been spilt upon it. Here, in 1400, Sir Robert Umfreville gained a victory over the Scots; and in 1575, it was the scene of another serious affray.[a] On the 5th of July, in that year, Sir

[a] As this affray is still narrated with much traditionary embellishment by the Northumberland fire-sides, and still continues to excite much local interest, we subjoin* the following letters, selected from several others in the Cotton. MS. Calig. C. V. and for transcripts of which we are indebted to the kindness of W. C. Trevelyan, esq. :—

* " The state of the late disordre chaunced att the Redd Swire the vii^th of July att a meeting betwixt the Lord Wardein of the Midle Marches of England, And Jhon Carmichell deputie keapar of Liddisdale.

" It appeareth that the said wardein and Carmichell did meete att the tyme and place aforesaid for execution of justice onlye w^thout any pretence of mallice or discord for so they both affirme and agrey, wch the rather seameth to be trewe bicause they, and almoste all the people on both sides cam̃ unarmed, and after accustomed manner did scatter and go abroad either into others companye.

After their meeting and frendlye salutac̃ons paste, they chose a fytt place in the Englishe grownd to do justice, therein proceading orderlye and quietlye in sondrye Billes of attemptats, &c. w^thout any difference or disagreement, saving for the deliv̉ey of Willm Fenwick charged with receipt of a Scottishe fugitive, and demaunded therefore to be delivered, wch Bill passed over, They proceaded forewardes, aud after did curteouslye drincke together.

" After their drincking togethers they beganne againe to execute justice, calling a Bill againste Henrye Robson englisheman, who att a former meeting was fyled condicionallye and being then called, awnswere was made for him that he was sicke: The wardein of England willed suche as made that awnswere to make othe thereof, and bicause they refused to sweare and that the partiē made not apparence, the wardein fyled that bill thwart out, that is, condempned the partie by default. Whereuppon Carmichell asked deliverye for the same, and the warden of England offered to make deliverey att their next meeting: But Carmichell again demaunded present deliverey accordinglie as he had at this meeting and in like case before done: The wardein stille stoode to make deliverey att the next meeting alledgeing unto us, that the same agreeth with thordre of the Marches. Then Carmichell not contented herew^th said, that no more can I make further deliverey to yowe, and it will appeare that you cloke justice and are not willing yt should proceed. And as the wardein of England affirmethe, Carmichell then further said, that so long as his nowte and the keap^rs doe go quyettlye on the Borders, there is nothing but maintennce of fugitives Rebelles and Traitors: wch wordes Carmichell denyeth to be spoken by him att that tyme, but that before theire drincking the like wordes were merelye spoken, wheratt the wardein tooke none offence: Hereuppon the wardein of England audience. But there are exceptions. Darwin's *Voyage of the Beagle* is an account of a five year journey, but it is filled with his botanical and ethological observations, and some footnotes. Sir Richard F. Burton's (1821–1890) extraordinary *Personal Narrative of a Pilgrimage to Al-Medinah and Meccah* is an enormous and detailed account of his trip and all that he discovered along the way. Its two volumes run almost a thousand pages and culminate in an impeccable 65 page index. This is a popular travel account but with a strong scholarly bent. Thus, the sometimes extremely long, detailed, and even illustrated scholarly notes that adorn the foot of almost every page are not merely warranted; they are mandatory, since they present bibliographic, referential, lexicographic, historical, descriptive, and explanatory information that otherwise would only be available to the reader in hundreds of other sources or not at all. Burton's *Narrative* is an extraordinary hybrid that presents a real adventure[1] within a groundbreaking scholarly context. The profuse and informative notes astonish because, unlike some of the tedious and sometimes superfluous material presented by Pope or Bayle, for example, they are as enticing as the narrative text.

The mention of an Alexandrian obelisk brings forth a long multi-lingual note (in a reduced typeface):

> 1 Cleopatra's Needle is called by the native Ciceroni 'Masallat Firaun,' Pharaoh's packing needle. What Solomon, and the Jinnis and Sikandar zu'l karnain (Alexander of Macedon), are to other Moslem lands, such is Pharaoh to Egypt, the 'Caesar aut Diabolus' of the Nile. The ichneumon becomes 'Pharaoh's cat '... [and so on for 15 additional lines] [I, 10].

Jubbah elicits more than a mere definition:

> 1 The jubbah is a long outer garment, generally of cloth, worn by learned and respectable men. The za'abut is a large bag-sleeved black or brown coloured robe ... [I, 17].

Some of the notes are both quite long and extremely informative. One, on the etymology of "moor" with an aside on "Saracen" including remarks on Sanskrit, Persian, and Greek (in both English and French), runs a full page (I, 187–188). Another, dealing with eye disease and Herodotus, is a page and a half in length (I, 385–387). And a third, presenting a taxonomy of Moslem secular studies, rambles along for two pages (I, 107–109). Unlike his accomplished fellow footnoters, most of whom reap all of the glory, Burton is a masterful story teller both in the text and in the wonderful ancillary material.

Many of Gustav Gruener's footnotes to "The *Nibelungenlied* and *Sage* in Modern Poetry" (1896) are purely bibliographic in nature, but a few are sometimes lengthy substantive comments (one goes on for more than a page); two include footnotes to the footnotes; in one example, the text reads:

> ... what shall we ... say to the poet who contemplates the dramatization of the old German epic?[1] [234].

The note begins:

> [1]This line of argument applies with equal truth to the dramatization of the modern novel.* [234].

The asterisk leads to a subsidiary footnote:

> Since writing this note the attention of the writer has been called to an essay by Brander Matthews ... [234].

This is unnecessarily complex but it jibes with traditional 19th and 20th century scholarly documentation.

Elliott Forbes's work is quite different. A most unusual and peculiar commentary is the intercalated material that one finds in *Thayer's Life of Beethoven*. The history of this work and its translation is extremely complicated, but of importance here is that it first appeared in print, in part, between 1866 and 1879 (Forbes, vi). It was completed by a series of editors and published in both German (1907–1917) and English (1921) (xxii). And there matters rested until 1964, when Forbes published a revised two volume edition. Forbes reworks and retains Alexander Wheelock Thayer's highly edited original but includes within the text his own brief (a sentence), detailed (a paragraph), or extremely lengthy (many pages) intercalations, which are always set off by two blatant printer's marks; thus, it is easy for the reader to distinguish between Thayer and Forbes:

> They were ordered, undoubtedly, as in the case of Mozart's Andante in F major (K. 616), by Count Deym, in whose museum there was a collection of mechanical instruments.
> ...✳✳(We return to the subject of Beethoven's friendship with the Countess Deym in 1804; on January 27 of that year the Count died, and the widow's friendship with the composer developed into an affair of the heart.)✳✳...
> The year 1800 is an important era in Beethoven's history. It is the year in which, cutting loose from the pianoforte, he asserted his claims to a position with Mozart ... [I, 237].

To add to the graphic confusion, some of the original footnotes are retained but Forbes also includes his own; the notes are either purely bibliographical or offer additional (corrective) commentary. The text,

> 'Apparently his mother was already dead at the time,[8]...' [I, 58]

leads to the following:

> [8]Error. Beethoven's mother did not die until 1787, long after he had left school. This story, however, supports the belief, mentioned earlier, that

the mother's care in externals was not always of the best. (TDR, I, 132, n. 2.) [I, 58].

A limited number of pages are entirely devoid of formal documentation but others contain as many as six often substantive notes. (See page I, 195, for an example.)

Although this is one of the most important Beethoven biographies, it is an annoying farrago and reads in a most disjointed manner. The halting 1136 pages (including nine appendices and an index) are further disrupted by occasional brief quoted jottings following upon each other in quick succession, thus:

> The doctor has allowed rice soup …
> .⁓.
> You may eat fruit.
> .⁓.
> Dr Wawruch's visits: on the 5th of December one time, on the 6th of December 2 times, on the 7th–14th once per day [II, 1022].

These textually intercalated entries continue in like manner with many more in this specific instance. Equally disconcerting in a narrative text are the listings of chronologically appropriate compositions and publications at the conclusion of most of the 40 chapters.

It is unusual to find texts with intercalated commentary set off graphically, but here is one more example. Louis Jacobs, in *Jewish Ethics, Philosophy and Mysticism,* collects 25 brief excerpts from the works of a group of medieval thinkers. A section of each text is printed in bold followed by Jacobs's commentary printed in Roman; there follows more text and then additional commentary. These sections vary in length from a sentence or two, to four pages. Here is what this looks like:

> **There arose in His simple will the will to create worlds and produce emanations in order to realize His perfect acts, His names and His attributes. This was the purpose for which the worlds were created.** In the "simple light of Én Sof" there emerged a will to create. (Note the way in which it is avoided saying that Én Sof willed directly, because this is considered as touching on a mystery too deep for human understanding [131].

This is preceded and followed by a series of similar alternating texts and comments. Both Forbes and Jacobs employ what amounts to an interlinear methodology to enhance, emend, or comment precisely and immediately. For these purposes, it is even more effective than footnotes, but mellifluousness is sacrificed and the overall result may be disjunctive and confusing for the reader.

A documentary spoof, along the lines of Pope's remarks in *The Dunciad,* but much more extreme and entirely fictitious, is Vladimir Nabokov's (1899–1977) *Pale Fire,* a 37 page poem followed by 229 pages of commentary (plus an index), all of which derive from Nabokov's creative imagination. His sometimes excruciatingly long and detailed exegetical remarks are specifically geared to the poem's numbered lines. It is not necessary to overemphasize the "scholarship," in what Nabokov terms a novel, so a very minor example will suffice:

> Line 501: L'if
> The yew in French. It is curious that the Zemblan word for the weeping willow is also "*if*" (the yew is *tas*) [222].

This type of preposterous semi-imaginative comparative philology appeals to a limited number of readers who either enjoy word games or who have an inherent stake in annotated texts. (The present author does not share either of these interests.) There can be little doubt that Nabokov liked this type of work and that his successful fictional foray inspired him to continue to labor on a real scholarly endeavor: Perhaps the most bizarre example of serious commentary ever produced is the enormous ancillary volume of annotations that supplement Nabokov's often quirky translation of Alexander Pushkin's *Eugene Onegin.* The two volume paperback abridgement (which I consulted) of the original four volume set eliminates the correlative lexicon, the appendices, and the original Russian, but includes 28 pages of preliminary matter, an 88 page introduction, the long poem including Pushkin's own notes (246 pages), and the commentary: 545 pages followed by 382 pages plus a 109 page index. Thus, the *abridged* edition runs a total of 1398 pages. This obviously borders on madness.

In order to fully appreciate the translation but especially the ancillary material, one should be aware of two important points. First, Nabokov was born in Russia into a family that also spoke English; additionally, he mastered French, so that he was fully trilingual. Many people, because of circumstance or predilection, study and learn a second or third language, and may use them on an ongoing basis. But very few people are truly trilingual; and even fewer master the languages as completely as Nabokov did. He reveled in the acquisition of ever more esoteric, obsolete, and archaic English terminology, but simultaneously maintained his competence in Russian and the etymological and connotative aspects of its vocabulary. For Nabokov, language was more than a mere handmaiden to be used pragmatically when required. Instead, he was a true wordsmith who liked playing with linguistic meanings, connections, alliterations, and other often annoying arcana. (One of his novels is entitled *Ada or Ardor,* another *Pnin,* both of which he found linguistically — esthetically — pleasing.) The second point is that Nabokov was befriended by Edmund Wilson, at that time the leading literary critic in the United States, and they developed a strong and lasting relationship. When the *Onegin* volumes appeared, Wilson wrote a critique for *The New York Review of Books*. In a long, scholarly and pedantic essay, he foolishly informed readers that Nabokov had produced a monstrosity and he proceeded to discuss the volumes' many faults (3-6). Nabokov responded in print and then broke off relations. Despite Nabokov's articulate defense, one that corrected Wilson's misconceptions, the truth is that this is an extremely peculiar work.

The English version is often stilted because Nabokov insisted on a literal (pedestrian, awkward, stilted, obsolescent) version ("only this is true translation" [I, viii)]), used inappropriate diction, and had a perverse and stubborn proclivity for choosing extremely arcane and often contextually bizarre vocabulary. There is nothing wrong with *ananas, crackbrain, cronking, doveling, kibitka, mollitude, phthisical, polyhedral, quitrent, tosh,* or *vernant*—although the first is never used by English speakers, though it means pineapple in a host of European languages, and the last was rare or obsolete when the first edition of the *Oxford English Dictionary* appeared in 1928 — they just do not belong in a poem, which brings up another necessity. Nabokov's translation is sadly but purposely lacking in two of poetry's major attributes: meter and rhyme, both of which can be found in the original Russian:

> XLII
> Capricious belles of the *grande monde!*
> Before all others you he left;
> and it is true that in our years
> the upper *ton* is rather tedious [I, 113].

For all of his knowledge and scholarly work, this is a mere trot.

But what concerns us here is the commentary. Set off originally in two separate volumes but later placed in one enormous compilation, it is meant to be consulted as one encounters difficulties in the text. It is similar to keys created for James Joyce's incomprehensible *Finnegans Wake* or Dylan Thomas's sometimes difficult poems. It is doubtful that even Nabokov thought that more than a handful of aficionados would read the commentary straight through. But since the remarks are not located in close proximity to the text, reading becomes an onerous chore, rather than a pleasure, when one is forced to constantly flip back and forth between the different volumes. So, Nabokov's annotations are really for scholars who are doing research rather than a true helpmate to readers diligently trying to understand some arcane reference or locution as they read the poem for pleasure. This is very different from texts in which a scholar provides annotations to truly help (rather than impress) readers, for example, *Gulliver's Travels, Alice in Wonderland,* and the Sherlock Holmes accounts, where the notes are found on the same page as the text. It is extremely dangerous to second-guess an author, but the possibility certainly exits that Nabokov was in the same playful mood that generated *Pale Fire*, and is both toying with the reader, whose ostensible ignorance he probably detested,[2] as well as showing off.

His extremely long and pedantic adumbrations, explanations, comparisons and contrasts, influences, linguistic and poetic discussions, and variant readings test one's patience because rather than helping, they often hinder, confuse, and annoy. For Pushkin's simple epigraph to book two, "O rus! O Rus'!" (I, 123), Nabokov helpfully indicates Horace's "O countryside!" which is followed by Oh Russia (II, part 1, 217–218). But he must then additionally quote Horace, partially in Latin, followed by Stendhal in French, and there is more. The epigraphs (which he terms mottos) to each of the chapters elicit the same type of detailed remarks, except for Byron's "Fare thee well, and if for ever, / Still for ever, fare thee well..." (I, 279), the epigraph to the eighth and final chapter, which leads to only the following brief sentence: "The beginning of Byron's famous and mediocre stanzas, *Fare Thee Well*, on his domestic circumstances, first published in the London *Champion*, Apr 14, 1816" (II, part 2, 129). To avoid belaboring Nabokov's methodology and frequent and interminable substantive remarks, I limit myself here to two additional examples. The note to lines 1–4 of chapter 4's 39th sonnet begins as follows:

> One of the best examples that one can choose to illustrate some of the special difficulties that Pushkin's translators should be aware of is this quatrain of st. XXXIX, which describes Onegin's life in the summer of 1820 on his country estate:
>
> *Progúlki, chtén'e, són glubókoy,*
>
> ...
>
> In the first line (which Turgenev-Viardot translated correctly as "La promenade, la lecture, un sommeil profond et salutaire"), *progulki* cannot be rendered by the obvious "walks," since the Russian term includes the additional idea of riding for exercise or pleasure [II, part I, 460].

This goes on for six pages! (And why is the Russian text transliterated? Anyone who can read Russian prefers it in Cyrillic script; those who cannot read it, profit little from this because the system of transliteration does not offer precise equivalents, so readers will of necessity mispronounce the words, and because one cannot derive meaning intuitively from an alien language.) Nabokov's disbalanced presentation and extreme pedantry can be observed in his remarks on the word "romanticism," which Pushkin mentions parenthetically in chapter 6's 23rd sonnet:

> 2/ romanticism: As happens in zoological nomenclature when a string of obsolete, synonymous, or misapplied names keeps following the correct designation of a creature throughout the years ... [II, part 2, 32].

and so on; he follows his sometimes offensive opinions with pages of interminable definitional remarks on the eleven meanings of romanticism and its allied terms. None of this is at all necessary or helpful. Nabokov, incidentally, is a perfect analogue to Pope: *Pale Fire* is Pope's *Dunciad* and *Eugene Onegin* is his Homer.

More typical is contemporary scholarship in some disciplines that insists that tangential substantive commentary appended in foot- or endnotes is essential for both the author's integrity and the reader's comprehension; to leave anything out could apparently lead to accusations of incompetence. Till van Rahden presents a parallel commentary to her article in the 101 notes that adorn her 24 page essay. Here is the way this frequently unfolds. The twelfth note reads in its entirety:

> Jacob Toury, *Soziale und politische Geschichte der Juden in Deutschland, 1847–1871: Zwischen Revolution, Reaktion, und Emanzipation* (Düsseldorf, 1977), 114. For a different view, see Stafanie Schüller-Springorum, *Die jüdische Minderheit in Königsberg, Pr. 1871–1945* (Göttingen, 1996), 32: the 'broad majority of Königsberg Jews could secure their economic survival in the middle of the nineteenth century, but they were not affluent or even rich'; even after the turn of the century the "majority of the Jewish minority [belonged] ... to the middle and lower-middle classes that earned a moderate income" (ibid., 57) [1026].

Other authors are not quite as circumspect in the details they provide and so their notes are much longer; sometimes even purely bibliographical notes can run on for half a page, but more reasonable is a substantive comment that extends for 17 lines, such as James Elkins's third footnote in his response to Michael Fried (939); more extreme is Jana Evans Braziel's fourth endnote to her essay on *Krik? Krak!*, which covers more than a page, thus:

> [4]Chancy, whose *Framing Silence* is one of the first book-length studies on Haitian women writers, describes a political poetics influenced by critical race theory and critical race feminism, especially "the critical writings of other scholars or writers of African descent like Derrick Bell and Patricia J. Williams..." [92].

And so on for 53 lines of diminutive type. Someone could have used a good copy editor.

Most documentation, regardless of whether it is located at the foot of the page, at the conclusion of each chapter, at the end of the book, in an appendix, or in a separate volume and regardless of whether it is purely citational or more generous in allusion, explanation, interpretation, or commentary, is naturally a necessary, often mandatory, part of scholarly work in all disciplines. Its precise structure, emphasis, and detail depend both on the requirements and conventions of the discipline (history versus physics, for example), and the precise scholarly and professional needs as well as personal predilections of the author. But as shown above, some novelists and poets also employ documentation. This is unusual and occurs only infrequently. Cowley and Swift and especially Pope and Nabokov are the outstanding examples, because their documentation, in the form of foot- or endnotes, is an integral and extensive part of their work, which would be very different indeed if the notes were eliminated. But a few other littérateurs, including George Crabbe, Thomas Grey, David Jones, Herman Melville, Marianne Moore, John Berryman, John Updike (Zerby, passim), Lawrence Sterne, Henry Fielding, John Barth, Adrienne Rich, and Carolyn Forché, have also employed notes, which some readers may consider superfluous. Indeed, Rodger Beehler argues vehemently even against heavily annotated scholarly editions of classical novels. He cites some recent examples in order to denigrate, e.g., in an edition of Dickens's *Bleak House*, the first two paragraphs engender 12 endnotes that either provide superfluous information or annoyingly reveal the plot's itinerary.

In 1922, T. S. Eliot published *The Waste Land*, which is arguably the single most influential English-language poem of the twentieth century. It concludes with a series of 50 endnotes in English, French, Italian, Latin, and German that proffer sources, translations, or explanations. But despite the need to understand every subtle allusion in a work of art in order to fully appreciate it both intellectually and esthetically, a poem should stand on its own inherent merits. Therefore, one might iconoclastically but timidly wonder whether the notes are really necessary. Knowing that a particular line is a translation from Dante connects literatures and traditions, but it may not truly enhance the reader's experience with *The Waste Land*. (On the other hand, it can be argued that the calligraphy that frequently adorns Chinese landscape paintings is an integral part of the work and its removal would alter the viewer's esthetic interaction and appreciation.)

Eliot's inclusion of his ostensibly helpful notes in order to facilitate the reader's understanding is in direct contradistinction to James Joyce's method in *Ulysses* (also coincidentally published in 1922), in which he purposely obfuscates with every manner of linguistic complexification, much to the reader's annoyance and frustration. (Despite this, *Ulysses* is often cited as the most important novel of the twentieth century.) Joyce provides no helpmeets whatsoever. In his barely readable and frequently completely incomprehensible *Finnegans Wake*, Joyce does offer a handful of footnotes, which, however, do very little to help. These notes only occur in a single 24 page interpolated section and their usefulness is herewith exemplified. The text reads,

> We recognise at once the seductive rhythm and head-reeling "little language" of the Temptress Isobel — "encuoniams here and improperies there[1]. With a pansy for the pussy in the corner[2]" [112].

mother, enters the text and swamps the footnotes. We recognise at once the seductive rhythm and head-reeling "little language" of the Temptress Isobel—"encuoniams here and improperies there[1]. With a pansy for the pussy in the corner[2]".

Bewise of Fanciulla's heart, the heart of Fanciulla! Even the recollection of willow fronds is a spellbinder that lets to hear.[3] The rushes by the grey nuns' pond: ah eh oh let me sigh too. Coalmansbell: behoves you handmake of the load. Jenny Wren: pick, peck. Johnny Post: pack, puck.[4] All the world's in want and is writing a letters.[5] A letters from a person to a place about a thing. And all the world's on wish to be carrying a letters. A letters to a king about a treasure from a cat.[6] When men want to write a letters. Ten men, ton men, pen men, pun men, wont to rise a ladder. And den men, dun men, fen men, fun men, hen men, hun men wend to raze a leader. Is then any lettersday from many peoples, Daganasanavitch? Empire, your outermost.[7] A posy cord. Plece.

We have wounded our way on foe tris prince till that force in the gill is faint afarred

INCIPIT IN-
TERMISSIO.

Uncle Flabbius Muximus to Niecia Flappia Minnimiss. As this is. And as this this is.

Dear Brotus, land me arrears.

Rockaby, babel, flatten a wall.

How he broke the good news to Gent.

MAJOR AND
MINOR

---

[1] Gosem pher, gezumpher, greeze a jarry grim felon! Good bloke him!
[2] And if they was setting on your stool as hard as my was she could beth her bothom dolours he'd have a culious impressiom on the diminitive that chafes our ends.
[3] When I'am Enastella and am taken for Essastessa I'll do that droop on the pohlmann's piano.
[4] Heavenly twinges, if it's one of his I'll fearly feint as swoon as he enter-rooms.
[5] To be slipped on, to be slept by, to be conned to, to be kept up. And when you're done push the chain.
[6] With her modesties office.
[7] Strutting as proud as a great turquin weggin that cuckhold on his Eddems and Clay's hat.

112

Above, opposite, and page 64: Footnoted pages from *Finnegans Wake.* From *Finnegans Wake* by James Joyce, copyright 1939 by James Joyce, copyright renewed ©1967 by Giorgio Joyce and Lucia Joyce. Used by permission of Viking Penguin, a division of Penguin Group (USA) Inc.

3. Commentary

> and the face in the treebark feigns afear. This is rainstones ringing. Strangely cult for this ceasing of the yore. But Erigureen is ever. Pot price pon patrilinear plop, if the osseletion of the onkring gives omen nome? Since alls war that end war let sports be leisure and bring and buy fair. Ah ah athclete, blest your bally bathfeet! Towntoquest, fortorest, the hour that hies is hurley. A halt for hearsake.[1]
>
> MODES COALESCING PROLIFERATE HOMOGENUINE HOMOGENEITY.
>
> [1] Come, smooth of my slate, to the beat of my blosh! With all these gelded ewes jilting about and the thrills and ills of laylock blossoms three's so much more plants than chants for cecilies that I was thinking fairly killing times of putting an end to myself and my malody, when I remembered all your pupil-teacher's erringnesses in perfection class. You sh'undn't write you can't if you w'udn't pass for undevelopmented. This is the propper way to say that, Sr. If it's me chews to swallow all you saidn't you can eat my words for it as sure as there's a key in my kiss. Quick erit faciofacey. When we will conjugate together toloseher tomaster tomiss while morrow fans amare hour, verbe de vie and verve to vie, with love ay loved have I on my back spine and does for ever. Your are me severe? Then rue. My intended, Jr, who I'm throne away on, (here he inst, my lifstack, a newfolly likon) when I slip through my pettigo I'll get my decree and take seidens when I'm not ploughed first by some Rolando the Lasso, and flaunt on the flimsyfilmsies for to grig my collage juniorees who, though they flush fuchsia, are they octette and viginity in my shade but always my figurants. They may be yea of my year but they're nary nay of my day. Wait till spring has sprung in spickness and prigs beg in to pry they'll be plentyprime of housepets to pimp and pamper my. Impending marriage. Nature tells everybody about but I learned all the runes of the gamest game ever from my old nourse Asa. A most adventuring trot is her and she vicking well knowed them all heartswise and fourwords. How Olive d'Oyly and Winnie Carr, bejupers, they reized the dressing of a salandmon and how a peeper coster and a salt sailor med a mustied poet atwaimen. It most have bean Mad Mullans planted him. Bina de Bisse and Trestrine von Terrefin. Sago sound, rite go round, kill kackle, kook kettle and (remember all should I forget to) bolt the thor. Auden. Wasn't it just divining that dog of a dag in Skokholme as I sat astrid uppum their Drewitt's altar, as cooledas as culcumbre, slapping my straights till the sloping ruins, postillion, postallion, a swinge a swank, with you offering me clouts of illscents and them horners stagstruck on the leasward! Don't be of red, you blanching mench! This isabella I'm on knows the ruelles of the rut and she don't fear andy mandy. So sing loud, sweet cheeriot, like anegreon in heaven! The good fother with the twingling in his eye will always have cakes in his pocket to bethroat us with for our allmichael good. Amum. Amum. And Amum again. For tough troth is stronger than fortuitous fiction and it's the surplice money, oh my young friend and ah me sweet creature, what buys the bed while wits borrows the clothes.
>
> 113

The notes explain:

> [1]Gosem pher, gezumpher, greeze a jarry grim felon! Good bloke him!
> [2]And if they was setting on your stool as hard as my was she could beth her bothom dolours he'd have a culious impressiom on the diminitive that chafes our ends [112].

	Coss? Cossist? Your parn! You, you make what name? (and in truth, as a poor soul is between shift and shift ere the death he has lived through becomes the life he is to die into, he or he had albut — he was rickets as to reasons but the balance of his minds was stables — lost himself or himself some somnione sciupiones, soswhitchoverswetch had he or he gazet, murphy come, murphy go, murphy plant, murphy grow, a maryamyriameliamurphies, in the lazily eye of his lapis,	WHY MY AS LIKEWISE WHIS HIS.

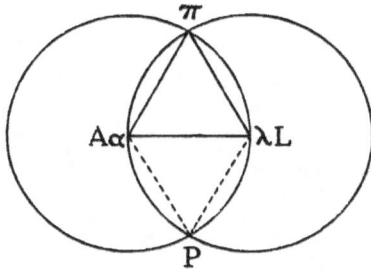

Uteralterance or the Interplay of Bones in the Womb.	Vieus Von DVbLIn, 'twas one of dozedeams a darkies ding in dewood) the Turnpike under the Great Ulm (with Mearingstone in Fore ground).[1] Given now ann linch you take enn all. Allow me! And, heaving alljawbreakical expressions out of old Sare Isaac's[2] universal
The Vortex. Spring of Sprung Verse. The Vertex.	of specious aristmystic unsaid, A is for Anna like L is for liv. Aha hahah, Ante Ann you're apt to ape aunty annalive! Dawn gives rise. Lo, lo, lives love! Eve takes fall. La, la, laugh leaves alass! Aiaiaiai, Antiann, we're last to the lost, Loulou! Tis perfect. Now (lens

[1] Draumcondra's Dreamcountry where the betterlies blow.
[2] O, Laughing Sally, are we going to be toadhauntered by that old Pantifox Sir Somebody Something, Burtt, for the rest of our secret stripture?

115

In order to make sense of this novel, one needs a key. Roland McHugh provides one in *Annotations to* Finnegans Wake. The layout is most peculiar because the explanations graphically mirror the original text. The result is a page that resembles nothing else in the history of book production:

3. Commentary

                                                                              Orion's

The Aeneid refers frequently to "Pious Aeneas"   fulminant: developing   firman: order issued
                                                                       suddenly; thundering   by Oriental sovereign

    tremulous   *F* terre
nychthemeron: period of 24 hours
G nicht: not

                                                                       U. was not protected by copyright in U.S. &
                                                                         pirated editions appeared [185]

                                                                      George Roberts: manager of Maunsel & Co, D, was to   185
                                                                   publish *Dubliners*, but after 3 years' delaying, the
                             public   printer, John Falconer, decided against it & destroyed
                           pulpit   the 1st edition
    L codex: book   *L* podex: posterior   (pulped)
                         L flammeus: flaming   benefaction   benediction

                         home rule   5
               ph wild goose chase   katharsis (J: *The Holy Office*)
                  Wild Geese: Ir. Jacobites who went to continent

             'where in Sam Hill': pop. C19 U.S. expression meaning 'where in the world'
                    The Sporting Times had hostile review of *U.* in April 1922

            P/K   cardinal & ordinal numbers   10
                                                The Anglican Ordinal
        ON Dönsk tunga: Danish tongue
        Rev 17:4–5: 'the woman was arrayed in purple & scarlet colour . . . & upon her forehead was a name written,
        MYSTERY, BABYLON THE GREAT, THE MOTHER OF HARLOTS'   *The Pink 'Un*: subtitle of *The Sporting*
        (Puritans applied to R.C. Church)   *Times*

        Luke 6:41: '& why beholdest thou the mote that is in thy brother's eye, but perceivest not the beam that is in thine
        own eye?'   *L* (translation): 'First the artist, the eminent writer, without any shame or apology,
        St Colmcille: *s* Altus Prosator   pulled up his raincoat & undid his trousers & then drew himself close to the life-
        Vulg Gen 3:7: 'et fecerunt   giving & allpowerful earth, with his buttocks bare as they were born. Weeping &   15
        sibi perizomata' ('& made   groaning he relieved himself into his own hands. Then, unburdened of the black
        themselves aprons')   beast, & sounding a trumpet, he put his own dung which he called his "down-
                                                castings" into an urn once used as an honoured mark of mourning. With an
                                                invocation to the twin brethren Medard & Godard he then passed water into it
                                                happily & mellifluously, while chanting in a loud voice the psalm which begins
                                                "My tongue is the pen of a scribe writing swiftly". Finally, from the foul dung
                                                mixed, as I have said, with the "sweetness of Orion" & baked & then exposed to
                                                the cold, he made himself an indelible ink'
        Litany of BVM: 'vas honorabile' ('honourable vessel')   20

            St Medard & St Gildard are invoked to bring rain

        Vulg Ps 44:2: 'Lingua mea calamus scribae velociter scribentis' ('My tongue is the pen of a scribe writing swiftly')

                                                                                       Orion's   25

         The Aeneid refers frequently to 'Pious Aeneas'   fulminant: developing   firman: order issued
                                                                     suddenly; thundering   by Oriental sovereign
                                    tremulous   *F* terre
                              nychthemeron: period of 24 hours
                             G nicht: not
                                                                   U. was not protected by copyright in U.S. &   30
                                                                  pirated editions appeared
        Gr Ourania: 'Heavenly', muse of astronomy   *Du* dood: dead   *Gr* kopros: dung
        Supposedly Orion originally named Ouriôn because generated from *Gr* ouron, urine

        solution of gallic acid + solution of a ferrous salt = blue-black ink   firstly

                 lastly   Esau   *R* menshevik: Russian Socialist of moderate
                                                             party
        alchemist   35

                                                  corrosive sublimate: mercuric chloride

---

Above and following page: Key to *Finnegans Wake*. McHugh, Roland. *Annotations to* Finnegans Wake. ©1980 The Johns Hopkins University Press. Reprinted with permission of The Johns Hopkins University Press.

```
                    Adam & Eve's Church, D, beside r Liffey, on site of tavern of same name
G Erinnerung: remembrance
                    Commodus: Roman Emperor              Vico    Vico Road, Dalkey
                                                    L vicus: village
*'Sir Amory Tristram 1st earl of Howth changed his name to Saint Lawrence, b. in Brittany (North Armorica)'
              HCE
                    viola d'amore (musical instrument)                F pas encore: not yet
      *'viola in all moods and senses'      Naut Short Sea: Irish Sea      *'ricorsi storici of Vico'
The legendary Tristan (Malory's Sir Tristram) spent youth in Brittany, returned to Cornwall & thence to Ir. to fetch      5
Isolde for his uncle, King Mark                             North America
(Isthmus of Sutton [Gr isthmos: neck]       G wiederfechten: refight       Peninsular War (Napoleonic) (Howth
joins Howth to mainland)                                                   is a peninsula)
Topsawyer's Rock: formation on r Oconee       L exaggerare: to mound up
                                        *'themselse: another dublin 5000 inhabitants'
*'Dublin, Laurens Co, Georgia, founded by a Dubliner, Peter Sawyer, on r. Oconee.
Its motto: Doubling all the time'      It gorgo: whirlpool
*'flame of Christianity kindled by St Patrick'      *'bellowed: the response of the peatfire of faith to the windy words
                                    afar                          of the apostle'
G taufen: baptise    Matt 16:18: 'thou art Peter'          Moses, Moses (burning bush)                    10
      *'The venison purveyor Jacob got the blessing meant for Esau'
scad: trick     As a boy Parnell was called 'Butthead'
*'Parnell ousted Isaac Butt from leadership'
*Swift's Stella & Vanessa both had name Esther         two-one       Jonathan (Swift)
               F sosie: twin        U.76: Abraham's son Nathan in Mosenthal's Deborah
s Willie Brewed a Peck o' Malt      Jameson whiskey     Guinness brewery      *L roridus: dewy
*'Noah planted vine & was drunk'      C shen: god, spirit       *'At the rainbow's end are dew and
       G Regenbogen: rainbow       G ringsum: around                the colour red'
              (7 clauses; 7 rainbow colours)              Angl bloody end to the lie = no lie
                  (stuttering)        J kaminari: thunder                                             15
              Hin karak: thunder       Gr brontaô: to thunder       F tonnerre: thunder
It tuono: thunder        Sw aska: thunder                       I tórnach: thunder
         Port trovão: thunder    Old Rum tun: thunder       Da tordenen: the thunder
                Wall Street Crash           parr: young salmon      F père       retailed
                    Old Parr: Eng. centenarian accused of incontinence
early to rise                Christy's Minstrels

                              F chute: fall

'The Solid Man': W. J. Ashcroft, D music hall performer      (If Howth is head of a sleeping giant, his feet stick up in    20
                       Humpty Dumpty                          Phoenix Park)
          enquiring
                       (5 toes)                  Castleknock, W. of Phoenix Park
                   Turnpike in Chapelizod
               Orange & Green factions        Du rust: rest
Basque word for orange etymologised 'the fruit which was first eaten'

                                                                          *letter, 15/11/26, to HSW
```

And so on, since this represents but one sixth of the page on which it appears. Finally, Grafton points out that both Petrarch and Dante produced commentaries on their own poetry (28).

In addition to legitimate commentary in margins, notes, addenda, or separate volumes to non-fictional works as well as serious ancillary matter included in notational form in fiction and poetry, there exists a small but growing body of fictional and poetic work that emphasizes fictional documentation. Swift and Nabokov have been briefly discussed above. Some recent contemporary works also bear mention. First, R. M. Koster's novel *The Dissertation* (1975) is a fictitious study of one Léon Fuertes. The text covers 267 dense pages; the 100 elaborate and replete notes run an additional 168 pages, and they are the ostensible raison d'être for the work; it is after all entitled *The Dissertation*. Camilo Fuertes, its putative author, relegates the commentary to endnotes because unlike Zerby, who reasonably insists that notes belong at the bottom of the page so that they can be consulted as one rolls through the text, he holds that "[i]t is an abomination on one's reader to make him yo-yo down and up the page between text and notes. I have marshalled my Text in the van, my Notes in the rear" (Koster, xix). An even more elaborate, indeed bizarre, construct is Mark Dunn's *Ibid: A Life: A Novel in Footnotes* (2004). This work, which unfolds exclusively in a series of notes, is predicated on the destruction of the only extant copy of the text. The 261 pages of endnotes, however, have been saved, and these a publisher decides to offer to the public sans text. *Ibid* is the result. One might contrast this with Gottlieb Wilhelm Rabener's *Hinkmars von Repkow. Noten Ohne Text* (1743), which is a similar series of independent notes lacking even the excuse

Notes without an accompanying text (*Noten Ohne Text*, 1743).

that the text has been destroyed. A third example is an extremely long and detailed mystery entitled *The Meaning of Night: A Confession* (2006). The author, Michael Cox, creates an elaborate fictitious structure including a concluding two page bibliography of P. Rainsford Daunt's 16 published works, and this despite the fact that this character never existed. A meaningful percentage of the novel's 703 pages contain footnotes, as many as three per page (some of which offer factual information). A series of asterisks and daggers lead to definitions (laudanum: "A mixture of opium and alcohol..." followed by a long exegesis [435]); attributions; identifications; and comments. And then there is Marisha Pessl's much touted and elaborately titled novel *Special*

70 | BOOK: A NOVEL

Taupe accuses Sovrana Sostrata of rape

Silence, apprehension.

"I'll tell you what I think of Adam Snell's book. Adam Snell's book isn't just bad, it's *criminal*. I've read racist books and sexist books; but *Sovrana Sostrata* is a *rapist book*,[9] a violent, malicious offense against the female."

Gazza's face had suddenly taken on a deep cast of sisterly compassion. "You mean you feel raped by the book?"

"I feel violated, yes, violated. The book is like a weapon of violation. Of course, there's nothing overt. Snell's too cautious for that. He even makes it seem as though his heroine is sexually exploiting men. But lurking deep underneath is a radically phallocentric[10] Gestalt, the most irresponsible, heedless assertion of naked maleness I've ever been exposed to. I'm afraid there are no laws about this, so even if we found Snell we couldn't turn him in.[11] But I implore you all to visit justice upon him in the only way you can: Remand his file to the provost."

The footnotes are restless

A confused flurry of emotional conversation, replete with phrases like "rapist discourse," "deprivileging the female," "passive aggressive," and "there oughtta be a law," calmed again to silence as it became apparent that Sanford Eule had risen to speak. A slim, good-looking man with curly dark reddish hair and boyish looks and manners, he addressed his colleagues in a vaguely English accent and

---

[9] I must join Footnotes 6, 7 and 8 in questioning the propriety of remarks made by professors during this meeting. I have myself been a footnote for over two hundred years. I have loyally obeyed the conscience, and satisfied the whims, of humanists from the Augustan Age down through the twentieth century. But this is going too far. This sort of behavior jargonizes and ideologizes language to satisfy political interest and indulge personal neurosis, until language no longer makes sense. And if language loses its openness, its potential for impartiality, then culture will rot from within.

If this goes on much longer, we may have to take steps.

[10] OK, this is it. I'm mobilizing the gang. Footnotes may not be human, but they have a sense of justice nonetheless. "Phallocentric"? One of the most blatantly self-serving simplifications ever invented. It does no justice at all to the real history of male/female relationships. And it's also a gross flattery to the contemporary Western male, who lost his masculinity a long time ago.

But to my point. These ideologues cannot be allowed to continue their mad career. DOWN WITH TYRANNY! FOOTNOTES, UNITE! The world is about to see something it has never seen before, a revolution of the apparatus!

[11] Can you beat this outrage against common sense and decency? I know where I can find some more footnotes. If Eule's talk is as foul as this, we'll monkey-wrench him right enough.

Above and opposite: Marginalia and footnotes take over (Robert Grudin, *Book: A Novel*). From *Book: A Novel* by Robert Grudin, copyright ©1992 by Robert Grudin. Used by permission of Random House, Inc.

3. Commentary

THE PARLIAMENT IN TOUWHEE HALL | 7

with impeccable suavity. "Some years ago at a beach resort in southern France a friend of mine was sitting at a café when a strikingly beautiful figure, high-heeled, silk-stockinged, green-and-pink-print dress, great eyes, straw hat and parasol, appeared at his table and addressed him with the sort of look that with unspeakable clarity, even to a fresh-from-college kid like him, suggested its venerable professional intention.[12] His feelings, to put it mildly, were muddled. How does an American man, trained in chivalry, respond to an unabashed female demand for intimacy? But as he jock-eyed verbally with her in broken English and French, two intuitions bore down on him irresistibly: one, that this was not a courtesan but in fact a police agent; two, that this was not a woman at all but a female-impersonating man. These intuitions were substantiated by the waiter, who approached his table shortly after his exotic visitor had left.

Eule argu from a new-historicist perspectiv

The footnotes are rising!

"My experience in reading Adam Snell's *Sovrana Sostrata* is a direct parallel to this incident. At first sight, even at first reading, the novel looks pleasantly subversive.[13] After all, your truth-telling, free-living heroine, wrestling with academic and intellectual convention, has got to have destabilizing[14] implications, d[15]e[16]p[17]r[18]i[19]v[20] nsoiorybam, fk sajpqmeytsdhkld ptwnz spid.

What a gas!

[12]Friends, I don't like the sound of this. It's not real reasoning but rather argument via anecdote, conceived in paranoia and spiced up with adolescent sexuality, all in the name of self-aggrandizement and character assassination. When I give the word, we strike!

[13]You all ready? Good. At the count of three, now. ONE.

[14]TWO.

[15]THREE! We're going in!

[16]DOWN WITH JARGON!

[17]I AM MAD AS HELL, AND I'M NOT GOING TO TAKE IT ANYMORE.

[18]TAKE SOME OF YOUR OWN MEDICINE, YOU SUPEREROGATORY, SEMPITERNAL, HEAUTONTIMORUMENICAL SYCOPHANT!

[19]ARE WE DISRUPTIVE OR ARE WE?

[20]HEY I THINK WE'RE IN CONTROL. LET'S TAKE OVER THE WHOLE TEXT, AND RID IT FOREVER OF

Topics in Calamity Physics (2006). Here the attributions, see references, and comments are parenthetically intercalated into the text; some of them relate to reality, but others are fictitious:

After school, standing outside of Elton, I watched Péron making her way to the Faculty Parking Lot (see "Leaving Madrid, June 15, 1947," *Eva Duarte Péron*, East, 1963, p. 334) [415].

> ...
> I was a little afraid, but I made myself go after her. ("'Keep tightening the screws on those chippies,'" entreated Private Peeper Rush McFadds to his partner in *Chicago Overcoat* [Bulke, 1948].) [415].

There is no appended works-cited list to which one might refer if the need arose. The novel concludes with an examination. Another example is Robert Grudin's graphically complex *Book: A Novel*. The peculiarities take many forms. A long quotation on its own page may precede a chapter (13). Some pages contain brief marginal comments, (upside down) and footnotes, occasionally in blaring capitals; here, the self-referential footnotes assume a life of their own and attempt to take over the text (71). J. M. Coetzee's 2007 fictional construct, *Diary of a Bad Year*, presents two and then three simultaneous narratives on a horizontally divided page, one that resembles some of the graphically complex scholarly work created in the past. The secondary and tertiary texts are not glosses on the primary and more replete narrative, but rather ancillary accounts concerning the protagonist and a secondary character. The novel concludes with eight brief endnotes. This peculiar physical structure does allow the three distinct narrative voices to clamor for the reader's simultaneous attention, but it is also divisive and disconcerting, forcing one, in effect, to alternate among contiguous narrative streams. It is as if Faulkner had alternated the separate voices of *The Sound and the Fury* on a single page. These gimmicks are distracting and probably unnecessary, although Nabokovians would enjoy them.

4
Marginalia

> *The marginal notes, and not just because of the color*
> *of the ink, seemed to be written in blood.*
> — Gabriel García Márquez

The taxonomy of marginalia is bifurcate: In the first instance, an author or someone else such as an editor, commentator, or translator affixes a note to the margin of a text at the time of inscription of a manuscript or publication of an edition (as, for example, in *The Annotated Walden*) (or shortly thereafter in the case of medieval manuscripts) or in a subsequent edition (as in "The Rime of the Ancient Mariner"). In some unusual instances, Ben Jonson's *Sejanus*, for example (Slights, *Managing 32*), a first edition's notations are subsequently removed. These marginal adumbrations are similar in most ways to foot- or endnotes, although their precise proximity to the text allows for immediate visual connection, just one step removed from a textually intercalated parenthetical remark. They are, astonishingly, superior to hypertext links, since clicking away from the primary text is unnecessary, and in extreme cases, a secondary gloss on the original marginal notation could be included in an oversize margin, thus allowing for a secondary level of connection. (Naturally, additional levels of connectivity could only be effectively achieved in an electronic environment, although it should be noted that such ongoing interrelated pathways are often counterproductive in their complexity, and may lead a reader away from a text that is then difficult both intellectually and even physically to revisit).

The second possibility concerns hand-written marginal notations usually provided by readers for their own edification. Anna Kavan (1901–1968) was so distraught by her publisher's emendations in the first edition of *Ice* (her copy held by McFarlin Library, University of Tulsa), that she appended

SEIANVS.

Sab. I know not, for his death, how you might wrest it:
But, for his life, it did as much disdaine
Comparison, with that voluptuous, rash,
Giddy, and drunken *Macedon's*, as mine
Doth with my Bondmans. All the good, in him,
(His Valour, and his Fortune) he made his;
But he had other touches of late Romanes,
That more did speake him: [a] *Pompei's* dignity,
The innocence of *Cato*, *Cæsar's* spirit,
Wise *Brutus* temp'rance, and euery virtue,
which, parted vnto others, gaue them Name,
Flow'd mixt in him. He was the soule of goodnesse;
And all our praises of him are like streames
Drawne from a spring, that still rise full, and leaue
The part remaining greatest. Arr. I am sure
He was to great for vs,[b] and that they knew
Who did remooue him hence. Sab. When men grow fast
Honor'd, and lou'd, There is a trick in state
(which Iealous princes neuer faile to vse)
How to decline that grouth, with fayre pretext,
And honourable coulours of Emploiment,
Eyther by Embassy, the War, or such,
To shift them forth into another ayre,
Where they may purge, and lessen; [c] So was he:
And had his Secon'ds there, sent by *Tiberius*,
And his more subtile Damme, to discontent him;
To breede, and cherish mutinies; detract
His greatest Actions; giue audacious check
To his Commands; and worke to put him out
In open act of Treason. All which snares
When his wise cares preuented, [d] a fine poison
Was thought on, to mature their practises.
Cor. Here comes [e] *Seianus*. Sil. Now obserue the stoupes,
The bendings, and the falls. Arr. Most creeping base!

SEIANVS. SATRIVS. TERENTIVS. &c.

Sei. I note 'hem well, No more. Say you. Sat. My Lord,

cit. *Annal.l.*1.pag. 9.l.4.princip. et per tot. Suet. Tib. Dion. lib. 57. & 58. Plin. et Senec.

[a] *Vide, a-pud* Vell. Patercul, lips, 4°. pag. 30.32.35. 47. *istorum hominum caracteres*.
[b] *Vide* Tac lib. 2 *Annal.* pag. 28. & pag. 34. Dio. Rom. Hist. lib. 57. pag. 705. 706.
[c] Con. Tac. Ann. l. 2. p. 39. de occultis mandatis Pisoni, et postea pag. 42, 43 & 8. Oratio. Do. Celeris Est tibi Augustæ conscientia, est Cæsaris fauor, sed in occulto, &c Leg. Suet. Tib. cap. 52 Dio. p. 706
[d] vid. Tac. Annal. l. 2. pag. 46. & 47. lib. 3. p. 54. et Suet. Calig. cap. 1. & 2.
[e] De Seiano. v'd. Ta-

Above and opposite: Notes in early edition expunged in a later edition (Ben Jonson, *Sejanus*). Johnson, Ben. *Sejanus His Fall.* London, 1605. (B3r) RB 60659. Johnson, B. *Workes.* London, 1616. (2H2r). RB 600687. These items are reproduced by permission of the Huntington Library, San Marino, California.

Seianus. 363

The sonnes of Prince GERMANICVS: It shewes
A gallant cleerenesse in him, a streight minde,
That enuies not, in them, their fathers name.
  ARR. His name was, while he liu'd, aboue all enuie;
And being dead, without it. O, that man!
If there were seedes of the old vertue left,
They liu'd in him. SIL. He had the fruits, ARRVNTIVS,
More then the seedes: SABINVS, and my selfe
Had meanes to know him, within; and can report him.
We were his followers, (he would call vs friends.)
He was a man most like to vertue'; In all,
And euery action, neerer to the gods,
Then men, in nature; of a body' as faire
As was his mind; and no lesse reuerend
In face, then fame: He could so vse his state,
Temp'ring his greatnesse, with his grauitie,
As it auoyded all selfe-loue in him,
And spight in others. What his funeralls lack'd
In images, and pompe, they had supply'd
With honourable sorrow, souldiers sadnesse,
A kind of silent mourning, such, as men
(Who know no teares, but from their captiues) vse
To shew in so great losses. COR. I thought once,
Considering their formes, age, manner of deaths,
The neerenesse of the places, where they fell,
T'haue paralell'd him with great ALEXANDER:
For both were of best feature, of high race,
Yeer'd but to thirtie, and, in forraine lands,
By their owne people, alike made away.
  SAB. I know not, for his death, how you might wrest it:
But, for his life, it did as much disdaine
Comparison, with that voluptuous, rash,
Giddy, and drunken *Macedon's*, as mine
Doth with my bond-mans. All the good, in him,
(His valour, and his fortune) he made his;
But he had other touches of late *Romanes*,
That more did speake him: POMPEI's dignitie,
The innocence of CATO, CAESAR's spirit,
Wise BRVTVS temp'rance, and euery vertue,
Which, parted vnto others, gaue them name,
Flow'd mixt in him. He was the soule of goodnesse:
And all our praises of him are like streames
Drawne from a spring, that still rise full, and leaue
The part remayning greatest. ARR. I am sure
He was too great for vs, and that they knew

Hh 2   Who

countless hand-written, vitriolic marginal comments aimed at or correcting the text, which she wanted returned to its original pristine state. (It may seem unlikely to the uninitiated that a publisher would thoroughly alter the final copy of a manuscript submitted by a well-known author, but consider that Thomas Wolfe [1900–1938] presented his editor, Maxwell Perkins, with a milk crate containing 3,000 pages of text; it was Perkins who, with the author's approbation, divided this mess into Wolfe's three great novels. When Tolstoy [1828–1910] received the published version of his first story, he claimed that it was so altered that he did not recognize it!)

Marginalia[1] of any type serve precisely the same purposes that notes do: One can acknowledge, attribute, cite, refer, connect, correct, define, gloss, comment, clarify, explain, adumbrate, expatiate, enlarge, translate, or agree. In addition, especially in hand-written notations included by readers in their own or borrowed copies, one may find arguments against the text. These are all subsumable under three headings: simple glosses, definitions or explanations of words; citations or references to other works; and commentary of some kind.[2] All of these may be included in the original manuscript or publication or may be hand-written additions included subsequently by readers. Some people use a simplified system of marks, but these underlinings, asterisks, exclamation marks, abbreviations, and symbols may signify more to their inscribers than to subsequent readers. (Lawrence Lipking draws a major distinction between the commenting marginal note and the defining marginal gloss, but this hardly seems warranted or necessary. If it is valid here, then it must logically also have some importance in foot- or endnotes, and who would [and to what purpose] divide notes into these peculiar categories?) Finally, ongoing and replete marginalia may serve a secondary, unintended purpose: a reader could use the inscriptions as a running index similar to the headings and subheadings now featured in scholarly material, which certainly do make skimming, as opposed to perusing, a more efficient and profitable experience.

Marginalia's form and function, though, differ dramatically from that of other documentation methods. Formally, they are contiguous with their progenitors: The thought that produces the necessity for a citation or remark leads directly into the marginal notation. Functionally, they seduce with their immediate demand: Only a complete and unequivocal commitment to the text would allow a reader to skip over a marginal note, something that can easily be accomplished with a footnote, despite the superscript number's obtruding presence. Readers refer to endnotes during the course of their textual perusals only when absolutely necessary, abandoning them to a time after the chapter or book is completed, if they bother to consult them at all. Thus, from the documenting author's perspective, marginal notation is the preferred modality. The problem is that it entails a physically complex and therefore

192 THE COMMON WORLDS

(take the floor),
Inform, Codify,
Legalize, Authorize,
Refer (to a court).

world, always inclined to lapse into the *particular*, requires conscious and *active mobilization* if it is to hold together. Persons must be continually on the alert to avoid *splintering* and to preserve a collective character. *Representatives* must be "in close *liaison* with the workers"; *members* must "remain *in constant contact* with the *organizations*... and with their *policies*." They must "*come to terms* and *organize themselves*," launch *appeals*, debate democratically, pursue *discussions*, *publicize* their *policies*, inform, and, in order to be *heard*, *multiply explanations* as much as possible."

The democratic
republic (FIGURES)
Republic, State,
Democracy, Base,
Electorate, Institutions
(representative),
Parliament.

The civic world, which can develop only in the context of a State, finds its most perfected form in *republics* and in *democracies*, which ensure the *representation* of citizens united in *electoral bodies* (*electorate, electoral college, representative institutions, parliamentary democracy*). Thanks to such institutions, the *general will* can emanate from the *base*: "In the framework of these activities, union members know the pulse of the workers. They know what... *aspirations* come to light in the workplace. If the *chapter* has a tendency toward apathy, they can

Demonstration for a
just cause (TEST)
Assembly, Congress,
Council, Meeting,
Session, Movement,
Presence (manifest the
presence of), Dispute,
Recourse, Justice
(demand).

arouse it, spur *debates*, and so on. The *members* are truly at the *base* of the *union chapter*." Democracy is the most appropriate political form for the manifestation of the general will that constitutes the model test for the civic world. The peak moments in this world are thus moments of *unity*, *meeting*, and *membership* ("call a *meeting* of the *membership*") in which the reality of the collective person is confirmed by the physical presence of its members: *demonstrations*, movements, *assemblies*, councils, *sessions, congresses*. These gatherings are particularly favorable to the development of collective worth when they aim at *demanding justice* by taking *recourse* to the *law* to settle a *dispute* or, better yet, when they provide the opportunity for a *reconsideration* that appeals to the judgment of all against institutions and against *judges* accused of *monopolizing* the *law* and bending it in favor of the particular interests of certain parties.

The verdict of the vote
(JUDGMENT) Voting,
Election, Consultation,
Mobilization, Cause
(support a) Awareness
(achieving).

Judgment is the expression of the general will that may be manifested in the inner self of each person through the *achievement of awareness* ("it is within the company that workers begin to *become aware* that they have *common interests*"); this may be manifested by a *collective reflection* or in the form of a *mobilization* around

Above and page 76: Superfluous marginalia (Luc Boltanski and Laurent Thévenot, *On Justification*). Boltanski, Luc; *On Justification*. Princeton University Press. Reprinted by permission of Princeton University Press.

THE SIX WORLDS 193

a *cause*, or it may use democratic instruments: *voting, elections*, the *designation* of *representatives*.

The form taken by evidence is the *law* in which the expression of the general will is inscribed. Its reality is clear when it is embodied in texts that can be invoked and in *legal rules* that can be applied: "The new *delegates* . . . will find useful information here on the *legal rules* that are applicable in such circumstances."

The polity comes apart when it yields to the *particular*. Whatever *dilutes, splinters*, or *restrains* is unworthy: "What would the *chapter* be if it were limited to a *restricted* number of *members*?" Thus the domestic bonds of *corporatism* are constantly denounced because they *divide* workers: "*corporatist* demands that only contribute to *dividing* the workers still further into different *categories*." To put an end to this divided state, it is necessary to "break down the trade structure that has splintered the working class." Beings, when they are not strongly held together by bonds of *solidarity*, go astray and allow themselves to be led into *deviations*. They dissolve into subgroups, or, worse, into self-serving *individualism*: "*Democracy* cannot be improvised in this world shaped by *individualism*." People left to *themselves*, prey to their own appetite for *personal power, monopolize speech* and, "practiced in *influencing assemblies*," "make decisions along lines that have very little to do with the *interests* of *all* the others." *In the minority*, they form a *tight inner circle*: "There is a great risk that a hierarchy will be constituted among the *militants* and that a *tight inner circle* will be created, one that cannot really use the existing possibilities." They are finally *isolated* and *cut off* from the *base*, and this absence of grounding in the general will gives them an *arbitrary* character contrary to the rule (*irregularity*) that leads them toward *a fall* and *annulment* (qualities that characterize the greatest deficiency imaginable in the civic world): "salaried workers who have been *removed* from their union functions"; "*irregularities* that may lead to the *annulment* of the *elections*."

The legal text
(EVIDENCE) Law (the),
Rules (legal), Statutes.

Division (THE FALL)
Divided, Minority (in the), Particular,
Isolated, Cut off (from the electoral base),
Individualism (self-serving), Deviation,
Subgroup, Irregular,
Arbitrary, Annulled,
Removed.

The Market World

The market world must not be confused with a sphere of economic relations. We have tried to show, on the con-more expensive page (even in an electronic typesetting environment). It was eliminated long ago in favor of footnotes, which eventually also succumbed to financial exigency. Although some houses, presses, and journals still allow or even require footnotes, their demise is inevitable. And only the most pressing circumstances now allow an author (generally a famous one such as Derrida) to publish marginalia adorned material. An unusual exception is Lawrence Lipking's 1977 *Critical Inquiry* piece in which he discusses marginal annotation and offers asides in the broad margins. Occasionally, contemporary marginalia appear to be entirely superfluous: Luc Boltanski and Laurent Thévenot's *On Justification* contains eleven chapters, eight of which reflect normal page layout; three, however, are composed of narrow texts and wide margins that proffer indexical lists that seem to serve no necessary purpose. "The polity comes apart when it yields to the *particular*..." leads to

> *Division (THE FALL)*
> *Divided, Minority (in the), Particular,*
> *Isolated, Cut off (from the electoral base),*
> *Individualism (self-serving), Deviation,*
> *Subgroup, Irregular,*
> *Arbitrary, Annulled,*
> *Removed* [193].

The Derridean influence (marginal annotation, italics, capitalization, peculiar locutions) is annoying and lamentable. A final bizarre example can be found in the margins of a David Horowitz–Michael Bérubé dialogical exchange. Whenever one of the discussants mentions something that appears unclear to the editor, it is highlighted in a specific color (green, orange, blue); this leads to a similarly colored boxed comment in the margin ("Breaking Bread"). This is pragmatically unnecessary, but this type of graphic gimmickry certainly catches one's attention. There is, additionally, a secondary type of marginal notation, one that does not usually concern the reader. Included here are various marks created during the production of the book: point holes, fingerprints and other printing anomalies, proof corrections, proofreaders' and binders' marks, cancellations, and so on (*Marks,* passim).

Hand-written Marginalia

Although a comprehensive overview of written (rather than printed) annotation is well beyond the parameters of this study, a glancing look at a few examples will confirm that marginalia of any kind are a functional subset of documentation. Students as well as intellectually scrupulous readers underline, emphasize, star, notate, criticize, and comment on and in their own or others' texts. Galileo's (1564–1642) personal annotated copy of his *Dialogo di Galileo Galilei ...* (*Dialogue Concerning the Two Chief World Systems*) is the most prized possession in the extraordinary history of science collection at the University of Oklahoma. Just as modern and contemporary readers dis-

Galileo's hand-written annotation in the margin (Galileo, *Dialogo*, 1632). Image copyright History of Science Collections, University of Oklahoma Libraries.

respect the physical, relatively inexpensive, mass-produced book and deface it, so too did the contemporary reader of religious and secular works annotate or comment on the text in the wide margins of medieval and Renaissance manuscripts—some of which now exist in unique copies such as the *Book of Kells* or the *Lindesfarne Gospels* and are either priceless or worth many millions of dollars. Contemporary (medieval) owners as well as Renaissance, Enlightenment, and Victorian collectors, though respectful or obsessed with their manuscripts and books, did not hesitate to deface them with their names and comments, and this marginalia was (and is) often considered an enhancement, a desirable feature of a specific copy. Jennifer Howard, echoing H. J. Jackson, observes that there is a "modern taboo against marginalia," which derives from the early circulating library ("Scholarship" 16). Of course, most people know that it is unacceptable to deface another's property, e.g., volumes borrowed from a friend or a library, but Jackson generalizes this by insisting that though readers were encouraged to annotate during the Romantic period, this habit is now "almost universally condemned" among English speakers (*Romantic* 299). But in fact, today, only purists and bibliophiles object to scribbling in the margins of their own (inexpensive) volumes; this is even the case for textbooks that a student plans to sell at the conclusion of the course (although now some readers may input summaries of their studies directly into a computer and concomitantly make remarks on the content in the electronic "margins"). Shortly after writing this defense, I came across an undergraduate student whose book was extensively marked in five distinct colors; she explained that the color-coded underlining indicated specific things to her as she studied. At the same time, I received some annotated material from Elizabeth Buchanan, a colleague, who during her studies and career deliberately and repletely marked pages with underlining and brief or detailed annotations. In one case, a comment, "Discipline—Think of Story of O, Marquis D'Sade" [sic]) is superimposed on the text, perhaps on a paste-it note. And on a single page of an (admittedly bizarre) letter that Franz Kafka wrote to his fiancée, Felice Bauer, Buchanan has nine sometimes lengthy underlinings, three encircled or boxed words or phrases, one cross-reference, and eight separate comments (almost filling three of the four margins) including "K has no sexual desires." This is the kind of scrupulous and responsive reading that most people are unwilling or unable to accomplish. Some readers are inordinately proud of their marginal comments and blatantly defend their habit: "...I find it difficult to respect books as objects, and see no harm whatsoever in abusing them" (Schott 31). Early hand-written marginal notations are the forerunners of the printed footnote, and it should be recalled that the earliest footnotes began in the margins, circled down to the bottom of the page and then curled back up on the other side, seeking empty space wherever it tricks, it's a lawyer's letter. And in doing so never forget your big Nevertheless.

I somehow can no longer write of anything but what concerns us, us in the turmoil of the world, just us. Everything else is remote. Wrong! Wrong! But the lips are mumbling and my face lies in your lap.

The most beautiful of your letters (and that means a lot, for as a whole they are, almost in every line, the most beautiful thing that ever happened to me in my life) are those in which you agree with my "fear" and at the same time try to explain that I don't need to have it. For I too, even though I may sometimes look like a bribed defender of my "fear," probably agree with it deep down in myself, indeed it is part of me and perhaps the best part. And as it is my best, it is also perhaps this alone that you love. For what else worthy of love could be found in me? But this is worthy of love.

And when you once asked me how I could have called that Saturday "good" with that fear in my heart, it's not difficult to explain. Since I love you (and I do love you, you stupid one, as the sea loves a pebble in its depths, this is just how my love engulfs you—and may I in turn be the pebble with you, if Heaven permits), I love the whole world and this includes your left shoulder, no, it was first the right one, so I kiss it if I feel like it (and if you are nice enough to pull the blouse away from it) and this also includes your left shoulder and your face above me in the forest and my resting on your almost bare breast. And that's why you're right in saying that we were already one and I'm not afraid of it, rather it is my only happiness and my only pride and I don't confine it at all only to the forest.

But just between this day-world and that "half hour in bed" of which you once spoke contemptuously as "men's business," there lies for me an abyss which I cannot bridge, probably because I don't want to. That over there is a concern of the night, thoroughly and in every sense a concern of the night: this here is the world and I possess it and now I'm supposed to leap across

271

Reader's heavily annotated text. Author: Franz Kafka, *Basic Kafka;* annotator: Elizabeth Buchanan.

was available. (As noted above, the calligraphic descriptions and remarks that adorn both Chinese and Japanese paintings — smaller scrolls but also large landscapes and portraits — are an integral esthetic part of the artistic work.)

Early medieval annotation begins with the gloss, and the most extensive gloss is a word for word interlinear translation. Two wonderful examples of this are found in the *Lindisfarne Gospels* (ca. 725) (held by the British Library) and the *Book of Mac Regol* (ca. 775) (held by the Bodleian Library, Oxford University). Both of these manuscripts contain Old English equivalents neatly intercalated above the inscribed Latin words in the generous white space left by the scribe (*Book of Kells*, 155, 158). Evelyn Tribble points out that the medieval *Glossa Ordinaria*'s commentary was so complex, so replete, and so overdone that it represents everything negative concerning mere reliance on tradition and authority, the result of which are "abuses of Scholasticism" and "intellectual aridity"("Like" 230). The same valid accusations could be leveled at any (sacred) text that generates vast quantities of commentary, which in turn result in additional attributions and remarks, the Talmud or Torah for example, whose pages (discussed above) resemble the *Glossa's* in some respects, though the former are often far more complex. A typical *Glossa* manuscript page contains a text with interlinear notes in a smaller, less ornate hand running down the narrow center of the page. This column is surrounded by commentary in a variety of hands. (Graphic variations exist; e.g., another version presents two small, central columns surrounded by their respective marginal commentaries.) A synoptic description of Mary Dove's printed edition of the "Canticum Canticorum" ("Song of Songs") will give the reader some idea of what is included, and what led Tribble to her negative evaluation. The right hand page presents a box containing two or three and infrequently a few more lines of text thus:

**Osculetur me osculo oris sui quia meliora sunt
ubera tua uino** [83].

Below the line cited, the first five words (osculetur...) are repeated (in bold) and then glossed via a series of numbers:

I Synagoga, congregatio, quod et lapidum ... [83].

And so on. The foot of the page contains two series of notes: attributions and some remarks. The facing page presents an English translation of the text and commentary. The footnotes are not translated. This process continues until the commentary in the boxed text is completed; it then recommences with the next line. This small Biblical book thus fills a 455 page volume. It may appear to the casual reader that "synagogue" and "congregation of stones" have very little to do with "Let him kiss me with the kisses of his mouth," and he or she would be correct. As in much theological commentary, the allusions or interpretations are not necessarily logically connected. They follow a path designed by the annotator, one that furthers his interest regardless of relevancy. (Indeed, the entire *Glossa* and all related commentary on the Old Testament in terms of Christian theology makes very little sense, since the text came into being thousands of years before the advent of Christianity.)

Margination in the *Glossa* is representative of the medieval manuscript

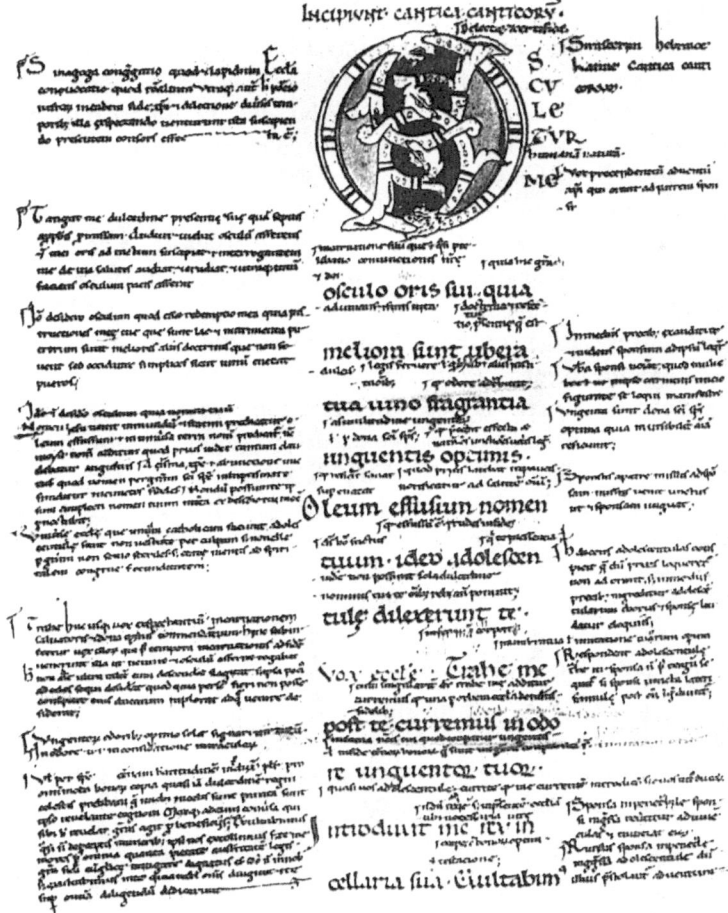

Glossa Ordinaria. Ms 74 fol. 84v. Used by permission of Laon, Bibliothèque Municipal.

generally: Replete commentary often swaddled or choked the text. Thus, an unmarginated manuscript might give one pause. The easy solution is to claim that the scribe (like some later Renaissance printers) took potential margination into account and left generous blank space available, but this may not be a valid deduction. Discussing the wide but unsullied margins found in some 13th century manuscripts, Alfred Pollard insists it is wrong: "...I do not think that 'to leave room for notes' can be considered one of the reasons for wide margins..." (68).

Although early translators who glossed manuscripts must remain anonymous, we do know that many well-known writers vigorously annotated their

Glossa Ordinaria, 1479–1481. ffIG4.S87R8.1479b. leaf VAULT 1st leaf (b4R). Used by permission of Bancroft Library, University of California, Berkeley.

reading material. The list is extensive and includes Kepler, Gabriel Harvey, Jonson, Milton, Walpole, Blake, Austen, Coleridge, Wordsworth, Hunt, Keats, Poe, Twain, Peirce, Valery, Olson, and Zukofsky. Indeed, it might be more useful to mention those who did not. Chris Matthew Sciabarra, the Ayn Rand scholar, refused to annotate because he wanted to be able to return to a text unhampered by earlier reflections. As he moved forward in his career, he found that he did not have the time to put his thoughts directly into a notebook or computer, so now he does make marginal notations (personal comments).

Scholars have scrupulously studied the marginalia of many of these people. For example, there are two substantial volumes devoted to the minor Renaissance figure Gabriel Harvey, whose extensive annotations in different scribal hands fill the white space in his many books. Another serial annotator worth noting is Voltaire, whose comments on Rousseau are revelatory. The latter's remark (in the *Contrat Social*), "Le raisonnement de ce Caligula revient á celui de Hobbes & de Grotius..." leads to Voltaire's marginal observation: "lauteur [sic] se trompe. hobbés [sic] reconnait le droit du plus fort non comme une justice mais comme un malheur attaché a la misérable nature humaine" (Havens 41). Indeed! Or Rousseau (in *Emile*) observes, "Je n'envisage pas comme une institution publique ces risibles établissemens qu'on *appelle collèges*." And Voltaire responds (in bastardized English): "those reverend bedlams colleges and scools" (Havens 77).

In two incisive studies,[3] H. J. Jackson examines written marginalia in order to discover how they relate to reading habits and social interactions. Casual though sophisticated British readers between 1790 and 1830 annotated because they were taught to do so, since it was a useful means of learning and recording (and from the many extant examples, it is apparent that they could barely control their annotating impulses). Well-known authors during this same period had similar motives, but their annotated books would also serve to enhance their reputations when passed along to coevals or future readers (*Romantic*, passim). Jackson cites a lovely example of a warning written in a library volume (which was contrary to the regulations): "A profane Book, unworthy of being read...." A second reader counters: "A very sensible book *well worth reading...*" (47). A bizarrely extreme instance of marginal notation can be found on the pages of *Facts and Observations relating to the Temple Church ...* (1811) (Jackson, *Romantic* 114–115). The annotator, Francis Hargrave, seems to have lost control and is apparently composing a book in the margins: Virtually every empty space on these pages is taken up with his comments, minuscule and indecipherable, though viewed through a high powered magnifier; they sometimes obscure the text and make it difficult to read. Even Hargrave must have found his scrawling annoying upon reexamination of the volume.

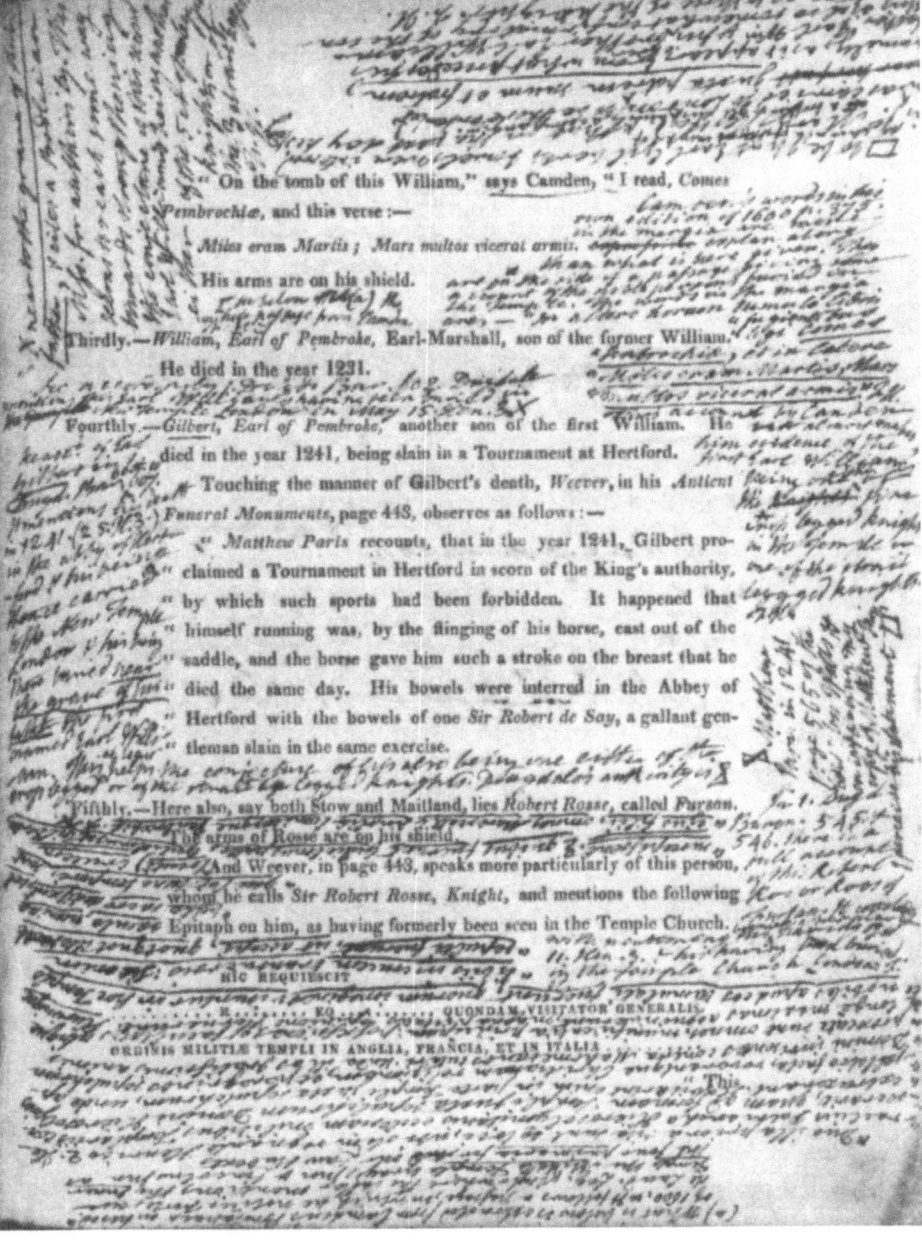

Above and page 86: Francis Hargrave's extreme marginal notation in *Facts and Observations relating to the Temple Church ...* (1811). 577.K.21 (6). Used by permission of the British Library.

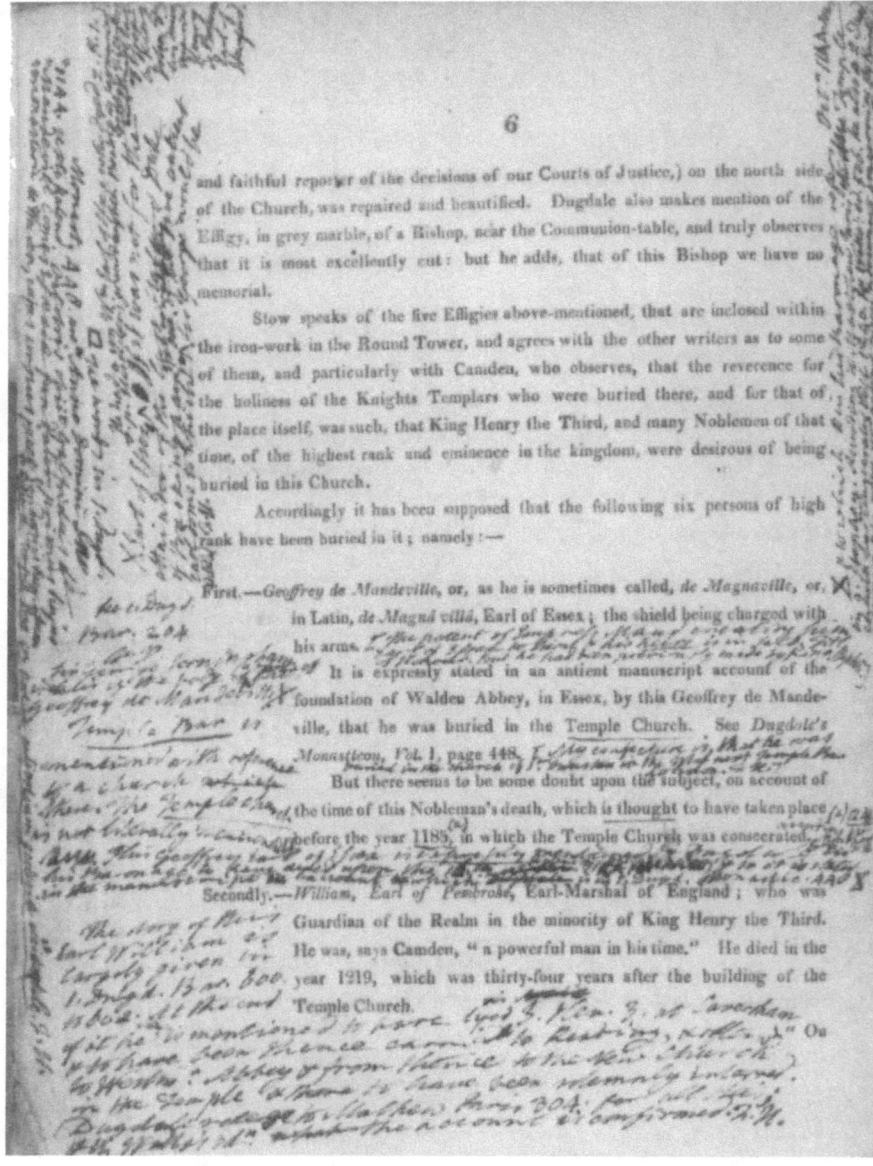

For those authors whose earliest thoughts on their creations appear in the margins of works they have read, the recovery of their annotations may be invaluable to scholars interested in etiology, development, and alternative possibilities. This is especially the case with Melville's (1819–1891) *Moby-Dick*, since the author was an inveterate annotator. Lamentably, many of his per-

MELVILLE'S MILTON

> BOOK VI. 193
>
> At first, that angel should with angel war,
> And in fierce hosting meet, who wont to meet
> So oft in festivals of joy and love
> Unanimous, as sons of one great Sire, 95
> Hymning th' eternal Father; but the shout
> Of battle now began, and rushing sound
> Of onset ended soon each milder thought.
> High in the midst exalted as a God
> Th' apostate in his sun-bright chariot sat, 100
> Idol of Majesty divine, enclos'd
> With flaming cherubim and golden shields:
> Then lighted from his gorgeous throne, for now
> Twixt host and host but narrow space was left,
> ╳ A <u>dreadful interval</u>, and front to front 105
> Presented stood in terrible array
> Of hideous length: before the cloudy van,
> On the rough edge of battle ere it join'd,
> <u>Satan, with vast and haughty strides advanc'd,</u>
> <u>Came towering, arm'd in adamant and gold</u>: 110
> Abdiel that sight endur'd not, where he stood
> Among the mightiest, bent on highest deeds,
> And thus his own undaunted heart explores.
>   O heaven! that such resemblance of the Highest
> Should yet remain, where faith and realty 115
> Remain not; wherefore should not strength and
>   might
> There fail where virtue fails, or weakest prove
>
>   93 *hosting*] Johnson has cited this unusual word from Spenser on
>   Ireland. 'Leading of their own followers to the general *hostinge.*'
>   105 *dreadful interval*] 'a needful counterview.' z. 231. *Bentl. MS.*
>   VOL. I.   25
>
> ╳ " The deadly space between "
>   Campbell.

Above and page 88: Melville's annotations in his copy of *The Poetical Works of John Milton.* Rare Books Division. Used by permission of the Department of Rare Books and Special Collections. Princeton University Library

sonal books are lost and the annotations in some extant seminal volumes were erased. It was only with the most painstaking forensic work that these remarks have been partially recovered. One can view these marginal reconstructions at <www.boisestate.edu/melville> along with the current editor's explanatory annotations (Howard, "Call Me"). Melville was fairly consistent in his meth-

> Then lighted from his gorgeous
> Twixt host and host but narrow
> A dreadful interval, and front to
> Presented stood in terrible array
> Of hideous length: before the cl
> On the rough edge of battle ere
> Satan, with vast and haughty st
> Came towering, arm'd in adaman
> Abdiel that sight endur'd not, w
> Among the mightiest, bent on hi
>
> 93 *hosting*] Johnson has cited this unusual word
> Ireland. 'Leading of their own followers to the ger
> 105 *dreadful interval*] 'a needful counterview.' x.
> VOL. I.   25
>
> ⤫ " The deadly space between "
>   Campbell.

ods, and these are nicely illustrated in his copy of *The Poetical Works of John Milton*, where on page after page he indicates to himself, in a variety of marginal ways, that something is of especial importance For example, page 158 in Robin Grey's study shows underlining, single, double, and enclosing marginal lineation, a cross, and an erased annotation that begins "This is one of the many profound atheistical hits of Milton [reconstructed]." Crosses may lead to comments, and Melville additionally utilizes checks, quadruple lineation, and question marks.

A fine example of the marginal emendation run amok can be found in Henry James's alterations on the last page (208) of the published London edition of *The American* (held by the Harvard University libraries). James has partially or fully crossed out 16 of the 19 lines and rewritten the text for the definitive New York edition in the margins and at the foot of the page. His scrawling alterations cover virtually all of the generous white space and must be inserted in at least three different locations in the original text. Words are blotted out or struck in the new version, and as he approaches the bottom of the page, the lettering diminishes in size, because he realizes that he will run out of room (*Marks* 44). What James has done here is very different from the typical reader's annotations. In the latter case, a person scribbles in the margin in order to alert him- or herself to an important point or to argue with the text. Only the originator must be able to decipher the remarks. In James's case, he is writing for himself (in order to improve the novel), but he is also communicating with the typesetter, who must be able to fully understand what he has noted, which, though not written in an incomprehensible script such as *literaria inintelligibilis*, does nevertheless

4. Marginalia

MELVILLE'S MILTON

Your fear itself of death removes the fear.
Why then was this forbid? Why but to awe,
Why but to keep ye low and ignorant,
<u>His worshippers</u>; he knows that in the day

    ANNOTATION: [erased] This is one of the many profound atheistical
hits of Milton. A greater than Lucretius, since he always teaches under a
masque, and makes the Devil himself a Teacher & Messiah.

§

[Satan to Eve:]
The gods are first, and that advantage use   718
On our belief, that all from them proceeds;

§

                        But if death   760
Bind us with after-bands, what profits then
Our inward freedom? in the day we eat
Of this fair fruit, our doom is, we shall die.

§

Superior; <u>for inferior who is free?</u>   825

§

[Eve:]
Lest thou not tasting, different degree
Disjoin us, and I then too late renounce
Deity for thee, when fate will not permit.   885
    Thus Eve with countenance blithe her story told;
But in her cheek distemper flushing glow'd.

§

    O fairest of creation, last and best
Of all God's works, creature in whom excell'd
Whatever can to sight or thought be form'd,
Holy, divine, good, amiable, or sweet!
How art thou lost! how on a sudden lost,   900
Defac'd, deflower'd, and now to death devote!
Rather how hast thou yielded to transgress
The strict forbiddance, how to violate
The sacred fruit forbidd'n! some cursed fraud
Of enemy hath beguil'd thee, yet unknown,   905
And me with thee hath ruin'd, for with thee
Certain my resolution is to die:
How can I live without thee! how forego

THE POETICAL WORKS OF JOHN MILTON

Another example of Melville's annotations (retypeset in Robin Grey's study *Melville and Milton*). Used by permission of Duquesne University Press.

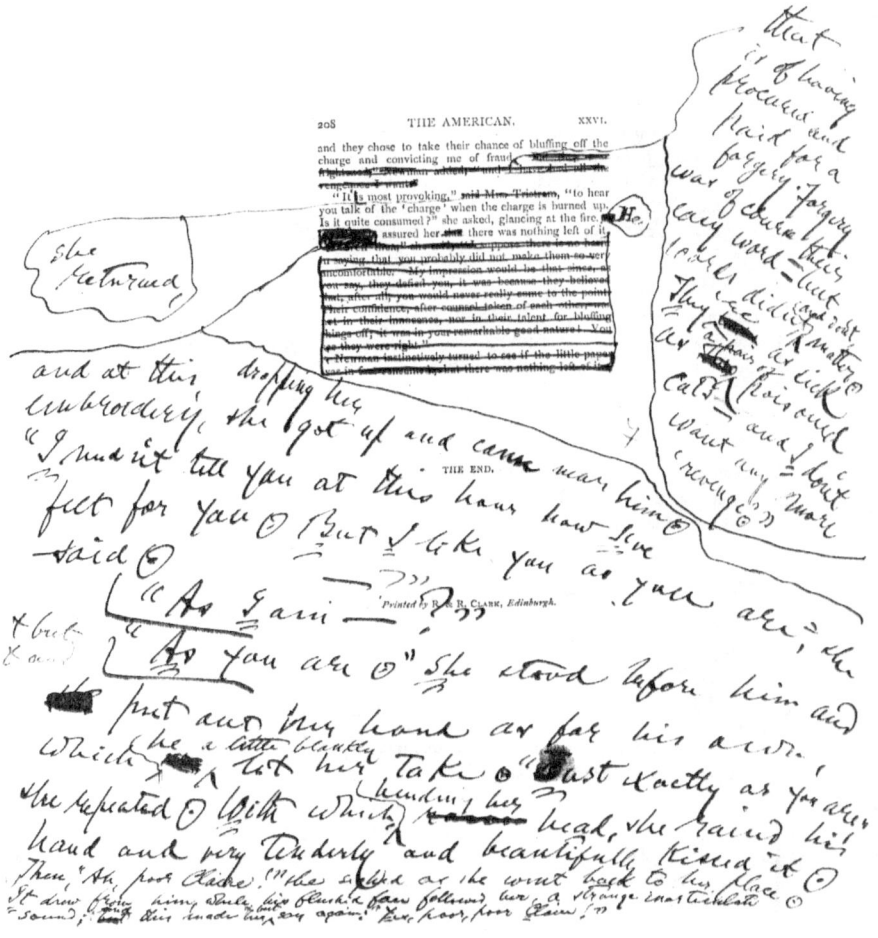

Henry James's marginal emendations of *The American* for the definitive New York edition. Ms Am 1237. Used by permission of the Houghton Library, Harvard University.

require some effort to decipher, and which when misinterpreted will result in inaccuracies in the new galleys or proofs. (One is reminded both of Tennyson rewriting his poems at the galley stage at the typesetter's table or of the *Ulysses* manuscript with which the Belgian typesetter had to struggle; that is why the first edition of Joyce's novel was so replete with errors.)

Ezra Pound (1885–1972) scrupulously perused and annotated a working recension of *The Waste Land*, improving T. S. Eliot's (1888–1965) first circulating version. His marginal annotations tell an astonishing story: Although Pound could be linguistically convoluted, arcane, and at times frustratingly incomprehensible in his own poetry ("The Cantos," for example), he was able to see through much (though not all) of the arcana that Eliot originally poured out and excise, alter, and emend so that the final version is considered the single most important and influential poem of the twentieth century in any language. Eliot recognized Pound's contribution in his dedication: "For Ezra Pound: Il miglior fabbro" ("the better creator"). Sometimes Pound excises almost an entire page, the third in "Death by Water" in the original recension, for example, or he may leave a page untouched; he may transpose a paragraph, add or delete a word, or make an acerbic remark: "make up/yr. mind/ you Tiresias/if you know/know damn well/or/else you/dont" (Eliot, *Waste Land: Facsimile* 47). Pages 10 (original) and 11 (transcription, with Pound in red) in the facsimile, the first page of what came to be called "A Game of Chess," shows Pound at his most complex: lineation, transpositions, strikes, brackets, snake trails, directions, dates, boxings, and comments in English, French, and his own bizarre locutions ("tum-pum," "penty") result in a manuscript that looks as if a crazed and messy chicken had pranced across its lines. As if this were not enough, the transcription facing the original manuscript also contains Vivien Eliot's markings (in black): lineation, comments, and parenthetical numbers that lead to notes at the end of the manuscript. This original recension does not contain Eliot's later notes to *The Waste Land*. More replete and complex examples of documentation exist (and have been noted above), but this nevertheless is marginal documentation with a vengeance. Pound's emendations can be examined in the facsimile copy of the annotated manuscript, published in 1971, almost 50 years after the original first appeared.

Richard Ellmann, the Joyce scholar, heavily annotated his copy of *Ulysses* (held by McFarlin Library, University of Tulsa). In some cases, all four margins are covered with glosses (for words such as *jalap* or *oxy*); long comments (Joyce's "cracked looking glass of a servant" leads to Ellmann quoting Wilde at the foot of the page, or Ellmann summarizes walkers' routes listing various physical locations); and interpretations in a small, tight hand. These are supplemented by sometimes extensive underlining, lineation, boxing, and question marks. Variations in script and ink indicate that the annotations were made at different times and may represent two separate and complete readings. All of this serves two purposes: The annotations are immediate and spontaneous reactions to scrupulously careful readings of the novel as well as helpmates to full comprehension; and they also act as aids for Ellmann's scholarly work on Joyce, which ultimately resulted in many monographic studies on the author and his circle. Thus, these marginal notations were of a personal, private nature, intended primarily if not exclusively for Ellmann rather than for an editor, reader, or colleague. Because of the complexity, such notations are not unusual for Joyce's readers. Hugh Kenner remarks that

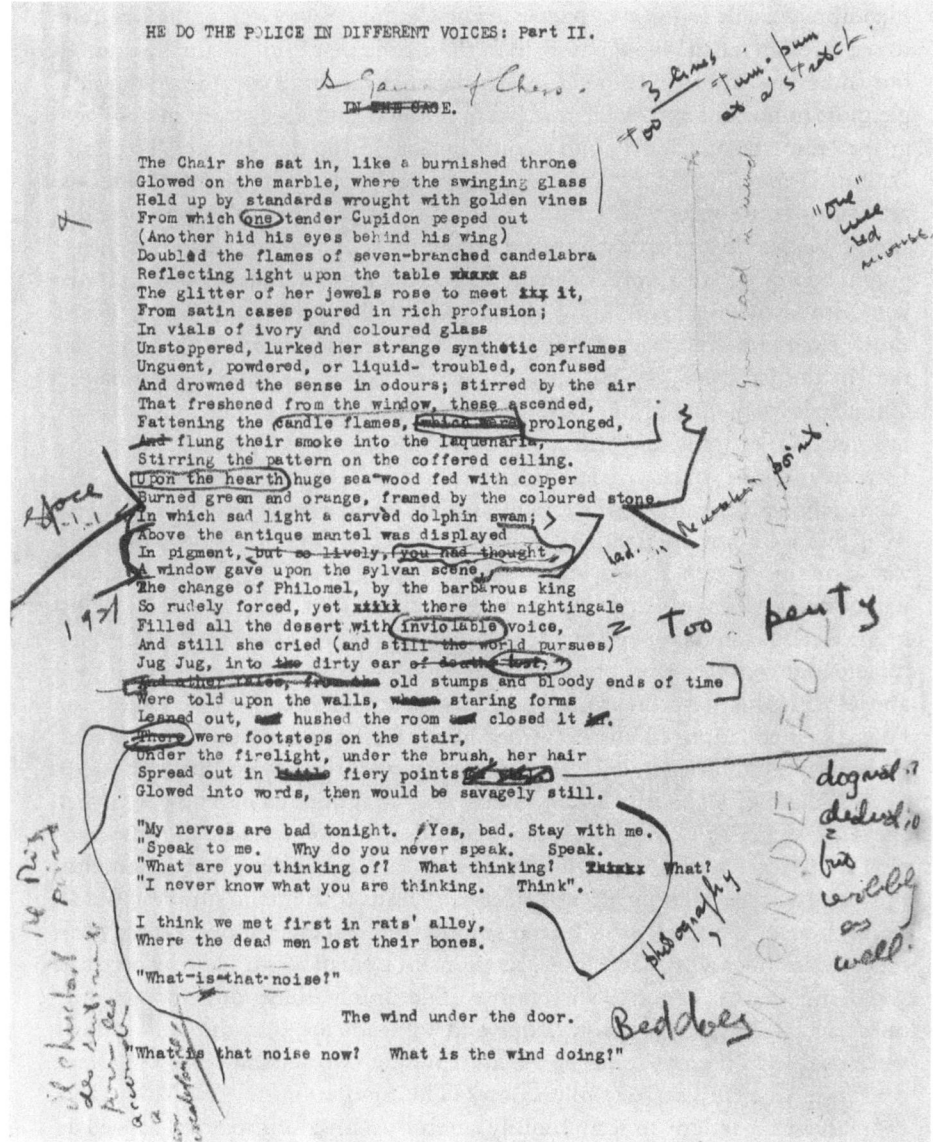

Above and opposite: T.S. Eliot, *The Waste Land*, with Ezra Pound's and Vivien Eliot's additions. *The Waste Land Facsimile* by T.S. Eliot, ed. Valerie Eliot. Used by permission of Faber and Faber Ltd., publishers.

4. Marginalia

HE DO THE POLICE IN DIFFERENT VOICES: Part II.

A Game of Chess.
~~IN THE CAGE.~~ (1)   3 lines
                                         Too tum-pum
                                         at a stretch

```
            The Chair she sat in, like a burnished throne
            Glowed on the marble, where the swinging glass
            Held up by standards wrought with golden vines
    a       From which one tender Cupidon peeped out (2)        "one"
            (Another hid his eyes behind his wing)               wee
 5          Doubled the flames of seven-branched candelabra      red
            Reflecting light upon the table where as             mouse (3)
            The glitter of her jewels rose to meet it, it,
            From satin cases poured in rich profusion;
            In vials of ivory and coloured glass
10          Unstoppered, lurked her strange synthetic perfumes
            Unguent, powdered, or liquid—troubled, confused
            And drowned the sense in odours; stirred by the air
            That freshened from the window, these ascended,
            Fattening the candle flames, which were prolonged,
15          And flung their smoke into the laquenaria,
            Stirring the pattern on the coffered ceiling.
            Upon the hearth huge sea-wood fed with copper
   Space    Burned green and orange, framed by the coloured stone,
            In which sad light a carved dolphin swam;
20          Above the antique mantel was displayed
            In pigment, but so lively, you had thought           had is   the weakest point
            A window gave upon the sylvan scene,                          here
   1921     The change of Philomel, by the barbarous king
            So rudely forced, yet still there the nightingale
25          Filled all the desert with inviolable voice,     too penty (4)
            And still she cried (and still the world pursues)
            Jug Jug, into the dirty ear of death; lust;
            And other tales, from the old stumps and bloody ends of time
            Were told upon the walls, where staring forms
30          Leaned out, and hushed the room and closed it in.
            There were footsteps on the stair,
            Under the firelight, under the brush, her hair
            Spread out in little fiery points of will,
            Glowed into words, then would be savagely still.             dogmatic
35                                                                       deduction
    Re this "My nerves are bad tonight. Yes, bad. Stay with me.           but
    point   "Speak to me. Why do you never speak. Speak.                  wobbly
            "What are you thinking of? What thinking? Think What?         as
            "I never know what you are thinking. Think".                  well

                                          photography (5)
            I think we met first in rats' alley,         ?
40          Where the dead men lost their bones.

            "What-is-that-noise?"
```

Il cherchait   The wind under the door. Beddoes (6)
des sentiments
pour les   "What is that noise now? What is the wind doing?"
accommoder
a
son
vocabulaire (7)

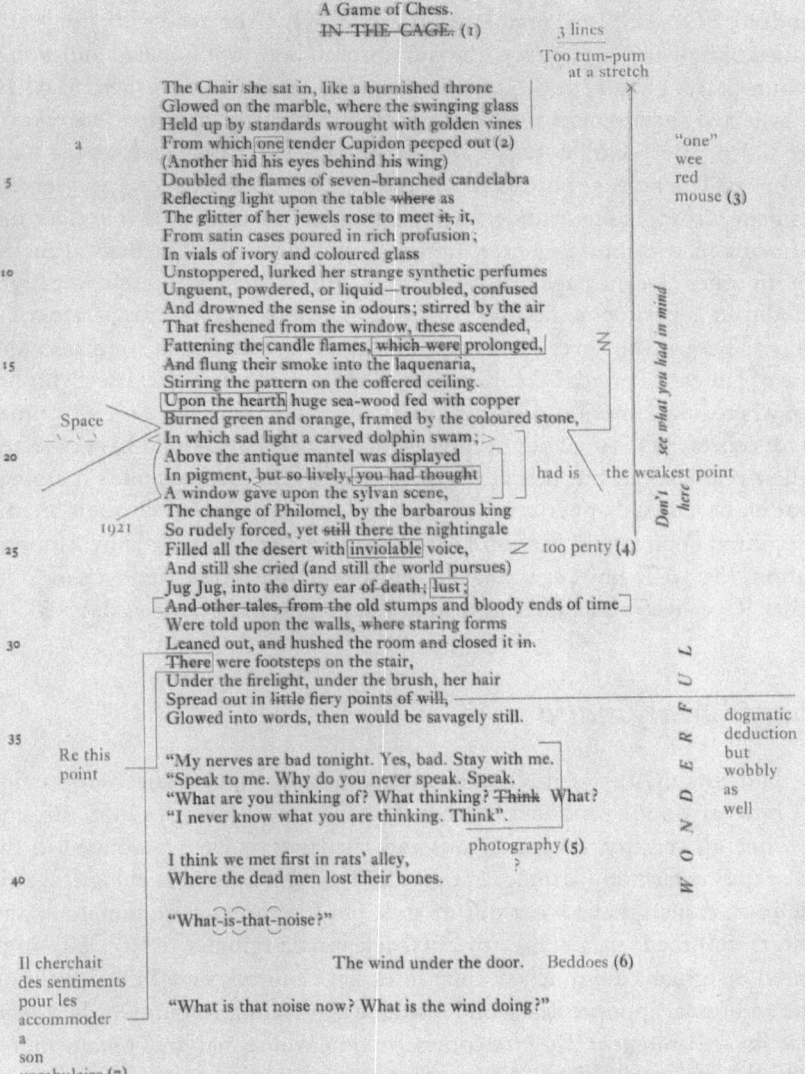

Typescript on three leaves of this section, with Eliot's additions, and Vivien Eliot's comments, in pencil.
Pound's criticism is in pencil and in ink. Line 16: laquenaria] laquearia.

[11]

[t]he Hanley Word-Index to *Ulysses* simply carries to an extreme of thoroughness the sort of marginal cross-references every student of the book pencils on page after page of his copy [32].

Ayn Rand, author of *The Fountainhead* and *Atlas Shrugged,* and the founder of Objectivism, annotated much of what she read with long and detailed marginal commentary. She was unforgivingly opinionated and would of course strongly affirm or attack depending on the text. Robert Mayhew has collected these remarks, and a typical example is revelatory: The text on page 123 of Barry Goldwater's *Conscience of a Conservative* ends at the halfway mark. The bottom portion of the page is covered with a long and fervent comment including many underlined words. This annotation is very clear and confined and with one tiny exception is unencumbered by additional markings. In other cases, a page may be covered with single and double lineation, underlining, question marks and exclamation points, and many separate comments. There is, however, a major difference between Rand's remarks and those of James or Pound: Like Ellmann's, Rand's were meant exclusively for her eyes, whereas in James's and Pound's cases the annotations were meant primarily for others'. (This does not necessarily mean that Rand would have objected to their publication, but it is at least a possibility. Sometimes one's marginalia are embarrassingly puerile or foolish, and, naturally, one often alters an initial opinion upon later reflection.) (See Baron for a series of essays by Anthony Grafton, Evelyn Tribble, et al. that accompany an illustrated catalogue of "The Reader Revealed," an exhibition held at the Folger Shakespeare Library.)

Printed Marginalia

Lamentably, the attitude and methodology of the *Glossa* were carried over into early book production, from the advent of printing in 1455 through the sixteenth century. Both religious and secular texts were annotated in the most extreme fashion (Tribble, *Margins* 230). Eventually, this eulogistic attitude toward marginalia went out of style, and authors, commentators, and printers colluded, in a sense, to cut back on marginalia (236). Although printed marginalia are touched upon in earlier chapters, here I must mention some additional apposite examples. A simple application is found in *An Admonition to the Parliament* (1572), a concise volume whose margins contain abbreviated Biblical attributions. A parenthetical alphabetic letter within the text ("y") leads to the correct location in the margin, thus:

y
I. Tim.3.8 [Hill 330].

Above and on page 96. Benjamin Pullen's hand-written copy of Richard Hooker's printed *Of the Lawes of Ecclesiasticall Politie* (1597). MS. Add. C.165, fol. 24r. Used by permission of the Bodleian Library, University of Oxford.

Monarchie. Pag. 3.

Where, he found him self courteously and very worshipfully enterteined. And at that tyme of his abode there, and after that, at sundry other tymes, of his Resort, thither, and to their Ships, he proceded so with them, according to his Intent: and pleasured them, so much according to their desire: That he finding them, quick of apprehension, and likely to remaine * Thankfull, for his pithy instructing of them: And they, finding him (aboue their expectation) skilfull: And (more then could be wished for) Carefully, for their well doing, in this their commendable and honorable Attempt: both the one and the other, became very sorry of their so late acquaintance and conference, for these their waighty affaires furdering: And greatly misliked their want of tyme, sufficient for the *Complement and principall pointes of the Perfect Art of Nauigation* learning at his hands. Such pointes, (I meane), as needed either great knowledge in the *Sciences Mathematicall*, and *Arts Mechanicall*: or expert Skill, of many *Causes and effects Naturall*; Such points (I say) to their affaires, and the *Perfect Art of Nauigation*, incident; he very aptly could, & right willingly wold haue dealt with them in: Yf that pinch of tyme, wold haue so permitted. For, it is very euident, by his description of the *Perfect Art of Nauigation* (in his foresayd *Mathematicall Praface*, declared) and also, common reason, and dayly experience, will confirme the same: that, not onely, such skill and furniture, as both here is rehearsed, and in that Praface is specified: But, other also, is most nedefull for him to be fraught withall, that shall be allowed for an exact *Hydrographer*, *Pylot-Maior*, *Arche-Pylot*, or *Grand-Pylot-Generall* of such an Incomparable *Ilandish Monarchy*, as, this BRYTISH IMPIRE hath bene: Yea, as it, yet, is: or, rather, as it may, & (of right) ought to be: As I haue bene informed by him, who can reasonably declare how:

* As (besides many other thinges) this letter, may seeme to be a sufficient witnes.

To the worshipfull and our approoued good freend M. Dee, giue these with speed.

This 26. of Iune. 1576. I ariued in Shotland in the Bay of Saint Tronions in the Latitude of 59 degrees, 46 Minutes.

[with M. Hall...] Your louing frend to vse and commaund Martin Probisher, Toures to commaund Ghristopher Hall.

The Complement of the perfect Art of Nauigation.

THE BRYTISH MONARCHY.

WHom, also, I haue heard, often and most hartily Wish, That all manner of persons passing or frequenting any our Seas, appropriate: and many wayes, next enuironing *England*, *Ireland*, and *Scotland*, might be, in conuenient & honorable sort (at all tymes,) at the Commandement and Order (by Beck or Check) of A PETY-NAVY-ROYALL, of Three score Tall Ships, (or more:) but in no case, fewer: and they, to be very well appoynted,

A.ij.

A very Commendable Wish of a faythfull Subiect.

A PETTY-NAVY-ROYAL

Extremely complex layout (John Dee, *General and Rare Memorials*, 1577). Dee, John. *General and Rare Memorials. London,* 1577. (p. 3) RB 82497. Reproduced by permission of The Huntington Library, San Marino, California

Hill also includes a reproduction of page 29 of Hooker's *Lawes of Ecclesiasticall Politie* (1597), whose text contains superscript letters that lead to three long marginal remarks. Two of them are so extensive that the typesetter was forced to partially insert them into the text. Because they are in a reduced italic, they are easily differentiated from the body, but their obtrusive (annoying) quality makes them very difficult to ignore (335). John Dee's *General*

The look with which they look'd on me
Had never pass'd away.

But the curse liveth for him in the eye of the dead men.

An orphan's curse would drag to hell
A spirit from on high;
But oh! more horrible than that
Is the curse in a dead man's eye!
Seven days, seven nights, I saw that curse,
And yet I could not die.

The moving Moon went up the sky,
And nowhere did abide;
Softly she was going up,
And a star or two beside—

In his loneliness and fixedness he yearneth towards the journeying Moon, and the stars that still sojourn, yet still move onward; and everywhere the blue sky belongs to them, and is their appointed rest and their native country and their own natural homes, which they enter unannounced, as lords that are certainly expected, and yet there is a silent joy at their arrival.

Her beams bemock'd the sultry main,
Like April hoar-frost spread;
But where the ship's huge shadow lay,
The charmèd water burnt alway
A still and awful red.

Beyond the shadow of the ship,
I watch'd the water-snakes:
They moved in tracks of shining white
And when they rear'd, the elfish light
Fell off in hoary flakes.

By the light of the Moon he beholdeth God's creatures of the great calm.

Within the shadow of the ship
I watch'd their rich attire:
Blue, glossy green, and velvet black,
They coil'd and swam; and every track
Was a flash of golden fire.

O happy living things! no tongue
Their beauty might declare:
A spring of love gush'd from my heart,
And I bless'd them unaware:

Their beauty and their happiness.

Curling marginalia (Samuel Taylor Coleridge, "The Rime of the Ancient Mariner").

and Rare Memorials (1577) presents instances of extremely complex layout. The primary text on page three is preceded by a secondary text (in a reduced font), which in turn is inscribed with an inserted box containing four separated notations. The right margin is used for a series of printed remarks, most of which are superfluous, since they merely repeat the text, thus serving as a running index or guide rather than a supplement. Both margins of the Huntington Library copy contain hand-written remarks (Slights, "Cosmopolitics" 212). Tribble reprints an elaborate example, the last I note from this early period. John Ogilby's *Virgil* (1654) commences with the "Bucolicks" (*Mar-*

The Rime of the Ancient Mariner from Coleridge's *Poetical Works*, 1834

It ate the food it ne'er had eat,**27**
And round and round it flew.
The ice did split with a thunder-fit;**28**
70 The helmsman steered us through!

And lo! the Albatross proveth a bird of good omen, and followeth the ship as it returned northward through fog and floating ice.

And a good south wind sprung up behind;**29**
The Albatross did follow,
And every day, for food or play,
Came to the mariner's hollo!**30**

In mist or cloud, on mast or shroud,**31**
It perched for vespers nine;**32**
Whiles all the night, through fog-smoke white,
Glimmered the white Moon-shine."

The ancient Mariner inhospitably killeth the pious bird of good omen.

"God save thee, ancient Mariner!
From the fiends, that plague thee
80   thus!—
Why look'st thou so?"**33**—With my crossbow**34**
I shot the ALBATROSS.**35**

an omission that intensifies the incident's role as symbolic of the ultimate crime, the crime of murder. Apparently the shooting was a premeditated, wanton act of cruelty. In an earlier (1800) printing of *Lyrical Ballads*, the "Argument" at the head of the poem speaks of "how the Ancient Mariner cruelly and in contempt of the laws of hospitality killed a Seabird . . ." The cruelty is heightened by the friendly behavior of the "pious bird," its apparent influence' in splitting the ice and bringing the

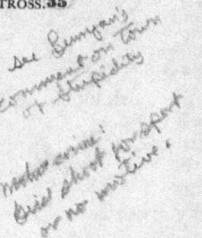

Text, notes, and printed, written, and illustrative marginalia (Coleridge, "Ancient Mariner"). Published by Bramhall House

gins, fig. 1). As is so typical of the period, there are some decorations, titles, an epigraph, a very short text of seven lines and an extraordinarily long and detailed set of marginal annotations, numbered 1–5 and a–b in Roman and italic and English, Latin, and Greek! It is not at all surprising that eventually those responsible for book production decided to cut back on annotation. One might also imagine that readers occasionally were satiated with the overwhelming (and sometimes annoying) scholarly apparatus (which in some cases may have been inserted merely to forward an ideological position held by the annotator who used the text as an excuse for his rambling remarks).

4. Marginalia

Lipking points out that Coleridge (1772–1834) was so hurt by the criticism that the first publication of "The Rime of the Ancient Mariner" engendered that he created a series of annotations to explain what his original readers found unclear or connect what they found dissociated (614). Subsequent publications of this famous poem contain these marginal comments, many of which are succinct notations (three or four words or a short sentence), but a few run on to such a degree that in some versions they curl around and continue under the stanza. In the 1965 *Annotated Ancient Mariner,* Gustave Doré's exquisite prints are included in the opposite margin (these are miniaturized versions of the much fuller images collected at the back of the volume); additionally, superscript, boldface numbers lead below or to the facing page where the editor, Martin Gardner, offers additional glosses and explanations. And in the particular University of Vermont copy that I examined, a reader has helped him- or herself and future borrowers by numbering, starring, underlining, and annotating ("See Bunyan's comment on town of stupidity" [Gardner 51]). Coleridge's annotations are very different from the succinct glosses that are sometimes printed in student copies of the classics, especially Latin, Greek, Middle English, and other linguistically challenging texts. These are inserted by contemporary editors in order to facilitate the study of the works; they are not an integral part of the texts, and can be removed, restructured, replaced, or resettled in future editions. Coleridge's explanations are now an integral part of the "Mariner" and are ignored at the reader's peril; in reality, they are very difficult to ignore, since they obtrude physically as one moves down the short trimeter and tetrameter lines. Lipking insists that "[t]he activity of the reader's eye, skipping back and forth between the margin and the text, now performs the work once left to the imagination" (615). Despite the incisive quality of this observation, it may not be entirely true. The text is not as complex as the poem's original critics believed. The notes may clarify, enhance, and assure, but the text still works its wonders and the imagination can still create a powerful mirror image despite the intrusive if helpful apparatus. Poetry is often by its very nature abstruse and some poets — Mallarmé, Pound, Thomas, Montale, Ungaretti — are purposely arcane, forcing the reader to work extremely hard to ferret out a meaningful gestalt. Even Pope could be referentially incomprehensible. Thus, it is something of a surprise that this ostensibly simple narrative account caused such a problem for many of its early sophisticated readers. The proof that this is not merely a reflection based on hindsight is that Charles Lamb (1775–1834) was upset that Coleridge (and Wordsworth) capitulated to the outcry: "I am hurt and vexed that you should think it necessary, with a prose apology, to open the eyes of dead men that cannot see..." (Lipking 620). These published "Mariner" annotations are also very different from Coleridge's extensive marginalia with which he decorated his many books; they fill six volumes in their Princeton University edition.

Now and again, a contemporary editor may choose to marginate a text. An example can be found in Jacques Barzun's "Artist as Prophet and Jester," which appears in a 2000 issue of *The American Scholar*, where the marginal quotations flow over into the text:

> Whether or not the younger talents admired any of these older figures, they were driven in other directions by the cult of the new. It was an imperative so ingrained that it was not even discussed: the nineteenth century had seen to it. But in that century, the new was a departure by a number of geniuses who soon generated a school of able exploiters. In the 1920s, originality produced the spectacle of many overlapping styles at once. The apparent gain was an actual loss: it not only deprived the age of what might have been its characteristic style, it also subjected each competing group to the accidents of vogue. By the end of the twentieth century it was commonly said that the lifespan of a style is three months. For such creators the ancient maxim is reversed: life is long and art is short [20].

> **The great geniuses of the past still rule over us from their graves they still stalk or scury about in the present, tripping up the living, mysteriously congesting the traffic, confusing values in art and manners, a brilliant cohort of mortals determined not to die, in possession of the land.**
> —WYNDHAM LEWIS (1915)

But this type of typographical aberration now occurs most infrequently. A concluding special case concerns the work of Derrida, whose "marginal" constructions are among the most complex ever attempted. In "Tympan," for example, he provides a main text that covers two thirds of the vertical page, a narrower parallel text (by Michel Leiris) on the right side, and numbered or signed, sometimes lengthy and illustrated footnotes; in the English version one finds additional notes provided by the translator. Very little of this makes sense, confusing rather than helping the reader. But this is a very simple instance of Derrida's extreme constructions. *Glas* obfuscates to the point of incomprehensibility. Few pages in the history of scholarly book production are as graphically complex as those found in this bizarre compilation, where text and documentation, body and marginalia are so purposely confused that Kant or Heidegger, by contrast, appear lucidly clear. The first oversize page begins with the following paragraph: "what, after all, of the remain(s), today, for us, here, now, of a Hegel?" (The initial *w* is a minuscule.) This left hand column continues to the bottom of the page with two insertions in a smaller, bolded typeface. The right hand column is a different text in a larger typeface. It contains some one word paragraphs. Things get considerably more complex: Some pages contain five separate "texts" in different fonts and sizes in Roman, italics, or bold including quotations, bizarrely lengthy lexicographical entries, and insertions. Each page is a bit different from its neighbors. (In this English version there are, additionally, lots of helpful bracketed intercalations of the original French term, e.g., "fall [*chute*].") This goes on for 262 tortuous pages. This type of madness may appeal to the extreme postmodern mind but for the normal reader it is frustrating and ultimately devoid of any real connected meaning, even if one is willing to work hard at ferreting one out. In an essay, Derrida confirms the reader's reasonable reaction:

> *Glas* is a book ... in which the logic of *stricture* substitutes itself for the logic or dialectic of opposition.
>
> ...
>
> Before *Glas*, I had often tried to destabilize the order of annotation by proposing typographical layouts, topographies that prohibited one from deciding what was the principle text and what was secondary ("This" 203).

In *Glas*, he succeeds admirably, to the point of total confusion.

Images

Now we arrive at a most unexpected point in this overview of marginalia, which for most readers — even sophisticated scholars who may have some general knowledge of documentation history — will be limited to verbal annotation. With the exception of medievalists, one tends to forget that prior to the invention of printing in 1455, manuscripts were produced by hand and subsequently illuminated, and in many cases diminutive images were added to the margins prior to binding or transmittal to a patron, commissioner, or buyer. (Indeed, it is possible that the more explicit and complex verbal annotations that one finds in the sophisticated texts of the Renaissance, encyclopedists, and post–Enlightenment authors ultimately trace their etiology back to these peculiar little drawings.) The figures, which appear in both religious and secular documents, run an extraordinary gamut and include real and imaginary humans (jugglers, dancers, hunters, musicians, servants, lovers, supplicants, grotesques), animals (apes, dragons, babewyns, grylli), and botanical and natural objects (tendrils, shells) (Camille, *Image*). These figures are often extremely small and may get lost on the sumptuous page of a Bible, book of hours, literary text, or bestiary. Thus, when first seen and recognized, they are often taken as mere decoration, and in some cases this is perhaps a valid conclusion. But often they have precisely the same functions that verbal annotations offer: Despite their frequently linear or cartoonish demeanor, they illustrate, clarify, emend, parody, amuse, and deny, but also horrify and stimulate. Since physical images often carry symbolic meanings (and this was especially the case during the late middle ages, when many of these marginalia were drawn or painted), it was very easy for an artist to present a second-

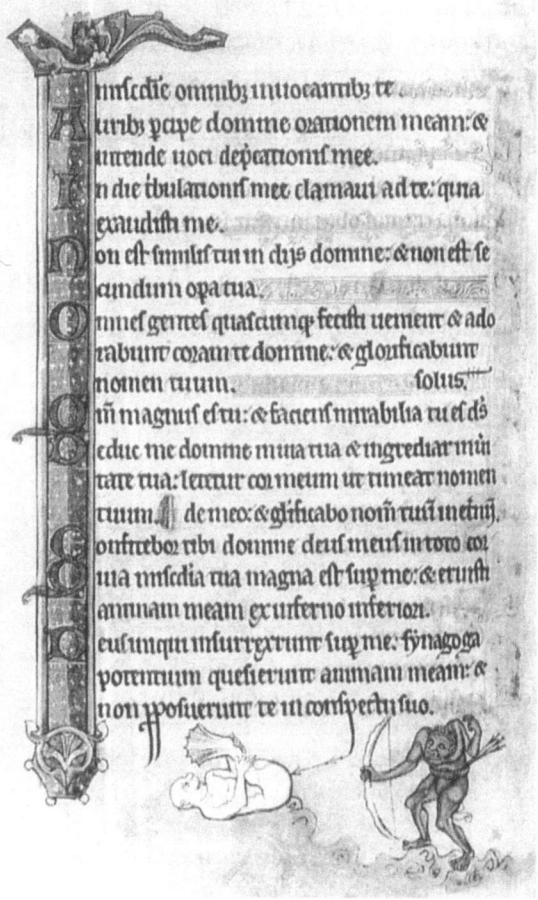

Archers shooting at bared bottoms (*The Rutland Psalter*). Add.62925. Used by permission of the British Library.

ary meaning in his countervailing depiction. For it is in the margin that he was able to indicate something that the author or scribe could not: Even religious texts are adorned with scatalogical, erotic, and sexual imagery that would make a twenty-first century liberal blush. Body parts and bodily functions were apparently as amusing to the medieval (religious) aristocrat as they are today to *The Village Voice* or *Playboy* reader. Examples include fornicating animals and people or archers shooting at bared bottoms, although these are counterbalanced by St. Augustine pointing to the text and saying "not me," mocking monkeys, and a little man pulling up a misplaced paragraph and indicating where it belongs (Camille, *Image*, passim). This type of sometimes sophisticated iconic marginalia may trace its etiology back to earlier intercalated text (script and imagery), out of which these little creatures eventually crawled into the margins. *The Book of Kells* (between 775 and 825) (held by the library of Trinity College, Dublin), often considered the world's most beautiful book, incorporates diminutive animals, birds, fish, people, and arabesques within the text. Occasionally, someone has appended a marginal comment, but generally the margins are unadorned.

An excellent example of diverse and extensive visual marginalia can be found in *The Hours of Catherine of Cleves* (1440), a divided manuscript held by the Guennol Collections and the Pierpont Morgan Library. Some pages consist entirely of text or illustrations, but many contain eight lines of text below a small, colorful illumination. The margins are decorated with various floral designs and no two are precisely the same. Interspersed among the botanical tendrils are diminutive depictions of grotesques (dragons), people (milking, turning a spit, firing an arrow), animals (monkeys, lions, hounds), vegetables, insects (butterflies), birds, and fish. These images may mirror, counter, or ignore the textual message offered in the center of the page.

The wealthy individuals who or organizations that commissioned or purchased illuminated, rubricated, or marginally illustrated manuscripts were willing to pay more for these lavish productions because they were impressive and esthetically pleasing. And this is still the case today. The more frequent and ornate the visual imagery, the more valued is the manuscript. But Camille points out that at least one influential purist and bibliophile disagreed: Richard de Bury (1286–1345) maintains in his *Philobiblon* that he dislikes marginal adornment and additionally, and bizarrely, rails against bodily pollutants (nasal effluvia, spittle, sweat), chewed food, folded pages, insertions, and anything else that might harm the precious volume. His discussion is couched in highly eroticized language ("Glossing" 245–246).

Printed marginal illustrations also exist, and the many large images of individuals found in the margins (but also within the text) of *The Nuremberg Chronicle* (1493) exemplify the extremes to which early printers would go. In a Biblia Pauperum (Paupers' Bible), the images almost supplant the minimal text, since these works were aimed at the illiterate. Here the text succumbs and the images cover much of the page.

Pulling up a misplaced paragraph and indicating where it belongs (Psalm 127 from a book of hours). The Walters Art Museum, Baltimore.

ANNUNCIATION

"Annunciation" (from a *Biblia Pauperum*). C.9.d.2. Used by permission of the British Library.

TEMPLATE OF THE NINE TEXTS
ON A
Biblia Pauperum BLOCKBOOK
PAGE

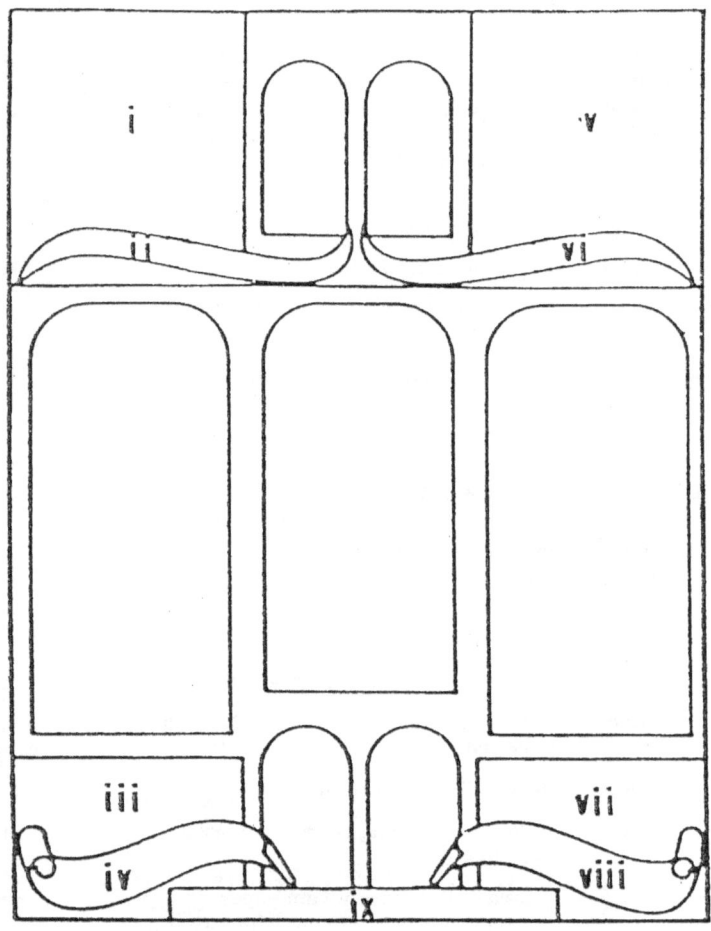

Template. Used by permission of Duquesne University Press.

Most of the marginal images, found primarily in manuscripts, were produced at about the same time that the text was inscribed or shortly thereafter. But there is a small class of marginal images that were drawn or painted by readers in printed books after their publication. Jackson includes a superb example, one that makes a great deal of sense for it is a series of detailed draw-

Latin Transcription

A   *Template*
                                                  i–ix

    Legitur in Genesi, iii capitulo, quod dixit Dominus serpenti super pectus tuum gradieris et postea ibidem legitur de serpente et muliere. Ipsa conteret caput* tuum et tu insidiaberis calcaneo ejus. Nam istud in Annunciatione Beate Marie Gloriose Virginis adimpletum est.   i

Isayas vii

	Ecce Virgo concipiet et pariet filium.	ii
Versus	Vipera vim perdit sine vi pariente puella.	iii
Ezeciel xliv	Porta hec clausa erit et non aperietur.	iv

    Legitur in Libro Iudicum, vi capitulo, quod Gedeon petiit signum victorie in vellere per rorationem irrigandam quod figurabat Virginem Mariam Gloriosam sine corruptione impregnandam ex Spiritus Sancti infusione.   v

David

	Descendet Dominus sicut pluvia in vellus.	vi
	Ave gratia plena Dominus tecum—Ecce ancilla Domini fiat mihi.	[scroll, center]
	Dominus tecum virorum fortissime.	[scroll, right]
Versus	Rore madet vellus permansit arida tellus.	vii
Jheremias xxxi	Creavit Dominus novum super terram femina circumdabit virum.	viii
Versus	Virgo salutatur innupta manens gravidatur.	ix

---

* caput] capud

Latin transcription. Used by permission of Duquesne University Press.

English Translation 99

A   *Template*
                                                         i–ix

[ANNUNCIATION]

[Eve and the Serpent]

Genesis 3.14	We read in Genesis, chapter 3, that the Lord said to the serpent, "Upon your breast you shall go," and in the next verse we read about the serpent and the woman, "She shall crush your head, and you will lie in wait for her heel." For indeed this event is fulfilled in the Annunciation of the glorious Blessed Virgin Mary.	i
Isaias 7.14	Behold a virgin shall conceive and bear a son.	ii
Verse	The serpent is ruined, the maiden giving birth without pain.	iii
Ezechiel 44.2	This gate shall be shut, and it shall not be opened.	iv

[Gedeon's Fleece]

Judges 6.36–38	We read in the Book of Judges, chapter 6, that Gedeon sought a sign of victory in a fleece filled with dew. This event prefigured the glorious Virgin Mary made pregnant without violation by the infusion of the Holy Spirit.	v
David, Psalm 71.16	The Lord shall come down like rain upon the fleece.	vi
	Hail, full of grace, the Lord is with you—Behold the Handmaiden of the Lord; may it be done to me.	[scroll, center]
	The Lord is with you, the strongest of men.	[scroll, right]
Verse	The fleece is filled with dew; the ground remained dry.	vii
Jeremias 31.22	The Lord created a new thing upon the earth; a woman shall compass man.	viii
Verse	The Virgin is saluted; she is impregnated remaining a virgin.	ix

English translation. Used by permission of Duquesne University Press.

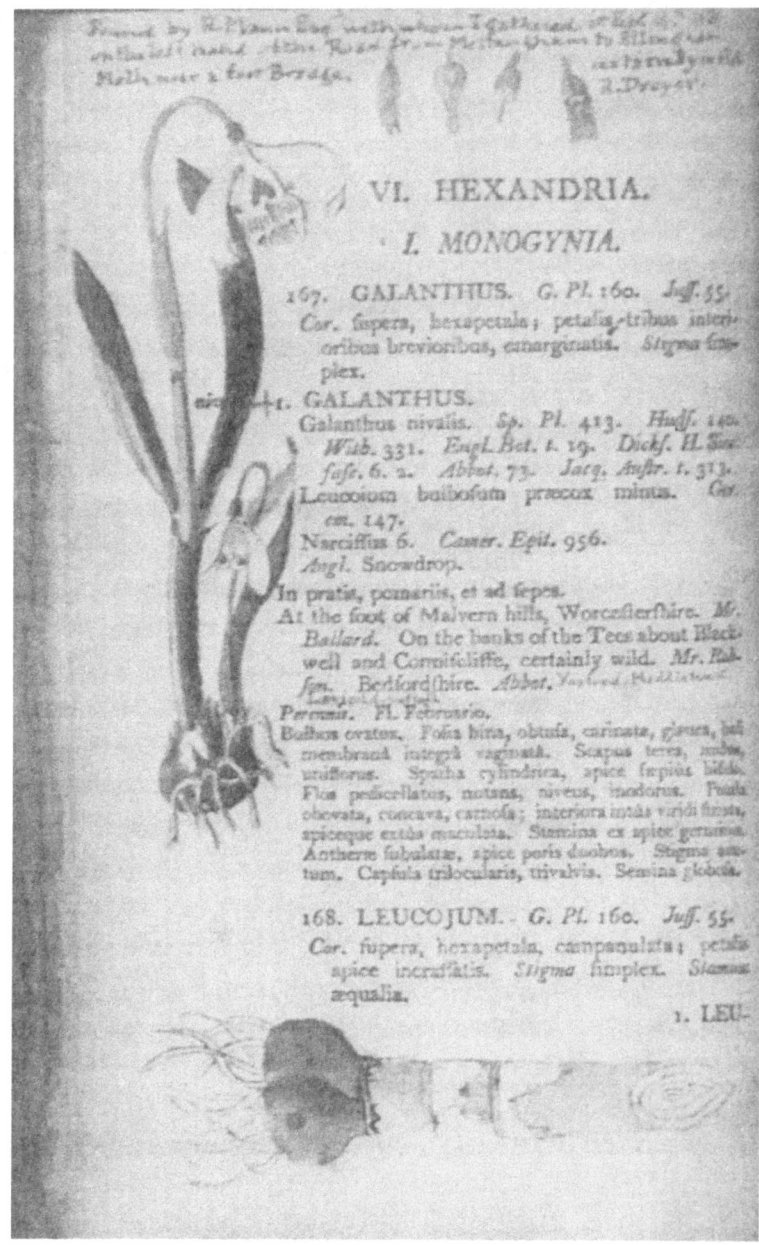

Marginal annotation and image added by reader to James Edward Smith's *Flora Britannica*, 1800–1804). Annotator and artist, Richard Dreyer. Used by permission of the Linnean Society of London.

ings of flowering plants in the margins of *Floria Britannica* (*Romantic* 80), which supplements the printed illustrations found on separately located plates.

Theory

Marginalia take diverse physical and intellectual forms and do different things for different people: the author, annotator, artist, contemporary or future reader, historian, critic, and theoretician each have a different perspective and therefore a different experience. Thus, an overriding "theory of margination," as William Slights (*Managing* 61) puts it, is very difficult to envision. Nevertheless, one can agree with Slights (whose entire monographic study of printed marginalia in a plethora of books published in England during the Renaissance is predicated upon this thesis) that marginal annotation manages or controls the reader, and this despite the fact that it may be irrelevant, confusing, annoying, chastising, or coercive (*Managing* 8): "...printed marginalia did more than any other material feature of book production in the period to determine ... the nature of the reading experience" (*Managing* 3). This makes a great deal of sense since the marginal annotations may have been written by an author who disagrees with himself or by another person who would thus emphasize or object in such a way that the reader's conclusions will differ dramatically had he or she read a naked text (*Managing* 11). Slights observes that the text (at least in this period but probably generally) is rhetorically and substantively expansive while marginalia is spontaneous, contracted, and abbreviated (passim). This and the graphic layout organize the visual and reading experience and may refer the reader outward beyond the limits of the page (*Managing* 76). The primary author controls the reader's response to the text; the annotator (who, naturally, might be a contrarian who vehemently disagrees with the author) concomitantly manages the reader's intellectual processes. What this obviously means is that the reader will have two or more simultaneous and often divergent responses to the text and its annotations. (I have no quarrel with Slights, whose insights are incisive and on target. But one should keep in mind that he is dealing with a limited number of English language volumes (ca. 2,000) in a proscribed chronological period (*Managing* 23). Much of what he offers is extrapolatable to material in other languages and periods, but there are exceptions, e.g., the Talmud (and the Torah as well) which may present a single word of text surrounded by vast quantities of verbose, unabbreviated marginalia.

Material that is devoid of any documentation or apparatus (parenthetical remarks, marginalia, notes) functions very differently from a mediated text, which does control both the reader's physical orientation as well as his or her intellectual reactions. On the other hand, Edgar Allan Poe, who observes that a generous margin allows him room to make various comments in close proximity to the thought that engenders them, which appears to be a serious and meaningful business, goes on to insist, teasingly perhaps, that "marginal jottings" have no purpose at all, and it is this that "imparts to them a value" (1–2). He holds that in this type of marginal remark, since "we talk only to ourselves," we are able to say things we might avoid under other circumstances; additionally, limited space forces the annotator to scribble succinctly (2), perhaps too much so because his general conclusion is that "nonsense [is] the essential sense of the Marginal Note" (4). Camille could not disagree more; discussing printed marginal remarks or images, he insists that "[t]he centre is ... dependent upon the margins for its continued existence" (*Image* 10). Somehow, though, the center continues to hold its preeminent position despite the extirpation of marginal imagery both because printing costs outweigh intellectual need and also, as Camille observes, because the margins of printed books were reduced dramatically, which left less room for iconic displays and, in any case, since the Renaissance, scholars have favored the substantive text over ancillary imagery (*Image* 158).

A theoretical construct that attempts to account for marginal accoutrement in all of its diversity may overstep its limits and unfairly increase its import. For example, it is tempting to draw an analogy between social outsiders on the one hand and marginalia on the other: Just as society produces pariahs who live in the borderlands, so too do texts engender verbal and visual marginalia that cannot survive in the body of the work but thrive in the margins as anti-social articulations and images. Camille affirms this point of view now and again for visual marginalia in medieval art (*Image*) — as does Slights for textual adumbration (*Managing* 15) — but I think that this superimposes misleading baggage especially on the superficial relationship between the text and its sometimes unrelated illustrations. It is highly improbable that the artists who created these sometimes playful and humorous drawings intended to distinguish in any meaningful way between the wealthy aristocrats who paid their wages and those who fell outside of the social sphere: the beggar, the grotesque, and the sexually aberrant. These were merely playful, discordant, but important participants on the margins of medieval society. They just happened to turn up in the margins of manuscripts and books because the artists enjoyed countering or undermining a text that they sometimes did not bother to read (Camille, *Image* 42). And Tribble insists (in succinct summary here) that her work on printed (rather than iconic) material does not "equate margins and marginality." Margins do not necessarily subvert; they may stabilize in a primary (rather than secondary) way (*Margins* 6).

A second example of theoretical connectivity that may at first seduce with its ostensible incisiveness, but upon reflection bears little connection with reality and does even less to help one understand marginal annotation and its influence on readers, is Slights's application of Tobin Nellhaus's idea that post–12th century literacy (in simplified concision) resulted in linearity and linguistic subordination, whereas orality necessitates concreteness and verbal formulae (presumably reducing Walter Ong's synthesis as filtered through other scholars). The text is a paean to literacy but the annotation is "a testimony to the survival of orality" because marginalia are direct and syntactically simple (*Managing* 6–7). Even if this is sometimes the case, how do these manifested characteristics of orality (and there are others) indicate its survival? In order to read these annotations one must be literate. Members of an oral culture, e.g., peasants who depended on pauper Bibles, are excluded. This thesis actually makes very little sense. A much stronger case could be made if marginal images were substituted for verbal annotations.

5
Footnotes

The footnote, which evolved from the abuses of the medieval gloss and extreme marginal annotation, solved the documentation problem for the printed book, although marginalia hung on for some time. Robert Connors observes that when publishers first brought out the classical writers (during the early years of the icunabula period, 1455–1481), marginal and footnoted material was abjured; the peripheral matter was placed "...in separate printed signatures or appended after the works themselves" ("Rhetoric I" 9). And eighteenth century printers and readers found the footnoted page more esthetically appealing (Tribble, "Like" 233, 231). So, scholars who wished to acknowledge or track their sources, offer a translated text in the original language, or indicate their command of their disciplines, placed a small mark or number to the side of or above the text and thereby referred the reader to the bottom of the page, where, sometimes in a smaller point size, a source was cited or an explanation or clarification was offered. (An historical survey of footnote usage and the Latin abbreviations that adorned them can be found in Pollak, and a similar detailed overview is available in Connors ["Rhetoric I"].) This system continued in use in most disciplines until the late 20th century, when, in the humanities and social sciences, it was partially replaced by in-text documentation and an accompanying reference list. Substantive notes can and do appear at the end of a work, although Francis Burkle-Young and Saundra Rose Maley claim (somewhat erroneously despite advice from MLA that discursive notes should be extirpated) that these notes no longer contain detailed information, which decreases "[t]he reader's ability to understand fully the whole journey that the author had taken..." (12). This is an intellectually annoying and esthetically displeasing system that is favored primarily because it is less expensive for publishers. (For this same indefensible reason, even scholarly presses may entirely expunge comprehensive bibliographies.) Betsy Hilbert laments the passing of the mellifluous prose made possible by the footnote: Consider a graphically and aurally horrific passage —

> The readers, those, at least, who could afford Murcheson's book, according to Fleemurscher's intricate statistical analysis of buying patterns during that period (426–91), were confused (Ottenbacher, trans. Hoffenpffeffer 398), enraged (Mishkeit 39) and appalled (Fleegle and Barnes, *Opposition of Insight* 93).

This could have been replaced with "Readers[1] were confused,[2] enraged,[3] appalled[4]" (402). Lipking holds that the footnote is imperiled for many reasons; he prefers the marginal annotation (638–639). Since his essay is now 30 years old, and a renaissance in printed marginalia has not occurred, it seems fair to conclude that the footnote (or endnote and in-text documentation) will continue to serve those scholars who choose to embellish their texts with ancillary material including attributions.

Key points in the historical development and application of the footnote are covered in other chapters; additionally, it is not necessary to rehearse the development that both Grafton and Zerby have already sketched in such exacting detail, though it must be noted that Grafton's work in *The Footnote*, with some few exceptions, emphasizes the contributions of historians. Here I would merely indicate that Leopold von Ranke (1795–1886), "supposedly the alchemist who created the modern historical apparatus," did not favor annotation; he appended footnotes to the body of his work only because he had to prove himself; he apparently did a poor job, because his notes sometimes did not precisely relate to the text (Grafton, *Footnote* 228, 64, 66). Bayle overused (perhaps even misused) notes and created a bizarrely intricate page; Swift, Pope, and Gibbon included lots of notes for legitimate definitional, historical, and interpretive reasons, but also because they wished to castigate or parody their historical or contemporary adversaries or amuse their readers. (Gibbon too was accused of misuse in his footnotes [Grafton, *Footnote* 100].) In classical studies, Ulrich von Wilamowitz (1848–1931) provided such complete and onerous apparatus that Steve Nimis refers to what he terms the "Wilamowitz footnote" (115). In "Fussnoten: Das Fundament der Wissenschaft,"[1] Nimis reproduces, in its entirety, a single bibliographic note that runs on for half a page; its author provides multiple citations in English, German, Latin, Italian, French, and Greek to five separate interpretations of a single line of Pindar's verse (128–129). The overused and overdone (historical) note, so popular in nineteenth century German scholarship, slowly eroded. Although it has certainly lost its former cachet, I recall picking up a newly bound historical dissertation, less than 40 years ago, and being stunned to discover that a substantial portion of this enormous document was given over to 800 endnotes. Even today, diligent or overly zealous historians as well as scholars in other disciplines overwhelm the reader with apparatus. This is painfully the case in legal scholarship, where the material is adduced in ludicrous profusion: Scholars, lawyers, jurists, clerks, and ingenuous law review editors continue to believe that it is possible to convince by piling on vast quantities of citational data. But occasionally, one encounters an antithetical case: a study that fails to include footnotes (or any documentation for that matter). Cited excuses for this are discussed elsewhere in this study. Here I include only a single controversial work that may have something to hide. In 1988, Arno Mayer published *Why Did the Heavens Not Darken? The "Final Solution" in History*, which David Henige briefly discusses. Although it contains a bibliography, there are no notes, and thus it is difficult and perhaps impossible to validate Mayer's controversial contentions. Henige heaps "opprobrium" on Mayer and insists that "his arguments [should] be ignored" (Henige, "Being" 112–113).

Current footnote usage is complex: Purely citational footnotes continue to flourish in the sciences, where intellectual acknowledgment is stressed, as well as in history, where substantive comments are often added, though the popularizer sometimes dispenses with all scholarly apparatus, as if he or she is creating the past *ab ovo*. In literature, citations are banished to parenthetical referrals and footnotes are limited to substantive commentary, which is much more important here than it is in the sciences, where it generally is abjured; the arbiters suggest that these remarks be intercalated into the text, but the more esoteric and committed scholars continue to place them in footnotes. In many publications, they are turned into endnotes, unless the publisher is following the *Chicago Manual of Style*, in which case footnotes are likely to appear. As observed above, footnote usage is carried to a sometimes ludicrous extreme in legal analysis and exegesis, where articles in law reviews routinely run on for 100 pages, half of which may be allocated to notes referring the reader to various statutes, cases, and precedents. Endnotes seem to be footnotes moved to the conclusion of the paper, but they have a very different effect and influence on the reader's cognitive processes and therefore the intellectual path he or she follows. Gertrude Himmelfarb dislikes the inconvenience that page flipping entails and additionally claims that endnotes result in author negligence in documentation style as well as in accuracy and relevance of content (124, 125). Hyperlinks in scholarly papers mounted on the Internet are similar. Additionally, it is possible that the footnotes in a traditionally published essay that is subsequently mounted on a database will metamorphose into endnotes, especially in hypertext format. PDF files will maintain the essay's graphic integrity.

Footnotes serve important and precise purposes. A work would be very different without them: It would lose credibility and not allow a reader to track down sources either intellectually or physically. Anne Stevens and Jay

Williams show that, despite countervailing trends, footnote usage has increased quite dramatically in the pages of the influential cultural journal *Critical Inquiry* during the second half of its ca. 30 year existence. They insist that footnotes are not necessarily insignificant or digressive; rather, they "are the mark of the author's status as a professional" (215, 220, 211). But not all notes are truly useful. Sometimes they are purposely overdone, parodic, confusing, or annoying. Legal notes, especially when the citations flow on interminably, are aggrandizing and impressive, but not necessarily helpful. And those who are obsessed with complexification, borders, and gimmickry rile the reader with structural superfluities that confuse rather than clarify. Pope, Joyce, and Nabokov come to mind. The most egregious example is Derrida, whose marginal antics in *Glas* are discussed above. But a more apposite case can be cited: In 1979, the Yale Deconstructionists (at one point disparagingly called the "Yale Mafia")— Bloom, de Man, Hartman, and Miller — along with Derrida published a collection of essays entitled *Deconstruction and Criticism*. Four of the authors offer brief traditional pieces. Derrida extends himself in "Living On/Border Lines," whose main text offers one account while along the bottom of each page is a series of lines (often seven) in a smaller typeface: This is a single footnote running the entire length of the 102 page work and telling a different story. I insist that it is impossible to read both of these simultaneously with complete comprehension. Therefore, if one reads the text first and then returns to the note, the structure is, for all practical purposes, unnecessary. The note could have been placed after the main text. Naturally, there are those who will insist they have managed the impossible feat mentioned above, but they may be the same geniuses who claim to fully understand *Finnegans Wake*. The present author is not one of them. Derrida is fond of notational gimmicks, which do not serve the reader well.

Footnotes continue to prosper in the hard sciences and in some university press monographs, but they have been banished by fiat in those humanistic disciplines controlled by the MLA and in the social sciences that are influenced by the APA. Thus, even scholars who would prefer to undergird each page with a foundational structure composed of footnotes are dissuaded by editors and publishers who will demand lots of time-consuming and aggravating changes in the manuscript. So, they capitulate to in-text documentation. But there is another class, a group of people, some of whom, as historians, could continue to use footnotes but who do not. There are many reasons set forth for this barbaric dismissal not merely of the note but of all scholarly paraphernalia. Well-known authors, those who have already made their reputations, dispense with documentation because they are omniscient and therefore do not require it or because they wish to capture the lay reader rather than alienate with apparatus or because they are acting fraudulently or because they just choose to abjure its use. Sometimes the documentation does not exist at all; sometimes it is available in unusable form (innumerable sources cobbled together in the text and all listed under one note), on a Web site, in a subsequently published volume of its own, or in a unique manuscript held by an archive. One might surmise that all of these peculiar variations would be anathema to legitimate scholars, except that legitimate scholars perpetrate them.

A Theory of Footnotes

Academicians like to gather their materials together and place them in a tidy box that they label theory. But despite the work done, no comprehensive theory of documentation or even of the footnote exists. In 1983, Walter de Gruyter published a small, 23 page pamphlet that was presented to the publisher's authors and friends. Though *Vorstudien zu einer Theorie der Fussnote* must have been widely distributed, it found its way into only two collections; thus it is extremely difficult to access. Interestingly, an English translation, *Towards a Theory of the Footnote,* is available (although no translator is mentioned). This strange compilation gives every appearance of being a work of genuine scholarship, but it is so exaggerated that one must conclude that Peter Riess, its author, is spoofing his legal colleagues who are notorious for abusing the footnote. Riess offers a complex and detailed taxonomy. The categories are helpfully numbered and lettered in excellent pseudo-scientific form, which I condense thus:

> II Footnote typology
>   2. Morphological (external) typology
>   c) apocryphal footnotes
>   aa) textual footnotes
>   aaa) interpolations in parentheses

This excerpt offers some idea of how this works; it goes on for five pages! Everything makes some sense and all of the permutations probably do exist, but it really helps very little. A taxonomic structure is not a theory, not even a prolegomenon to one. And some of Riess's remarks, in the concise text and the 66 verbose footnotes, strongly imply that the author is playing with his readers: "...the concept of the footnote can under no circumstances be limited to that which presents the outward appearance of a footnote..." (10); he prefers an "intersubjective consensus-based pragmatistic concept of the footnote" (12); and considering the legibility of type size, he observes, "[i]f the purpose of footnotes does not consist in communication, then it does not matter whether one can read them or not" (22, n65). That certainly puts documentation in an awkward position!

Notes serve the annotating commentator, who clarifies matters in poetry, for example, that the reader might find elusive; nevertheless, it is possible to enjoy and even understand without the help of an overweening apparatus. A. C. Hamilton makes this point in his lengthy disquisition on annotation and glossing, which is titled "The Philosophy of the Footnote," but this replete overview does not result in a comprehensive theoretical structure, despite the unusual claim that Stephen Booth's eccentric interpretation of Shakespeare's *Sonnets* "...should help free commentary from its traditional preoccupation, to clarify verbal and syntactical obscurities in a text" (153). For Hamilton, a philosophy derives from or perhaps controls "...the critical assumptions that determine what they [annotators] choose to gloss..." (158). He calls for less factual annotation and more relevant help in making the work truly comprehensible (159). This is useful advice, but it can serve only as an extremely proscribed philosophy, since these notations are not limited to critical glossing; as has been noted above, they serve a host of other purposes as well. W. Speed Hill takes a different tack: "There is no philosophy of the footnote..." (323). He is probably correct, but Frank Palmeri offers an excellent possibility for further development. Though his short discussion is more complex and is liberally peppered with allusions to Foucault, Bakhtin, and Derrida, it basically indicates that medieval and Renaissance marginalia consists of resemblances and commentary, whereas the footnote presents representation and criticism (245). Though these paradigms would not hold in every case (medieval marginalia sometimes surprises in its countervailing attitudes and footnotes are often purely attributive or banal), they do make sense and indicate that the alteration in form brought along with it a change in substance; for Palmeri, this is highlighted in the satiric notes of Swift and Gibbon. David Henige offers a similar and more powerful construct: "From at least the seventeenth century ... it began to become *de rigueur* to rely on argument and justification rather than authority and imitation..." in citation practices ("Being" 113). And in his discussion of scientific citation behavior, Blaise Cronin titles a chapter, "The need for a theory of citing[.]" He holds that scientists take little interest in citation as such and settle for a metaphysical rather than empirical explanation of its practices (*Citation* 25, 23, 24). Nevertheless, no comprehensive theory emerges even here where citation practices are comparatively simple, limited as they frequently are to bibliographic references, whereas in the social sciences and especially the humanities, they can be extremely complex in their extensive, interconnected, and convoluted commentaries. More recently, in a replete historical discussion of scientific citation and citation analysis, Loet Leydesdorff confirms this: "...a complete theory of citation is still lacking" ("Theories" 6).

In an excellent overview, Jeppe Nicolaisen discusses the reasons that scientists cite (which may differ from those that motivate humanists) and summarizes two theoretical perspectives. The first claims that citational practices derive from normative behavior: students learn from teachers, mentors, common practice, and perhaps through some limited instruction. A citation's primary function is to acknowledge that an idea derives from someone else (615–616). Some critics claim that scientists do not reference those who have contributed to what they are offering (618), but despite the fact that this conclusion is based on a (limited) empirical study, it seems farfetched as a generalization; authors cite the most important and pertinent influences and sources applicable to the specific study. Manfred Kochen notes that

> A paper that conforms to the norms of scholarly perfection would explicitly cite every past publication to which *it* owes an intellectual debt [54].

But striving for such perfection is counterproductive: It is not necessary to include every related item ever read on a subject in which one has become an expert. The basic constituent experiments, discoveries, and readings in genetics, for example, are an integral part of the scientist's mindset. Indeed, he or she would be condemned for padding a bibliography with real intellectual but irrelevant influences such as Mendel or Watson and Crick, when all this butterfly researcher is doing is reporting the results of an analysis of the genome of *papilio glaucus*, the yellow swallowtail. Another commentator surveyed 26 researchers and discovered that credit allocation was "...the least important motivation for citation" (Nicolaisen 619). If this is true generally, it helps to explain some of the scholarly and ethical problems that continue to crop up despite the major alterations that have been introduced into graduate education as well as the implementation of stricter rules and regulations that govern research and publication. The second possibility is functional (and is termed the social constructivist theory); here the claim is that one cites in order to persuade (Nicolaisen 619–620). It is difficult to understand why it is so compelling for some thinkers to theorize and thus compartmentalize citational behavior; even more disturbing is their insistence that purposes, functions, necessities, and desires are reducible to a single possibility. No legitimate reason can be adduced to show that citations do not acknowledge and concomitantly persuade (among a host of additional possibilities), although Stéphane Baldi's statistical analysis of papers dealing with celestial masers indicates that for this proscribed field the normative approach obtains and the social constructivist theory is disconfirmed, i.e., authors cite recent and relevant material and not authors whom they know in order to persuade (843); furthermore,

> ... citations in the social [rather than the natural] sciences may be influenced less by the intellectual content of articles and more by characteristics of their authors [844].

Norman Kaplan suggests that nationality influences citation practices; for example, American psychologists do not cite distant historical sources whereas British and French practitioners do (181). This may be coincidental or non-correlational but if it is the case (or was in 1965), it is indeed indicative that citational behavior varies along some type of normative continuum, whereas ideally it should be consistent and etiologically comprehensible across all disciplines, although it certainly is not.

Charles Bazerman analyzes a group of articles on spectroscopy published between 1893 and 1980 in *Physical Review*. He draws many valid conclusions including some concerning the references (their numbers change, early citations are undated, they serve very different purposes at different times [164–167]), but I am not certain that any of this is extrapolatable even to other physics publications, let alone to periodicals in unrelated disciplines. Furthermore, I am not certain that this offers any useful insights. It is obvious that an analysis of any (cohesive) group of publications over an extended period will result in some valid generalizations (e.g., in this case, the references imply "a loose cognitive structure in the early years" [167]); and these conclusions may differ dramatically from those derived from analogous studies, but does it really matter if in physics in 1890, articles contained 11 citations, but in metaphysics in 1920 they may have contained 22? Or that the references in the early publications in this study are often undated, but that that might not be the case in analogous chemistry, geology, or psychology articles? Collated and codified data is sometimes merely data with few meaningful or pragmatic implications, though I suspect that Bazerman and especially many scientometricians would scoff at this.

Henry Small is not satisfied with a simple and pragmatic explanation for citational practices. Naturally, authors cite in order "to persuade, to curry favor, to publicize, to avoid offending, to favor one approach over another, to give credit" ("Cited" 337), but their citations have (Letter 144) and lead to texts that have a symbolic function: "...[C]itation of a document [is] an act of symbol usage. ... [T]he document is viewed as symbolic of the idea expressed in the text. ... In citing a document an author is creating its meaning, and this, I will argue, is a process of symbol making" ("Cited" 327, 328). And rearticulated 20 years after his initial foray, Small claims that "...the author uses the cited work to symbolize a particular idea inherent in that work..." (Letter 144). Based on his remarks, I am not certain that Small really understands what a symbol is or how it functions. At any rate, his deconstructive extrapolation is both far-fetched and probably superfluous, because it sheds little additional light on citational practice, behavior, or meaning, although he would certainly argue vehemently with this, since he has devoted at least two works to defending his point of view.

The most detrimental comment that might be adduced against citational behavior is that it may result *exclusively* from social pressure, i.e., one cites because one wants to curry favor or repay an unrelated debt. Naturally, social citation may be interconnected with valid intellectual attribution, but in specific cases, a particular citation would not appear if the work had not been produced by a colleague, mentor, or friend. A reasonable assumption is that social citation (like self-citation) does occur but, within the broad array of all disciplines, less frequently and less blatantly than one might think. Three scholars investigated this phenomena in a longitudinal (though proscribed) study and discovered that social connections do influence citation patterns, but "intellectual affinity" is what really matters (White et al. 124):

> Who you know pays off only if the people you know have something worth knowing — something plainly relevant to your own claims [125].

Finally, it is necessary to observe that though references, citations, and annotations historically developed across disciplinary boundaries for similar reasons (to acknowledge, attribute, and comment), they have taken different forms with different emphases. The most blatant disparity exists, on the one hand, between current social science practice, where (despite scholars' desire to emulate their colleagues in the hard sciences) articles are frequently extremely long and detailed and the in-text references are sometimes multiplied and repeated beyond endurance, and the extremely concise articles usually (though not always) presented in the scientific literature, in *Nature* or *Science* for example, on the other. Arguably the single most important and influential paper published in the twentieth century in the long run, James Watson and Francis Crick's "A Structure for Deoxyribose Nucleic Acid," runs what amounts to one page; since it is so short it contains only six citations. This is generally how things work in the hard sciences: brief papers cite a limited number of forebears or influences. Naturally, there are exceptions and different (editorial) conventions dictate different necessities over time, e.g., papers in the biomedical field are now often replete with long lists of citations. But it is fair to conclude that social scientists (and humanists) overcite whereas hard scientists do not, perhaps because science editors will not accept 30 or 40 page disquisitions. Obviously, in legal periodicals, which encourage authors to submit 100 page diatribes, both convention and editorial demand often necessitate many hundreds of references in each paper.

Henk Moed summarizes the attempts of various scholars to theorize citational behavior; here the emphasis is exclusively on scientific citational practices, and the physical nature of the reference (footnote vs. endnote) is of no relevance. At least 15 scholars have come up with different ideas concerning precisely what a reference or citation measures, and these Moed summarizes in a useful chart. For example, Paul Wouters holds that references derive from the scientist and citations are "the product of the indexer" (194). Moed claims that all of these possibilities are subsumed under five disciplinary approaches: physical, sociological, psychological, historical, and informational (193). Despite all of these enticing ruminations, no general theory of scientific citational behavior, let alone footnoting, emerges.

Contrarians

Scholars who take an intellectual interest in documentation usually concentrate on the footnote, which they tend to eulogize, while ignoring all other methods of attribution and commentary. They adulate these diminutive inclusions that begin at the bottom of a page but may ramble on for hundreds of lines. Most of these people provide general panegyrics or comment on Bayle, Gibbon, or one of the other great footnoters. But Edward Heron-Allen remarks favorably on his own exaggerated applications. In 1940, in a short piece in *Notes and Queries,* he preens that he is the last "addict to this infuriating practice" and compares himself favorably to the greats, because when, in 1886, he translated *La Science de la Main,* half of his 431 pages were allocated to 468 footnotes, which in turn contained signs for references to eight languages including French and German, but also Arabic and Turkish. He apparently was not fully satisfied, because in 1928, he did it again, this time in a concise volume he composed on barnacles, although here his 125 page text concludes with 50 additional pages containing 300 "(foot)notes," as he puts it, being unable to admit that his foot has become a mere end. Perhaps he was correct: In 1983, G. W. Bowersock insists that "the art of sophisticated annotation is so rarely practiced these days" (54).

But only occasionally does anyone observe that the material presented in footnotes is inferior, lessened, pawned off, or degraded, sometimes purposely because it is of less value according to its author. This is especially the case with *obiter dicta* excursuses in legal pieces. Tribble explains that footnotes have this advantage over the marginal annotation: The material in the text is primary, truly important, and appears so to the eye; the tangential, the "degraded" content of the footnote is of secondary importance ("Peopled" 119), and may be ignored if one chooses to do so, though for some, this is psychologically difficult or impossible.

The Chicago Manual of Style does not sympathize with the serial annotator's compulsion to create long and detailed notes on every page. Thus, the editors offer some "remedies for excessive annotation": Verbose substantive material should be integrated into the text or, in some cases, placed in an appendix; citations can be combined into a single note, but one must be mindful to avoid the (inevitable) ambiguity and confusion that such long strings of data will cause (602). Neither Bayle, Pope, nor Gibbon would have fared well under *Chicago*'s tutelage. So, *Chicago* wisely wishes to diminish the plight of the reader overburdened by too many long-winded notes, and yet its arbiters hesitantly sanction a two-tiered, "cumbersome" system in certain instances: Numbers lead to bibliographical endnotes, while those grating little signs (asterisks, daggers, crosses, section markers) draw the reader's eyes to the bottom of the page for real substantive footnotes (609). Very few serious commentators derogate the footnote. Now and again, though, one discovers an adversary, a scholar or layperson who dislikes them for their own sake and not because they burden the publisher with additional costs or displease esthetically. Mary Cowden Clarke (fl. 1860), an early feminist, was apparently really angry when she described footnotes as "mere vehicles for abuse, spite and arrogance" (qtd. in Thompson 92). Rogelio Reyes begins a letter to the editor with the following remark:

> It is certainly refreshing to read an academic article without having to wade through all the appurtenances of scholarly writing — footnotes, references, citations, etc. ... [B17].

The bizarre attitude that attributive and explanatory documentation is somehow annoying and superfluous is confirmed by Supreme Court Justice Stephen Breyer, who does not tack footnotes onto his opinions:

> [T]he major function of an opinion is to explain to ... readers why it is that the Court has reached that decision.... If you see the opinion in this way, either a point is sufficiently significant to make, in which case it should be in the text, or it is not, in which case, don't make it [39].

When one considers that the legitimacy of the law depends on footnoted citations, this is a stunningly eccentric position. It is seconded by Judge Abner Mikva, who observes that "The use of footnotes ... has spread like a fungus...." Or to put it more blatantly, "I consider footnotes in judicial opinions an abomination" (647). They distract, waste time, present typesetting problems, are hard to read, and their style is governed by "byzantine rules" (648). Mikva cites some extreme cases in which as many as 1247 or 1715 notes are appended to a text (650). The goal here can not be elucidation; rather, all of this referential and tangential rubbish obfuscates and confuses. Like Breyer, Mikva does not use footnotes (651). For thousands of years, one of the most pressing problems of western scholarship has been the inability of authors to strike a fair and just balance between no documentation at all and an overabundance of superfluous logorrhea. One perhaps should be grateful to Breyer and Mikva for attempting to ameliorate the current state of legal scholarship.

If only Arthur Austin had listened. In 1987, he wrote a long and tedious piece, whose many pages and 107 notes attempt to convince the reader that it is the footnote that differentiates one article from another, and the more citations and comments one squeezes into one's essay (generally speaking), the more impressive it will be, and this will lead to encomiums and promotions. This is rather puerile, but it is undoubtedly taken seriously by many unwary or ingenuous readers.

A second class of critics use parody and humor to denigrate the footnote, which they feel is sorely abused. More than 50 years ago, John Updike published a pseudo-scholarly essay in *The New Yorker* in which he pokes fun at poets who append notes to their works; John Berryman, Marianne Moore, Richard Wilbur, Pound, and Eliot all feel his wrath. He insists that "self-exegesis" will breed "spoon-fed" readers as well as poets who prefer creating notes to composing their songs. He concludes with a series of 14 extremely esoteric and witty notes (including an illustration of a shadoof) to a non-existent sonnet (28, 29). And more than 65 years ago, Frank Sullivan had the same reaction to two of Van Wyck Brooks's studies including *New England: Indian Summer*, which he greatly admires, but claims have been "rendered cockeyed by the footnotes" (263). He creates a series of exaggerated numbered and interspersed signed footnotes which essentially supplant "A Garland of Ibids," his humorous essay. For example, the 16th note reads in its entirety:

> [16]Edward Gibbon, English historian, not to be confused with Cedric Gibbons, Hollywood art director. Edward Gibbon was a great hand for footnotes, especially if they gave him a chance to show off his Latin. He would come sniffing up to a nice, spicy morsel of scandal about the Romans and then, just as the reader expected him to dish the dirt, he'd go into his Latin routine, somewhat as follows: "In those days vice reached depths not plumbed since the reign of Caligula and it was an open secret that the notorious Empress Theodoro *in tres partes divisa erat* and that she was also addicted to the *argumentum ad hominem!*" Gibbon, prissy little fat man that he was, did that just to tease readers who had flunked Ceasar [265].

Much of this parodic humor will be lost on contemporary readers who not only never studied Latin, but did not even bother with Caesar in translation, nor Gibbon for that matter. But they will understand that a few people including scholars dislike the obtrusive footnote.

Two Minor Considerations

Futurists like to present optimistic technological auguries. These are usually much rosier in prediction than in reality five years hence. Nevertheless, it is true that the Internet has allowed people to mount vast quantities of useful data and information, which even today is often interconnected. Kevin Kelly predicts that a text's internal hyperlinks will solve humanity's logistical documentation problems. Soon, online texts and citations will lead directly to additional texts and citations, many of which have been tagged, or annotated, by readers. One will be able to move along, "traveling from footnote to footnote to footnote..." (45). This sounds as if it might be helpful, but it may turn out to be a never-ending, circuitous bibliographical nightmare. One may recall that Blake points out that everything in the universe is interrelated: Complete interconnectivity will confuse completely.

Finally, here is something that may not have occurred to Swift, Pope, or Gibbon. It is apparently much easier for some people to listen to an audiobook while driving to Fargo at 75 miles an hour than to relax with a volume of Bentham propped on their knees. Non-fiction has always incorporated citational and substantive notes; in the past some fiction has as well. Recently, more novelists are including annotated remarks in their works, either parenthetically or in foot- or endnotes. Andrew Adam Newman wonders how these asides can be translated into mellifluous verbal articulation: David Foster Wallace (reading his essays) alters his voice; another speaker says "footnote" just before he reads one (35). Annotation, marginalia, and notes do not lend themselves to integrated verbal performance. Hugh Kenner confirms this:

> You cannot read a passage of prose aloud, interpolating the footnotes, and make the subordination of the footnotes clear, and keep the whole sounding natural [39–40].

This is just one of many good reasons to read the book in the traditional way.

Codified Notes: Bibliographies

In the early ecstatic days of the World Wide Web and subsequently, some publications decided to relegate documentation to a Web site; thus, a person reading a hard copy issue of *Online,* or Robert Kaplan's *The Nothing That Is: A Natural History of Zero,* published by Oxford (Carvajal, "Book" A1), is forced to go to an externally networked computer, log on, access the Internet, locate the site, and find the list of sources, in the latter case at <www.oup-usa.org/sc/0195128427/> (which does still work). A more dismal idea has not been implemented since footnotes were eliminated in favor of in-text documentation. These Web-mounted bibliographies have the horrific advantage of being alterable, which is conducive to fraud, as well as the nasty habit of disappearing. MIT has also perpetrated this hoax on the readers of its superb books, as has Rutgers. Astonishingly, some authors favor this barbarism (Carvajal, "Book" A12).

In APA and MLA, the in-text system is the required modality; in order to indicate a complete citation, a list of the works cited must be appended to the article, chapter, or book. There is no question of eliminating this. But for those who present full citations in foot- or endnotes, which are not acceptable in these systems but are in *Chicago* style and in many disciplines including biology and history, it is possible to entirely expunge a comprehensive bibliography (see Hauptman, "Whatever"). Very few legitimate scholars would choose this extremely unsavory option. The bibliography summarizes sources and apportions credit in a single, comprehensive listing. In many cases, it is the intellectual summation of all of the seeking, locating, researching, collating, thinking, and writing that has gone into the preceding work. A bibliography appended to a text is sometimes the most important part of the study. One may care little for the author's discussions, clarifications, pronouncements, or arguments, but the intellectual sources for the work may lead to new avenues and help the reader immeasurably. In the past, few serious studies lacked a bibliography. When one occasionally encounters such a work, one is confused: Joseph Wood Krutch's excellent *Modern Temper* (1929) is devoid of references, probably because the publisher wished to pander to the layperson. Erich Auerbach's massive and influential *Mimesis* also lacks most scholarly apparatus, but this, astonishingly, is because he wrote it during the Second World War in Istanbul primarily from memory: He did not use any secondary source material! An extended piece of scholarship that lacks a bibliography appears naked and unjustified despite the innumerable (and sometimes confusing) bibliographic notes that may adorn each page. The culprits responsible for this recent execrable habit are publishers that apparently care more about saving a few pennies than about the quality of their publications. And the publishers that appear most culpable are university presses. How the director at Harvard, for example, can justify expunging the bibliography in Anthony Grafton's masterful *Footnote*, a book that deals precisely with documentation, is a mystery that I will never fathom. Another superb study, Grafton's *Defenders of the Text* is a telling case. Here, Harvard included 73 pages containing almost 900 notes in English, German, French, Italian, and Latin, but did not include a bibliography. Locating specific or relevant titles using the notes is a nightmare, one that most people will abjure. If university presses at Harvard, Princeton, Yale, Cornell, Virginia, or Oklahoma hold that the works' intellectual sources do not require comprehensive codification, then why should Knopf, St. Martin's, or McGraw-Hill spend money on superfluous addenda?

Well, they do not: Ray Takeyh's *Hidden Iran* (2006), published by Henry

Holt, concludes with 18 pages of numbered endnotes, but the bibliography was expunged. For *A Grand and Godly Adventure* (2006), Godfrey Hodgson prepared 12 pages of numbered endnotes, but the publisher, Public Affairs, decided that a bibliography would be a burden. There is none. And here are some annoying variations. In 2007, the University of Chicago, ironically, published Piero Melograni's *Wolfgang Amadeus Mozart: A Biography.* The volume contains 19 dense pages of notes, but instead of concluding with a comprehensive, alphabetical listing, one finds a five page bibliographical overview. There are certain advantages to these run-on, sometimes classified listings, but most serious students of Mozart would undoubtedly prefer a traditional bibliography. Much worse is Dan Agin's *Junk Science*, especially since the author is a serious scholar. This study includes neither footnotes nor a bibliography; rather, its many quotations are precisely attributed, but in a chapter by chapter jumble. There is naturally a reason that apparently excuses this:

> Because this book is intended primarily for the general reader and is not a scholarly work, I have forgone the use of footnotes to identify references [293].

Agin does not even mention the missing alphabetical list. A most peculiar variation can be found in the fall and winter 2000 issues of *American Speech* (and, *mutatis mutandis*, elsewhere). Each number contains more than 30 Diamond Anniversary Essays, but the in-text referrals do not lead to the ends of the individual articles; instead, all of the citations are cumulated in a single alphabetical list at the conclusion of their respective issues ("References"). I am not alone in my condemnation. Abagail Zuger, reviewing Michael Stein's *Lonely Patient*, complains that "...Dr. Stein quotes extensively from sources like Oscar Wilde and Oliver Sacks without bothering to provide even a cursory bibliography" (D5).

Bibliographies should appear at the conclusion of all scholarly works.[2] This even holds for footnoted (scientific) journal articles, if they are extremely long and overburdened with innumerable citations. The entries should contain all of the elements included in the paradigms cited in the author's disciplinary manual or in the journal's or publisher's instructions, correctly ordered, and separated by the correct punctuation. Henige refers to an article that lacks these qualities, astonishingly, in *PMLA*, a journal in which one would expect the documentation to be letter-perfect: In Arturo Arias's "Authoring Ethnicized Subjects..." "...citation, even for quotes, is either shamefully absent or incoherently present" ("Being" 116, nt. 48). (My examination of this essay did not reveal these inconsistencies.) Henige also allows for some discretion in constructing an entry, but pragmatically he knows that it must conform to the editor's requirements ("Being, II" 78–79), although editors vary in their strictness and sometimes allow formats that their peers would shun. For example, as an editor of various collections and journals, I request APA style, but when I receive an excellent manuscript correctly documented according to MLA, for example, I do not request that the text and works-cited list be emended. Others are not so lenient: A journal sponsored and published by APA or a prestigious publication such as *Science* or *Cell*, would, I presume, never allow such an abomination. And now we have a new and most peculiar anomaly: Novels are being published with appended bibliographies (Bosman B1). These are not the kind of listings one might find in the bizarre constructions discussed in chapter 3, the parenthetically annotated or footnoted novels that derive their essence, at least in part, from the documentation. These, rather, are normal novels that their authors created, from historical precedent, and the authors wish to acknowledge or trace or preen. Very recent examples come from the pens of Martin Amis, Norman Mailer, and Thomas Pynchon, among many others (Bosman B8). Ironically, Zerby's study of footnotes does not include a comprehensive listing; instead, the volume concludes with the following brief note: "Readers desiring a bibliography to this work should look for my next book, *A History of Bibliographies*" (150). Lamentably, they will not find it: Zerby passed away in 2003.

6
Illustration

*The Illustrations are intended to keep the reader
from dwelling on the paucity of documentation.*
— Hugh Kenner

Ancillary or tangential data or information can be intercalated into the text or placed in the four margins or at the end of a chapter or the conclusion of the work. This material can attribute, affirm, explain, clarify, supplement, correct, or translate. Documentation is a broad and diverse category that, arguably, can also subsume graphic images, which serve many purposes in relation to a text. Iconographic catalogues of artistic works, discussions of paintings, prints, renderings, photographs, cinematic stills, or advertising illustrations take the image as a given; it is that which makes the text necessary. Without it, the text cannot come into being. Here it would be impossible to make a case for the illustration as an adjunct to the text in the way that an attribution or tangentially noted remark is. To be explicit, what this mean is that when the objective of the work is, for example, an overview of Rubens's painting or Steichen's photographs, it falls outside the pale of this discussion. But when an author graphically illustrates a complex, often incomprehensible point in any field but especially (and here I am being conservative) in mathematics, astronomy, physics, chemistry, biology, geology, cartography, anthropology, geography, literary studies, or music, it is similar to a supplementary comment within, for example, a footnote. Bert Hall tangentially affirms this: "[Conrad] Gesner was deeply aware of how pictures could supplement the printed word..." (17). And again, "As a rule, we expect images that appear in the company of texts to explicate the material covered in the text in some fashion or other" (21). Samuel Y. Edgerton, Jr., avers that "Historians of science ... tend to treat scientific pictures only as afterimages of verbal ideas" (qtd. in Topper 215). This is confirmed by Martin Rudwick, who claims that geologists have always depended upon illustrations but historians of geology relegate them to a decorative role or ignore them entirely (149). David Knight holds that "[s]cientific illustrations are pictures designed not to stand on their own but to accompany a text..." (qtd. in Topper 221). Bruno Latour inadvertently creates an analogy between the explanatory illustration and the evidentiary historical foot- or endnote:

> It is ... the unique advantage they [images] give in the rhetorical or polemical situation. "You doubt what I say? I'll show you." And without moving more than a few inches, I unfold in front of your eyes figures, diagrams, plates, texts, silhouettes ... [36].

Ann Shelby Blum insists that in the sixteenth century

> [d]espite the importance of picture printing to natural history ... text remained the primary vehicle of scholarly expression. Pictures illustrated text, not vice versa. Pictures served texts, supplemented it, completed it, remained subordinate to it ... [8].

Mutadis mutandis, this is a precise description of the roles that annotation or documentation play within or ancillary to the body of a work. In a lengthy discussion of the early development of the periodic table, Benjamin Cohen alludes more than once to the ancillary aspect of graphic display: "...[T]he tables of classification have always been elements of practice which were activated when read in the laboratory or when referred to in the text" (44). And again, "...[Tables] can be regarded as tools in much the same way as a laboratory balance, or a set of flasks, or perhaps a reference book" (47). Edward Tufte insists that

> [a]t their best, graphics are instruments for reasoning about quantitative information. Often the most effective way to describe, explore, and summarize a set of numbers — even a very large set — is to look at pictures of those numbers [*Visual* 9].

And Charlotte Tancin, in a personal communication, offers a different point of view:

> From our perspective in the history of botany, plant illustrations are scientific documentation and are crucial for botanical literature. They verify, attest to and vouch for the existence of a plant and the accuracy of its identification and description.... [W]hen illustrations are published with the written description of a new species, they are cited as permanent documentation.

The only unequivocally explicit affirmation and discussion of the illustration as a subset of documentation occurs in David Henige's overview of peripheral forms of annotation, under which heading he includes graphs, charts, maps, and facsimiles ("Being, II" 63), but the abandonment of the "charts and illustrations" in a recent publication to a Web site (Carvajal, "Book" A12) is an inductive indication that these images are somehow less important than and ancillary to the text and thus displaceable. Even Martin Kemp, an authority on art and science, in a book on this very topic, observes that

> [i]llustrations appear in books for many different reasons ... and they need not be structurally related to the main purpose of the text [9].

And again, in reference to the images he has chosen for his book,

> ... I have aspired to provide enough illustrations ... to support the argument ... [9].

This is a precise analogue to the evidentiary documentation (original texts, letters, translations) provided notationally, by historians, for example. For Tufte, images play an evidentiary and explanatory role (*Beautiful*, passim). Images clarify, verify, expand, and, by definition, illustrate. Perhaps the most pointed analogy between illustration and annotation, one that indicates a precise parallelism concerning purpose and structure, is tendered by Scott L. Montgomery:

> The visual dimension to science forms a language all its own, a kind of pictorial rhetoric, if you will. By this I mean that graphics are often much more than a handmaiden to writing. They don't just restate the data or reduce the need for prose, but offer a kind of separate "text" for reading and interpretation.... You will find that they tell their own story, in some manner parallel to that of the writing, but in other ways different, enriching, though also with notable gaps [qtd. in Goldbort 175].

An illustration can take the form of a typical textual annotation, regardless of where it is physically located. Tufte points out that Leonardo da Vinci integrates illustrative drawings within his surrounding hand-written text (*Visual* 182). Others place the image above, below, or to the side of the text, in the margin, on a separate plate, in a collection of plates distant from the text, or in a note of some kind. It may be impossible to understand the discussion without its accompanying visual explication. Here the text is an *a priori* given and the graphic an ancillary, explanatory adjunct. In many cases, even if a reader were willing and able to create a working mental or physical image for guidance, it might turn out to be extremely misleading. John L. Ridgway makes this blatantly clear: "It would be impossible to present a clear understanding of the physical characteristics of a bird or other creature based alone on measurements, color, and the usual diagnostic characters, or to describe adequately the form and details of many organisms, without illustrations" (1).

6. Illustration 131

To document, in the context of this study, is to provide sources (attributions) for material presented or to complement what is discussed through a gloss or some form of commentary. But the term has a less specific denotation: it means to provide evidence or proof (which is what it does in scholarship), and this is precisely what Sam Smiles means when he titles a study, *Eye Witness: Artists and Visual Documentation in Britain, 1770–1830*. For evidence to be meaningful or useful it must be true. In considerations of illustrations, especially those used in scientific works, the attitude has been one of skepticism. Indeed, since visual representations, some of which purposely fool the eye (as in trompe l'oeil), are mere simulacra, they have traditionally been mistrusted (although recent scholarship has come to their defense, e.g., James Robert Brown

Leonardo da Vinci's illustrations integrated into his text. "Codex Urbinas Latinus 1270." Used by permission of Princeton University.

for mathematics and Laura Perini for science, *inter alios*, show that visual imagery can be trusted). Nevertheless, images in scientific texts have long been treated as mere adjuncts, heuristic aids to help, but the binding evidence, the proof could only be found in the textual discussions, explanations, and equations. Yet, it is possible for an adjunct (an image found within a footnote, to cite an extreme case) to purvey a visual truth that leads to unequivocal proof. I have tried to make the case that illustration is indeed a reasonable subset of documentation, but since this is not a crucial aspect of this study, I prefer not to belabor the point. Appropriate images (illustrative and evidentiary) include those found in pauper Bibles (they are a simulacrum of the text); botanical and zoological illustrations (often in color); mathematical, scientific, and technical graphics including equations and geometric forms that clarify or supplement; as well as charts, tables, diagrams, figures, photographs of various types, drawings, and various notational systems (such as the one used in music) in any discipline, but especially in the hard and social sciences.

Examples

Euclid's (ca. 325–ca. 265) *Elements* is a good place to begin. It is very difficult to comprehend abstract geometric discussions; thus, illustrations make Euclid's remarks more easily comprehensible. The 1482 *Elementa Geometrica* produced by Ratdolt in Venice is the first printed Latin text and contains some 400 woodcuts. The 1499 edition that Aldus Manutius published,

Marginal illustrations (Euclid, *Elementa Geometrica*, 1482). Image copyright History of Science Collections, University of Oklahoma Libraries.

of Euclides Elementes.   Fol.314.

ward narower and natower, at length ende their angles (at the heigth or toppe therof) in one point. So all their angles there ioyned together, make a solide angle. And for the better sight thereof, I haue set here a figure wherby ye shall more easily conceiue it, the base of the figure is a triangle, namely, A B C, if on euery side of the triangle A B C, ye rayse vp a triangle, as vpon the side A B, ye raise vp the triangle A F B, and vpon the side A C the triangle A F C, and vpon the side B C, the triangle B F C, and so bowing the triangles raised vp, that their toppes, namely, the pointes F meete and ioyne together in one point, ye shal easily and plainly see how these three superficiall angles A F B B F C, C F A, ioyne and close together, touching the one the other in the point F, and so make a solide angle.

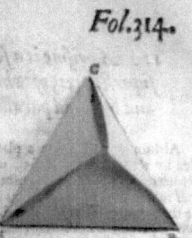

10. *A Pyramis is a solide figure contained vnder many playne superficieces set vpon one playne superficies, and gathered together to one point.*   Tenth definition.

Two superficieces raysed vpon any ground can not make a Pyramis, forthat two superficiall angles ioyned together in the toppe, cannot (as before is sayd) make a solide angle. Wherfore who thre, foure, fiue, or moe (how many soeuer) superficieces are raised vp fro one superficies being the ground, or base, and euer asceding diminish their breadth, till at the legth all their angles cōcurre in one point, making there a solide angle: the solide inclosed, bounded, and terminated by these superficieces is called a Pyramis, as ye see in a taper of foure sides, and in a spire of a towre which containeth many sides, either of which is a Pyramis.

And because that all the superficieces of euery Pyramis ascend from one playne superficies as from the base, and tende to one poynt, it must of necessitie come to passe, that all the superficieces of a Pyramis are trianguler, except the base, which may be of any forme or figure except a circle. For if the base be a circle, then it ascendeth not with sides, or diuers superficieces, but with one round superficies, and hath not the name of a Pyramis, but is called (as hereafter shall appeare) a Cone.

Of Pyramids there are diuers kindes. For according to the varietie of the base is brought forth the varietie and diuersitie of kindes of Pyramids. If the base of a Pyramis be a triangle, then is it called a triangled Pyramis. If the base be a figure of fower angles, it is called a quadrangled Pyramis. If the base be a Pentagon, then is it a Pentagonall or fiueangled Pyramis. And so forth according to the increase of the angles of the base infinitely. Although the figure of a Pyramis can not be well expressed in a playne superficies, yet may ye sufficiently conceaue of it both by the figure before set in the definition of a solide angle, and by the figure here set, if ye imagine the point A together with the lines A B, A C, and A D, to be eleuated on high: And yet that the reader may more clerely see the forme of a Pyramis, I haue here set two sundry Pyramids which will appeare bodilike, if ye erecte the papers wherin are drawen the triangular sides of the Pyramis, in such sort that the pointes of the angles F of ech triangle may in euery Pyramis concurre in one point, and make a solide angle: one of which hath to his base a fower sided figure, and the other a fiue sided figure. The forme of a triangled Pyramis ye may before beholde in the example of a solide angle. And by these may ye conceaue of all other kindes of Pyramids.

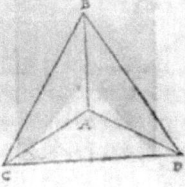

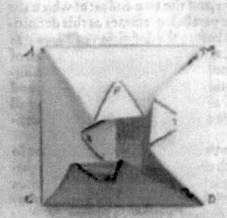
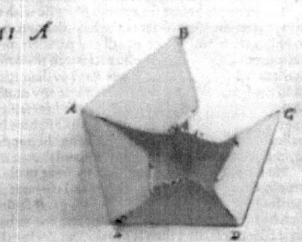

Three dimensional, pop-up illustrations (*Euclides Elementes*, 1570). Image copyright History of Science Collections, University of Oklahoma Libraries.

also in Venice, is the first printed Greek text and the first book to appear in italics. Many years ago, I was privileged to handle the first English edition; it was published in London in 1570 and is noteworthy because it contains three-dimensional illustrations (Magruder, passim). This is truly extraordinary because this is something that even today one only finds in children's pop-up books. These tactile images of the geometric discussion help to clarify precisely what Euclid means in the same way that an explanatory or exegetical footnote does verbally.

Ramon Llull (1232–1316) is not interested in attributing influences and sources, but documentation, in the form of illustration, plays a major role in his work, because he uses both small charts and tables to make his points. The former are clear; the latter are so complex that they are almost incomprehensible. His work is reminiscent of Spinoza's attempt to mathematize ethics. The answers to questions are aligned with specific word sets and symbolic letters (that correspond to the tables):

> 3. *Question*: Whether goodness has power eternally.
> *Solution*: [goodness eternity/AT/SV/ being perfection/majority end/justice generosity] [456].

But none of this solves any real problems.

Another superb example of illustrations that are an integral and necessary part of the text, though set off in the left and right hand margins, are those found in Copernicus's (1473–1543) *Revolutions of the Heavenly Spheres* (*On the Revolutions*). These many geometric diagrams, as well as a series of numerical tables, help to make the astronomical discussions more easily comprehensible. An excellent example is the simple illustration accompanying the two paragraphs of book IV's chapter 11, "Tabular Presentation of the Lunar Prosthaphaereses or Normalizations." It would be almost impossible to visu-

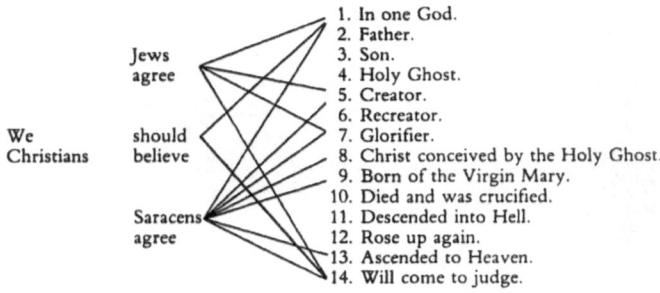

Ramon Llull, chart. Bonner, Anthony; *Selected Works of Ramon Llull 1232–1316, Volumes 1 and 2.* ©1985 Princeton University Press. Reprinted by permission of Princeton University Press.

DISTINCTION I

The Second Figure of A

```
good    great   etern   power   wisdom  will    virtue  truth   glory   perf    justice gener   simpli  nobil   mercy   domin
good    great   etern   power   wisdom  will    virtue  truth   glory   perf    justice gener   simpli  nobil   mercy   domin

good    great   etern   power   wisdom  will    virtue  truth   glory   perf    justice gener   simpli  nobil   mercy
great   etern   power   wisdom  will    virtue  truth   glory   perf    justice gener   simpli  nobil   mercy   domin

good    great   etern   power   wisdom  will    virtue  truth   glory   perf    justice gener   simpli  nobil
etern   power   wisdom  will    virtue  truth   glory   perf    justice gener   simpli  nobil   mercy   domin

good    great   etern   power   wisdom  will    virtue  truth   glory   perf    justice gener   simpli
power   wisdom  will    virtue  truth   glory   perf    justice gener   simpli  nobil   mercy   domin

good    great   etern   power   wisdom  will    virtue  truth   glory   perf    justice gener
wisdom  will    virtue  truth   glory   perf    justice gener   simpli  nobil   mercy   domin

good    great   etern   power   wisdom  will    virtue  truth   glory   perf    justice
will    virtue  truth   glory   perf    justice gener   simpli  nobil   mercy   domin

good    great   etern   power   wisdom  will    virtue  truth   glory   perf
virtue  truth   glory   perf    justice gener   simpli  nobil   mercy   domin

good    great   etern   power   wisdom  will    virtue  truth   glory
truth   glory   perf    justice gener   simpli  nobil   mercy   domin

good    great   etern   power   wisdom  will    virtue  truth
glory   perf    justice gener   simpli  nobil   mercy   domin

good    great   etern   power   wisdom  will    virtue
perf    justice gener   simpli  nobil   mercy   domin

good    great   etern   power   wisdom  will
justice gener   simpli  nobil   mercy   domin

good    great   etern   power   wisdom
gener   simpli  nobil   mercy   domin

good    great   etern   power
simpli  nobil   mercy   domin

good    great   etern
nobil   mercy   domin

good    great
mercy   domin

good
domin
```

Ramon Llull, table. Bonner, Anthony; *Selected Works of Ramon Llull 1232–1316, Volumes 1 and 2.* ©1985 Princeton University Press. Reprinted by permission of Princeton University Press.

alize or conceptualize what Copernicus describes without the subtended circles and triangles that accompany the text (and precede the tabular presentation).

Sir Isaac Newton (1642–1727) performed an experiment in which he refracted light into its constituent spectral colors. The schematic diagram he appended to his published letter helps the reader understand the precise alignment of the apparatus that showed the path of the light and its alteration as it emerged from the prism. Without the simple drawing it would have been difficult to envision what he had done; with it, the ray's path and its dissection are clear. He recapitulates this in his *Opticks,* where the path of the light is precisely described —

> At the right, sunlight (o) enters the prism through a hole in the window shutter, at F. The rays enter the prism ABC, and refraction by the prism generates the spectrum (p, q, r, s, t) that falls on the double-convex lens, MN. [And so on.] —

laxes [IV, 16]. Thus that distance of 48° 6' between the luminaries, which Hipparchus had obtained instrumentally, accords with my computation with remarkable closeness and, as it were, by agreement.

TABULAR PRESENTATION OF THE LUNAR PROSTHAPHAERESES OR NORMALIZATIONS   Chapter 11

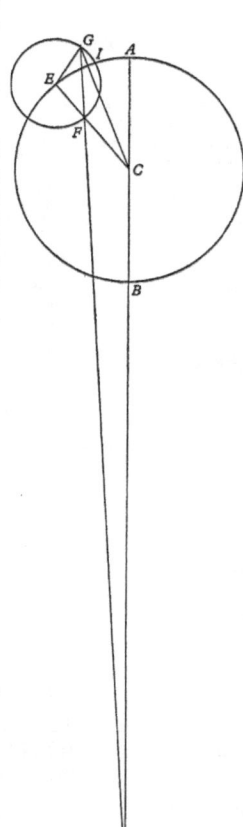

The method of computing the lunar motions, I believe, is understood in general from the present example. In triangle *CEG* two sides, *GE* and *CE*, always remain the same. Through angle *GEC*, which constantly changes, but nevertheless is given, we obtain the remaining side *GC*, together with angle *ECG*, which is the prosthaphaeresis for normalizing the anomaly. Secondly, when two sides, *DC* and *CG*, in triangle *CDG*, as well as angle *DCE* are determined numerically, by the same procedure angle *D* at the center of the earth becomes known [as the difference] between the uniform and the true motions.

In order to make this information even handier, I shall construct a table of the prosthaphaereses in six columns. After two [columns containing the] common numbers of the deferent, the third column will show the prosthaphaereses which arise from the epicyclet's twice-monthly rotation and vary the uniformity of the first anomaly. Then, leaving the next column temporarily vacant to receive numbers later, I shall concern myself with the fifth column. In it I shall enter the first and larger epicycle's prosthaphaereses which occur at mean conjunctions and oppositions of the sun and moon. The biggest of these prosthaphaereses is 4° 56'. In the next to the last column are placed the numbers by which the prosthaphaereses occurring at half moon exceed the prosthaphaereses in column 4. Of these numbers, the largest is 2° 44' [= 7° 40'– 4° 56']. For the purpose of ascertaining the other numbers in excess, the proportional minutes have been worked out according to the following ratio. [The maximum number in excess] 2° 44' was treated as 60' in relation to any other excess occurring at the epicyclet's point of tangency [with the line drawn from the center of the earth]. Thus, in the same example [IV, 10], we had line *CG* = 1123 units of which *CD* = 10,000. This makes the largest prosthaphaeresis at the epicyclet's point of tangency 6° 29', exceeding that first maximum by 1° 33' [+4° 56' = 6° 29']. But 2° 44' : 1° 33' = 60' : 34'. Therefore we have the ratio of the excess occurring in the epicyclet's semicircle to the excess caused by the given arc of 90° 10'. Accordingly, opposite 90° in the Table, I shall write 34'. In this way for every arc of the same circle entered in the Table we shall find the proportional minutes, which are to be recorded in the vacant fourth column. Finally, in the last column I added the northern and southern degrees of latitude, which I shall discuss below [IV, 13–14]. For, the convenience of the procedure and practice with it convinced me to preserve this arrangement.

195

Nicholas Copernicus, geometric illustration. Copernicus, Nicholas. Translation and commentary by Edward Rosen. *On the Revolutions: Nicholas Copernicus Complete Works*. P. 195. ©1978 Edward Rosen. Reprinted by permission of the Johns Hopkins University Press.

BOOK I CH. 14

II

Any arc of a triangle must be less than a semicircle.

For, a semicircle does not form an angle at the center, but proceeds through it in a straight line. On the other hand, the two remaining angles, to which arcs belong, cannot enclose a solid angle at the center, and consequently not a spherical triangle. This was the reason, in my opinion, why Ptolemy, in expounding this class of triangles, especially in connection with the shape of the spherical sector, stipulates that the assumed arcs should not be greater than a semicircle [*Syntaxis*, I, 13].

III

In right spherical triangles, the ratio of the chord subtending twice the side opposite the right angle to the chord subtending twice either one of the sides including the right angle is equal to the ratio of the diameter of the sphere to the chord subtending twice the angle included, on a great circle of the sphere, between the remaining side and the hypotenuse.

For let there be a spherical triangle *ABC*, in which *C* is a right angle. I say that the ratio of the chord subtending twice *AB* to the chord subtending twice *BC* is equal to the ratio of the diameter of the sphere to the chord subtending twice the angle *BAC* on a great circle.

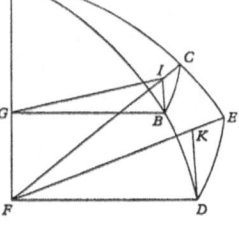

With *A* as pole, draw *DE* as the arc of a great circle. Complete the quadrants *ABD* and *ACE*. From *F*, the center of the sphere, draw the intersections of the circles: *FA*, of *ABD* and *ACE*; *FE*, of *ACE* and *DE*; *FD*, of *ABD* and *DE*; and also *FC*, of the circles *AC* and *BC*. Then draw *BG* perpendicular to *FA*, *BI* to *FC*, and *DK* to *FE*. Join *GI*.

If a circle intersects another circle while passing through its poles, it intersects it at right angles. Therefore *AED* is a right angle. So is *ACB* by hypothesis. Hence both planes *EDF* and *BCF* are perpendicular to *AEF*. In this last-mentioned plane at point *K* draw a straight line perpendicular to the intersection *FKE*. Then this perpendicular will form with *KD* another right angle, in accordance with the definition of planes perpendicular to each other. Consequently *KD* is perpendicular also to *AEF*, according to Euclid, XI, 4. In the same way *BI* is drawn perpendicular to the same plane, and therefore *DK* and *BI* are parallel to each other, according to Euclid, XI, 6. Likewise *GB* is parallel to *FD*, because *FGB* and *GFD* are right angles. According to Euclid's *Elements*, XI, 10, angle *FDK* will be equal to *GBI*. But *FKD* is a right angle, and so is *GIB* according to the definition of a perpendicular line. The sides of similar triangles being proportional, *DF* is to *BG* as *DK* is to *BI*. But *BI* is half of the chord subtending twice the arc *CB*, since *BI* is perpendicular to the radius *CF*. In the same way *BG* is half of the chord subtending twice the side *BA*; *DK* is half of the chord subtending twice *DE*, or twice angle *A*; and *DF* is half of the diameter of the sphere. Clearly, therefore, the ratio of the chord subtending twice *AB* to the chord subtending twice *BC* is equal to the ratio of the diameter to the chord subtending twice the angle *A*, or twice the intercepted arc *DE*. The demonstration of this Theorem will prove to be useful.

IV

In any triangle having a right angle, if another angle and any side are given, the remaining angle and the remaining sides will also be given.

43

Nicholas Copernicus, geometric illustration. Copernicus, Nicholas. Translation and commentary by Edward Rosen. *On the Revolutions: Nicholas Copernicus Complete Works*. P. 43. ©1978 Edward Rosen. Reprinted by permission of the Johns Hopkins University Press.

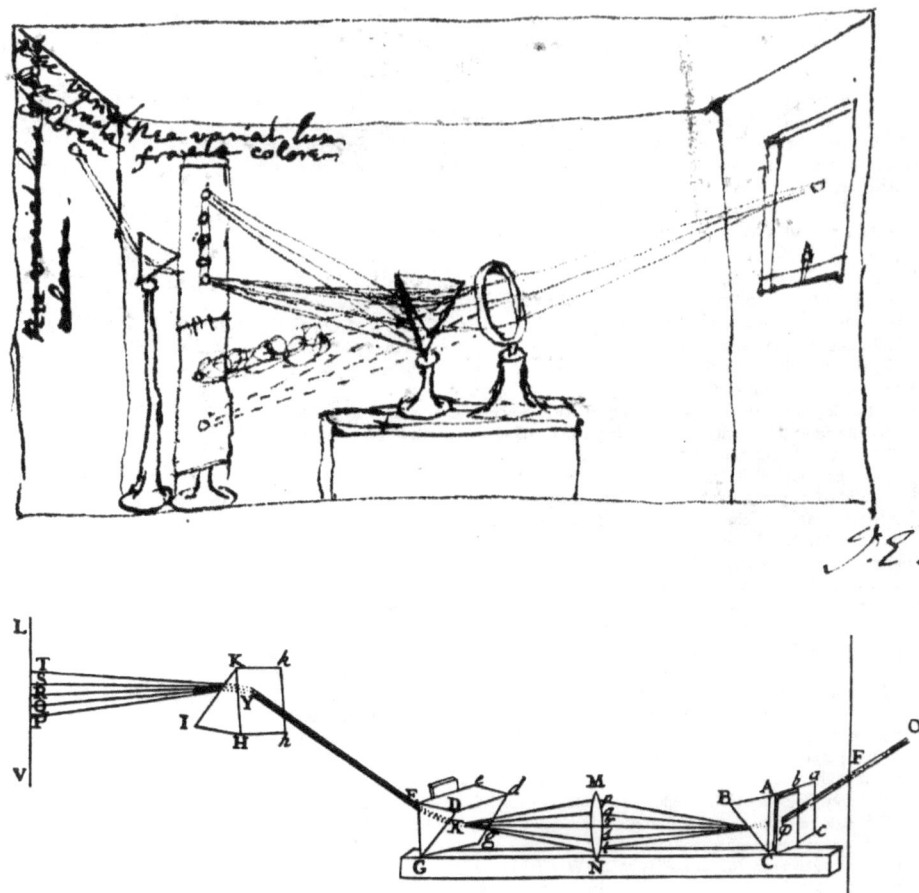

Top: Sir Isaac Newton, illustration accompanying a published letter. By permission of the Warden and Fellows, New College, Oxford. *Bottom:* Clarifying rendition of the Newton drawing. In Harry Robin, *The Scientific Image*, published by Abrams.

and concomitantly laid out in a more sophisticated diagram (Robin, *Scientific* 84–85). Though the verbal descriptions would make little or no sense without the graphics, the illustrations are appendages, explanatory footnotes as it were.

One of the great works of western thought is Denis Diderot's (1713–1784) *Encyclopedia.* The text and its footnotes are supplemented by many additional large volumes containing plates. The magnificent copper engravings illustrate common items, occupations, warfare, machinery, and processes. In some cases, it would have been possible to draw a verbose, comprehensible verbal picture

6. Illustration 139

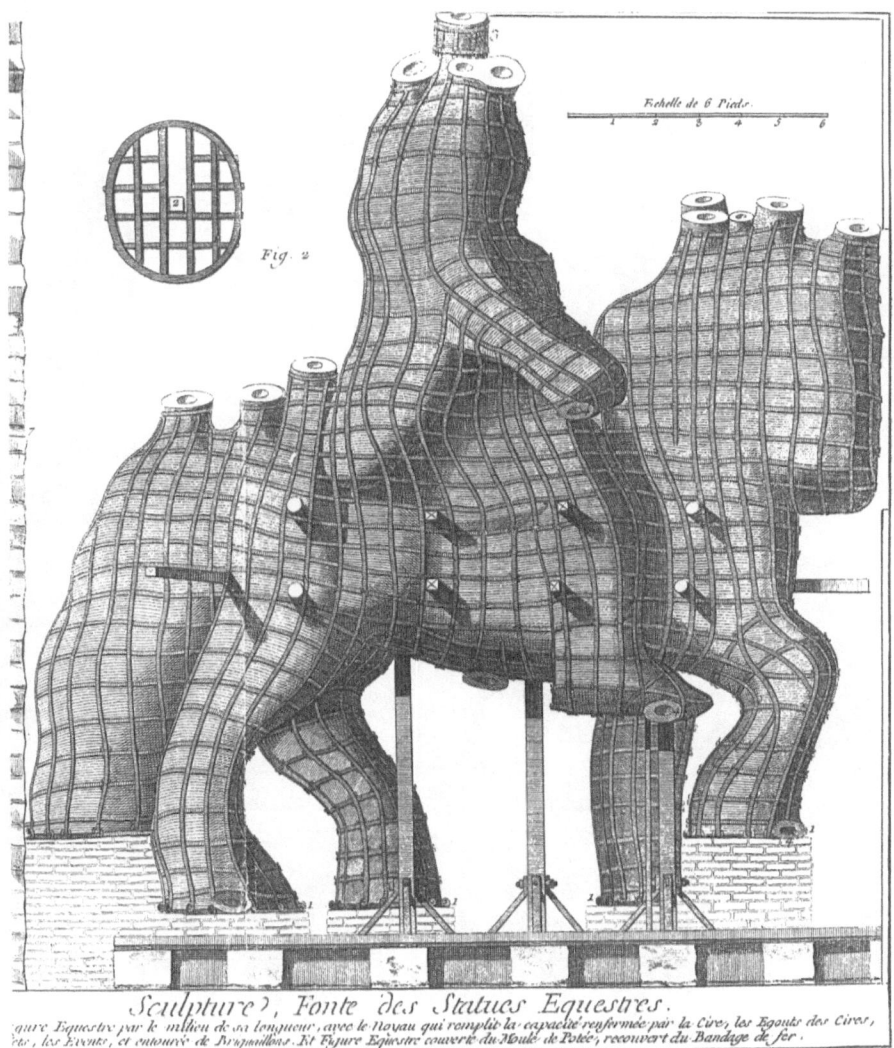

Casting a statue (Denis Diderot, *Encyclopedia*). Permission granted for Denis Diderot, *A Diderot Pictorial Encyclopedia of Trades and Industry*, published by Dover.

of what is being described, but in others, such as the fourth plate in the series "Casting A Statue" (pl. 120) or "Ironwork III" (pl. 167), words are incapable of bringing the image to life. Thus, the illustrations offer a supplementary clarification, one that makes something otherwise unknown or esoteric truly comprehensible.

140 Documentation

Vol. IX, Serrurerie, Pl. XII.

Ironwork (Denis Diderot, *Encyclopedia*). Permission granted for Denis Diderot, *A Diderot Pictorial Encyclopedia of Trades and Industry*, published by Dover.

A classic case of intuitive discovery in the history of science concerns Friederich August Kekulé's (1829–1896) dream concerning an interconnected ring of snakes (Harry Robin calls them chains of dancing atoms), which for him represented, at last, the structure of benzene, something that had eluded chemists for years. His explanation is illustrated through a simple drawing and his text makes it clear that the drawing is a mere appendage:

> This opinion concerning the structure, which consists of a closed chain (ring) of six carbon atoms will perhaps be still more clearly rendered through the following graphic formula, in which are shown the carbon atoms, around, and the four affinities of each atom through the four lines that extend from each of them [Robin, *Scientific* 213, my translation].

I am making a simple semantic distinction here, but it is crucial to my overall argument: Kekulé's brief text is not a description of the image; rather, the graphic clarifies the verbal explanation, and without this visual addition, the text would be almost as unclear as the structure of benzene had been, despite the great strides made in chemistry. This is annotation's precise function: to clarify parenthetically, marginally, or notationally.

It might be possible (though counterproductive and even foolish, I believe) to argue that in many disciplinary areas and cases, scientific and mathematical illustration is superfluous, unnecessary, misleading, or unreliable, since it may not provide evidentiary proof. But even the most avid dissenter

offene Kette.   geschlossene Kette.

Diese Ansicht über die Constitution der aus sechs Kohlenstoffatomen bestehenden, geschlossenen Kette wird vielleicht noch deutlicher wiedergegeben durch folgende graphische Formel, in welcher die Kohlenstoffatome rund und die vier Verwandtschaftseinheiten jedes Atomes durch vier von ihm auslaufende Linien dargestellt sind:

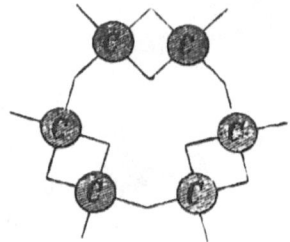

Friedrich August Kekulé's illustration of the benzene ring (from his *Organic Chemistry*, 1860).

(I think that this point of view obtained primarily in the past) would be unable to gainsay the necessity for anatomical illustrations including drawings, woodblocks, etchings, engravings, and photographs. The most intense and detailed verbal description cannot pretend to give a full picture of the layout, location, and interaction of various body parts. Da Vinci concurs:

> I counsel you not to cumber yourself with words unless you are speaking to the blind...[.] How in words can you describe this heart without filling a whole book? Yet the more detail you write concerning it the more you will confuse the mind of the hearer [qtd. in Roberts et al., 7].

Even the structure, curvature, texture, and configuration of a few small bones must be communicated visually. The soft tissues and organs, of the human body, for example, are so complex that it takes years to truly master their interconnections. A visual aid helps since it is impossible to perform a dissection or even refer to a preserved corpse every time some data is required, and only a genius with a photographic memory could recall every nuance of our internal body parts. (This is especially true for the beginning student of human anatomy and physiology, who struggles to memorize nomenclature, parts, and functions). Appended illustrations supplement the text and make it possible to learn the required material by recreating a visual map of the body in one's mind: One may simply refer to the mental image in order to ascertain where the neck arteries lie in relation to the muscles, lymph nodes, throat, and other cervical accoutrements.

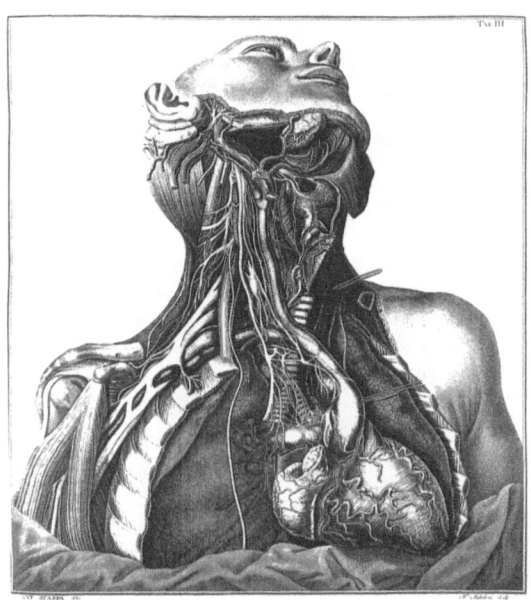

Nerves and other parts leading from the heart into the neck. A Scarpa, *Tabulae Neurologicae*, 1794. Used by permission of Wellcome Library, London.

A more extreme example is the mutually reciprocal documentation that occurs when a physical illustration (drawing, painting, photograph) works symbiotically with a text. Sometimes a single person such as William Blake creates both simultaneously. Here the "illustration" is not a subsidiary form. It is not meant to stand as a mere reflection of the words; rather, it is an autonomous but connected entity with equal stature: its full power is felt only when viewed in relation to the poem. At other times, word and text derive from separate people. The Bible inspired Michelangelo and da Vinci, whose Sistine Chapel frescoes and *Last Supper* are glosses on their respective texts; Dante inspired Daumier; and the fiction of Dickens, Carroll, and Doyle is reflected in the drawings of a host of graphic interpreters. It is also possible for a graphic image to inspire an author: Rosanna Warren, for example, wrote a series of 24 poems that derive from but do not merely describe or reflect James McGarrell's etchings, which in turn were inspired by Greek mythology. Steven P. Schneider offers an excellent if concise overview of *ekphrasis* (the mutual interaction of poetic texts and images) that includes its contemporary practitioners as well as a listing of scholarly resources.

In periodical articles and often in monographs, explanatory and illustrative images are intercalated into the text where required. Historically informative (rather than confirmative) photographs are sometimes treated differently, especially in monographs, where they may be bunched together in one or more inserts placed at various points in the book, as is the case in Tabitha Kanago's *African Womanhood in Colonial Kenya, 1900–50*, where a map and 12 photographs (x–xvi) follow the fore-matter. The difference between a color image in *Cell* and the photograph of Aidé Tito Romero at her fiesta clothing stall (109) (ironically, intercalated into the text) in Linda Seligmann's *Peruvian Street Lives* is that in the former case, the photograph is essential for both comprehension and confirmation, whereas in the vendor's case, it is merely a lagniappe, good to have but not truly necessary.

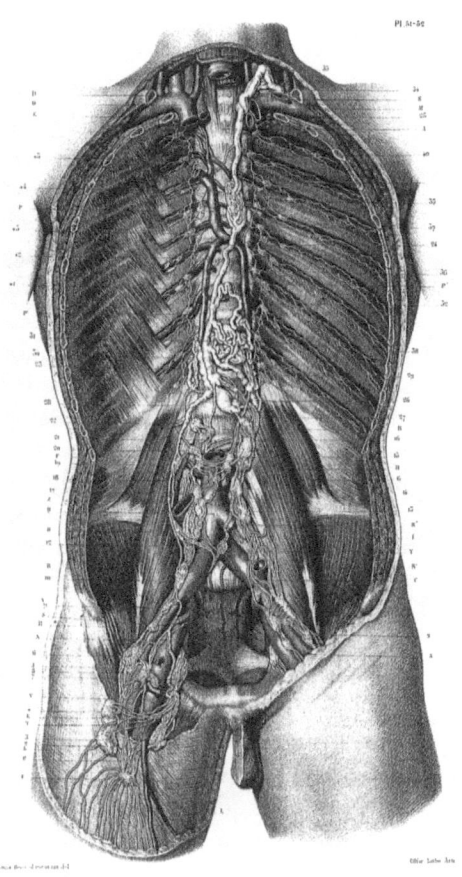

Lymph nodes and other internal body parts. Bonamy et al., *Atlas d'anatomie descriptive*, 1847. Used by permission of Wellcome Library, London.

Maps

A complex, descriptive text exists; the author or editor appends an explanatory parenthetical, marginal, or noted annotation, an excursus that clarifies, interprets, or refers to other possibilities. This notation comes into being only in relation to its text and complements it (although occasionally the annotation counters or parodies its progenitor). This is precisely the function of the illustrations that this chapter discusses. In this context, there is no appreciable difference between verbal and graphic excursuses. An iconic or cartographic image may be considered a non-verbal "text" (McKenzie 43), a perceptible, visual, comprehensible artifact (not to be confused with the text-annotation distinction maintained throughout this study). As such, it is an analogue to any type of verbal annotation. Conversely, though, if a specific image, e.g., a detailed ecological map of Siberia, is the text (and the data and information presented in purely visual form can be as complex as a verbal text), then brief appended verbal explanatory remarks constitute the annotations, which may appear marginally, or under superscript numbers or signs, or in overlays directly on the ice-encrusted surface of the Siberian tundra as represented on the map. Normally, though, a verbal geographical reference to or description of a location, for example, may be clarified by appending a visual, cartographic explanation: Bhutan is located east of Nepal, north of India, and south of China. But where exactly, and what shape does it take, and how large is it, and what about its general geographic features? A small topographic emplacement map that follows or is located in a note visually answers the above mooted questions, and many others as well. Even a professional physical geographer would have a difficult time envisioning specific esoteric cartographic features of a given area. A verbal description of the Grand Canyon, the Urals, the Orinoco, Idaho, Latvia, or Mongolia only goes so far.

Scott McEathron (University of Kansas), in an e-mail message sent in response to a query that I had posted on two map Listservs, confirms this through exemplification:

> ... [A]ny text dealing with U.S. Public Land Policy in 1850–60 may be totally incomprehensible without a cartographic adjunct to some. Also, any text dealing with a military campaign or battle wherein the reader was not a participant or familiar with the terrain.

A cartographic explanation clarifies in a way that words cannot, and the same holds true for a photographic image of a specific feature. Naturally, different types of maps — ecological, topographic, seismic, spatial, sociological, economic — yield different bits of data; and this is true for different types of photographs as well — wide-lens, composite, three-dimensional, computer-generated, radiographic — each tells its own story, one for which verbal articulation alone proves completely inadequate. Most supportive, however, is Ahmet Karamustafa, whose remarks are salient, incisive, and uniquely confirming:

> Almost all the extant Islamic maps are integral parts of larger manuscript contexts.... For those map artifacts that are found in texts, it seems safe to assume that they served a didactic or illustrative function subservient to the main textual narrative [4, 5].

A minor extrapolation would allow me to extend this to textually intercalated or referenced maps generally. But perhaps the most compelling evidence one can adduce to show that maps are often (unconsciously) considered a part of the same ancillary apparatus to which parenthetical adumbrations, marginalia, and notation belong is the fact that regardless of their crucial explanatory importance to a text, they often adorn a book's front and rear endpapers. Occasionally, an orienting map for the entire text is placed just before or after the table of contents.

Authors (sometimes influenced by their publishers) refer to maps (and other images) in different ways depending on the importance they allocate to them. Here are three hierarchical possibilities: Quite ironically, in a study entitled *The Mapmaker's Wife,* Robert Whitaker emphasizes the text to the exclusion of the various maps (and many images) scattered throughout the volume. First, he does not recognize them at all either in a preliminary list of illustrations (which does not exist) nor in the notes, bibliography, or acknowledgments that conclude the work (though credit is apportioned, in some cases, in the captions). Second, in chapter 12, "Lost on the Bobonaza," Whitaker makes no textual reference to the explanatory and validating map (and image) that are intercalated here. This appears to be his general modus operandi.

Maps are more important to John C. Behrendt, because in *The Ninth Circle,* an account of his life in Antarctica, he refers the reader to the cartographic collection at the back of the book thus: "After 8 more miles, we turned about west and drove on to 976 where we camped [see map 8]" (190). (He brackets his reference because this material is a quotation from his journal.) This is a referral to ancillary apparatus analogous to those found in Bayle or Gibbon. Other than captioned credits for the maps (and many photographs), Whitaker does not acknowledge his images. Finally, we find intercalated and referenced maps (as well as tables and photographs) in David Kornhouser's *Japan,* a study that reasonably does contain preliminary lists of photographs, tables, and maps. Here is how he alludes to his illustrative material. The text on page 12 refers directly and specifically to the contiguous table on page 13 and the map on the following page:

> Table 1.2 gives a rough indication of these circumstances....
>
> ...
>
> A glance at a physiographic map of east Asia, for example, allows an immediate visual comparison between the spacious North China Plain, and the Kanto Plain, Japan's largest and most important level area (Map 7).

This is precisely how textual matter is annotated, referenced, cited, or documented. Finally, maps play a crucial role in biological documentation (which is, admittedly, slightly different than the matter under discussion):

> ... [M]aps are also considered vital documentation in biology. They document the itineraries of explorers and collectors, and show locations where specimens were found. This is important not only for floras and other such enumerations but also for ecology and other aspects of biological study [Tancin].

On the other hand, cartographic images, like all visual representations of reality, can seduce, distort, mislead, or allow the viewer to perceive something that is not represented at all. One need only recall that we see what we expect; those who are not used to viewing visual images see nothing (a photograph of a cow is much too small to be — or represent — a cow, so it is not); and the blind, given sight, must learn to correlate an object with its verbal description (and mentally conceived image). But in tandem with its text, documenting illustration provides the best representational explanation possible in an imperfect world.

The claim that visual, and by taxonomic inference cartographic, images are sometimes subsets of documentation and have similar functions, appears to be a clear and tenable hypothesis. Thus, I was disconcerted to discover that some scholars disagree quite strongly. In an another e-mail message, Matthew H. Edney, of the University of Wisconsin,

> ... suggest[s] that it would be a mistake to consider maps as 'illustration' and therefore a "subset of documentation." ... Certainly, in many texts ... they are treated as ancillary to the written word.... But people in our modern society have been deluding themselves about the nature of maps for a long time. In particular, maps are integral components of the overall text; they have a symbolic role (just as footnotes signify erudition and highbrow writing) but more importantly also their content is read in concert with the written word.

I understand that a cartographic historian would of necessity take this position, and I sympathize with it. I certainly do not mean to relegate maps to a subsidiary physical or intellectual position. But I do think that just as some maps mislead or distort because their creators' intentions are impure (see Mark Monmonier's *How to Lie with Maps*), which does not disparage maps generally, so can some examples be mere explanatory adjuncts to a text. This, naturally, does not imply that in other cases, the map is not the "text" and the verbal description, commentary, or discussion not the adjunct.

Illustrations in their extraordinary diversity serve many purposes and do so in many different ways. Emily Marsh and Marilyn Domas White have created a simple but effective taxonomy for the ways in which images relate to their texts. Three major divisions (little relation, close relation, and extra-textual) are broken down into a series of subcategories (e.g., decorate, reiterate, interpret), which in turn yield precise functions (e.g., change pace, concretize, emphasize). This categorical breakdown shows how illustrations sometimes serve authors and readers in the same way that annotation does. Indeed, one of the functions included is to document (653).

7
The Major Systems

Little more than a hundred years ago, there was no single codified system for those who chose to attribute their sources or tangentially comment either within the text or in some type of note (in the margins or at the foot of the page). Even more recently, formats varied widely depending on the predilection of the scholar. They still do, but now the distinctions derive from innumerable formal organizations or independent controlling editors. Countless formalized systems exist: *RefWorks* lists 321. *EndNote* claims that it offers 2300 different styles. (See "Software," p. 166.) But naturally there are a handful that predominate in most venues or disciplines; these include *Chicago*, APA, MLA, and CSE; newspapers often follow AP. Many of the others are variations on these major systems and differ only minimally from their source. A few are the eccentric necessities of editors of individual journals. Below, I discuss and comment on the systems that encompass scholarly documentation generally in the humanities and social and hard sciences. The style guides or manuals are replete with much extraneous material: *Chicago*, for example, has an enormous section on bookmaking and another on production and printing. They all offer guidance and help with style and grammar. Documentation as such often only takes up a small (but crucial) portion of these volumes.

The earliest Modern Language Association (MLA) style guide was a succinct pamphlet (a mere 31 pages in its first recension, published in the April 1951 issue of *PMLA*); it served its purpose quite well and the present author used it to produce a research paper in his freshman English course. This occurred almost a half century ago, and during the intervening years, things have become more complex.

The current (sixth) edition of the *MLA Handbook for Writers of Research Papers* runs on for 361 pages. The same evolutionary processes have occurred with the *Publication Manual of the American Psychological Association*, which, now, in its fifth edition, is a generous 439 pages long. The 1974 second edition of APA managed to cover the same material in a mere 136 pages. The 15th edition of *The Chicago Manual of Style* contains 956 pages! (For an excellent brief historical overview and commentary on APA and MLA, see Connors, "Rhetoric II.") The Council of Science Editors (CSE, but formerly the Council of Biology Editors, CBE) manual is the general guide for the hard sciences, but as noted below, there is a great deal of variation even within specific disciplines such as biology. The 658 pages of the 2006 edition cover everything imaginable. A mere 86 pages are given over to documentation, which allows for three possibilities: the citation-sequence system (text numbers leading to a numerical list); the name-year system (these terms noted parenthetically leading to an alphabetical list); and the citation-name system (numbers leading to an alphabetic list, each entry of which is also numbered sequentially; the numbers do not necessarily appear in the text in numerical order). It is this last peculiar method that CSE emphasizes.

Robert Goldbort devotes a full chapter in his *Writing for Science* to a comparative analysis of the citational formats used in five systems: CBE (now CSE), American Chemical Society (ACS), *Chicago*, APA, and MLA. He presents many specific citations in all five systems in side-by-side comparisons, which allow one to immediately perceive the subtle distinctions (152–173). And in *Cite Right* Charles Lipson offers paradigmatic overviews from a host of systems including those discussed in this text plus those favored by the American Anthropological Association; the American Medical Association, which has a style guide; the American Institute of Physics, which also has a style guide; the Association of Legal Writing Directors, whose style guide is an alternative to the *BlueBook;* and others.

Some demographics will help the reader understand why I emphasize what I do. There are innumerable high schools as well as more than 4,200 institutions of higher education in the United States. Many millions of students attend these schools and they write tens of millions of papers during their secondary, undergraduate, and graduate careers. Most of these essays are documented in MLA or APA style (or in a handful of disciplines such as history, in a derivative format). Far fewer instructors (or pure researchers) exist, and only a small percentage of these actually write and publish papers. Thus, *Chicago*, which is required primarily of authors at university presses, is applied less frequently than MLA or APA; furthermore, my remarks on these latter systems would, in many cases, be applicable to *Chicago*, for which I therefore offer only some cursory comments.

University of Chicago Press ("Chicago")

It's a monument.
— Nicholas Frankovich

The first version of the *Chicago Manual of Style* appeared in 1906 and emphasized typographical rules. Since then, it has grown into a complex, 956 page compilation that has influenced most other documentation systems and formats. *Chicago*, which is in its 15th edition (2003) and has no immediate plans for a revision, is not discipline based, but rather guides monographic and journal publishers, especially university presses. Its documentation rules differ in various ways from the systems that are used in disciplines such as literature (MLA) or psychology (APA). *Chicago* does not necessarily advocate a specific and absolute format but rather simultaneously offers the parallel possibilities of the note, still favored by history and the sciences, and the author-date system of APA. The *Manual* offers the most complete overview and analysis: 162 of its 956 pages are allocated to documentation. It is now also available on CD-ROM and online at <www.chicagomanualofstyle.org>; there is a reasonable fee associated with its use.

Chicago presents formats and countless paradigms for its versions of the note and author-date systems, sometimes in side-by-side comparisons and contrasts. Notes can include all bibliographic data and are similar to the form that MLA once required:

> 1. Wendy Doniger, *Splitting the Difference: Gender and Myth in Ancient Greece and India* (Chicago: University of Chicago Press, 1999), 23 [*Chicago* 595].

The bibliographic entry for the note system looks exactly like MLA:

> Doniger, Wendy. *Splitting the Difference: Gender and Myth in Ancient Greece and India*. Chicago: University of Chicago Press, 1999 [*Chicago* 594].

The in-text reference for the author-date model is like APA except that no comma intervenes, e.g., "(Morris and Morris 1966, 1–24)" (*Chicago* 595). The works-cited entry for this resembles APA, although *Chicago* does not invert subsequent names, nor does it enclose the date in parentheses:

> Morris, R., and D. Morris. 1966. *Men and pandas*. New York: McGraw-Hill [*Chicago* 595].

Unlike other systems, Chicago offers possibilities rather than mandates; thus, one may choose a method and even make subtle alterations as long as he or she is consistent. This is not the case with other systems, the editors who require them, nor even with instructors of undergraduate or graduate students. Most, though not all, of the empowered, those who control academic environments and publication possibilities, are extremely strict in their demands for adherence to the stipulated format. It little matters that they sometimes do not have an excellent grasp of the system.

Scientific Citation

The five hard sciences (astronomy, physics, chemistry, biology, and geology, as well as their technological and professional offspring including computer science, medicine, and engineering) usually continue to rely on numbered foot- or, more frequently, endnotes, most of which resemble the form favored by *Nature*. There are sometimes minor differences among the thousands of journals involved, but they are mere stylistic variations. Herewith follows a typical citation from *Nature:*

> 61. Susin, S. A. *et al.* Two distinct pathways leading to nuclear apoptosis. *J. Exp. Med.* **192**, 571–580 (2000) [Bredeson et al. 802].

Other prestigious journals follow this paradigm. For example, a *Cell* citation is the same except that bibliographic references are not numbered; the date parenthetically follows the author's name; the abbreviated journal title is not italicized; but the unbolded volume number is. The same is true for *JAMA*, perhaps the world's most prestigious medical journal. Here, incredibly, the free-standing date precedes the unbolded volume number; a semicolon without a space separates them; and this is followed by a colon and the pagination (unspaced). Finally, the *Journal of Bacteriology* manages to come up with yet another variation (to distinguish it from its brethren): Authors' names are bolded; the date follows; italics are abjured; and the volume number is separated from the pagination by a colon without spacing. These are all minuscule variations with no appreciable difference in citation format, data, implication, or influence. They exist at the whim of powerful organizations and editors. The scientific disciplines all have style guides but obviously they do not control wanton proclivity as do APA and MLA in their respective domains.

With a single exception, most of the peculiar features manifested here are repeated in APA, and I will comment on them under that rubric. The abbreviated journal title is unique to the hard sciences (and law); it apparently saves space, though it confuses the uninitiated and may force him or her to consult *CASSI* (*Chemical Abstracts Service Source Index*, a listing of abbreviated and expanded titles) in order to decipher the cryptic notation.

The *Nature* citation presents an easy case and the title is undoubtedly the *Journal of Experimental Medicine*, but what is one to make of "*Cell Death Differ.*" or "Antimicrob. Agents Chemother." (not italicized in the *Journal of Bacteriology*)? Scientists do not cite monographs, broadcasts, DVDs, or Web sites very often. They continue to depend almost exclusively on the print version of the scholarly journal for scientific communication, at least in their own peer-reviewed print publications.

Legal Citation

Legal referencing is extremely complex because the sources are so diverse, numerous, and repetitive. The correct formats are scrupulously demarcated in *The BlueBook,* a substantial volume of rules, paradigms, and explanations. The reverse sides of the front and back covers and the following pages offer a concise summary of the major formats. In law reviews, citations are codified in footnotes, which adorn substantial portions of their many pages. I will not mention cases, constitutions, statutes, treaties, nor other esoteric materials. To begin to conceptualize just how truly fussy these legal editors are, consider that law reviews use specific typefaces (Roman, italic, and large and small capitals) for their citations (typefaces in substantive footnotes are governed by a different rule), whereas court documents and legal memoranda use others (ordinary type and italic or underlining). These variations do not sound very distinctive but when viewed, the citations look dramatically different. (Many tens of thousands of periodicals are published in the humanities and again in the social sciences and yet again in the hard sciences. It is inconceivable that even a small subset of editors in one of these groups would band together and agree to use a specific set of typefaces in their publications.)

There is a certain perversity in formatting evident in many of the major systems, but this streak is especially obvious in legal references. Here is a paradigmatic law review book citation (in context, it would be preceded by a footnote number).

> CHARLES DICKENS, BLEAK HOUSE 49–55 (Norman Page ed., Penguin Books 1971) (1853) [Editors, inside front cover f.].

It is as if the arbiters said, "Let's twist all other citation formats into something bizarrely different": There are no italics, no parentheses around pagination, and no location (this is perhaps the only format to indicate the publisher without a location, whereas others, e.g., history, do the reverse), the editor and publisher are intermixed, and the author and title are in large and small capitals while the rest is in normal Roman. (Incredible as it may seem, *Bleak House* is italicized — underlined — when cited in court documents and legal memoranda.) The periodical format is worse:

> Thomas R. McCoy & Barry Friedman, *Conditional Spending: Federalism's Trojan Horse*, 1988 Sup. Ct. Rev. 85, 100 [Editors, inside front cover f.].

How about that for perverse, idiosyncratic confusion? The title of the article is italicized (here italicized), but the journal title is in Roman and this despite the historical precedent that has obtained for hundreds of years of italicizing book and periodical titles (the title here, naturally, is abbreviated). The citation concludes with the first page of the work and the page on which the material cited is located. How would anyone unfamiliar with legal citation know that? (In the sciences 85 would be the volume number.) If there is a volume number, then it precedes the journal title and the date is shifted to the end of the citation:

> David Rudovsky, *Police Abuse: Can the Violence be Contained?*, 27 Harv. C.R.-C.L. L. Rev. 465, 500 (1992) [Editors, inside front cover f.].

These two journals are consecutively paginated. The *Harvard Business Review* is not:

> Barbara Ward, *Progress for a Small Planet*, Harv. Bus. Rev., Sept.-Oct 1979, at 89, 90 [Editors, inside front cover f.].

Note the transposition of the date and the pagination as well as the peculiar insertion of *at*, a preposition that often annoyingly obtrudes itself in articles on any topic written by legal scholars. The individual letters that comprise the authors and titles of books and the titles of law reviews are in large and small capitals, whereas an author entry in a collection is lower-cased (where appropriate), though the chapter is italicized and the collection title (but not its editor) are again in capitals. This is all extremely confusing and off-putting and there is much more, but it is not necessary to dwell on legal formats. (By the way, the editors of these publications are often law school students; law is the only discipline that allocates such responsibilities to naive, barely knowledgeable, uncredentialed youngsters.) And as it turns out, all of this bibliographic pilpul matters very little. Apparently, judges do not bother to read these disquisitions: "'I haven't opened a law review in years,' said Chief Judge Dennis G. Jacobs of the federal appeals court in New York. 'No one speaks of them. No one relies on them'" (Liptak A8). Imagine a doctor admitting that he does not keep up with the latest medical developments by reading *JAMA*! Nevertheless, legal scholars continue to concern themselves with citation format. Ian Gallacher, in a lengthy overview, discusses and clarifies two alternative systems to the *BlueBook:* the University of Chicago's *Maroon Book* and the Association of Legal Writing Directors' *Manual*. He indicates that the legal publisher West is against neutral citation format: "...it correctly identified citation as one of the most important impediments to the development of an alternative to West-based legal information" (526). Citation matters!

American Psychological Association (APA)

The earliest avatar of the autonomous *Publication Manual of the American Psychological Association* is a succinct, seven page guide published in the *Psychological Bulletin* in 1929 ("Instructions"). This is followed by a 32 page piece by John E. Anderson and Willard L. Valentine in a 1944 issue of the same journal. It deals with "the preparation of articles," but leaves the nuances of documentation entirely in the capable hands of the 1937 *Manual of Style*, i.e., the *Chicago Manual of Style*. Even in 1944, scholars were apparently careless or derelict in their attention to details. Anderson and Valentine point out that "...in a recent *Bulletin* article, 323 corrections were made in a bibliography alone" (363). The first edition of the *Publication Manual* appeared as a supplement to the *Bulletin* in 1952 and is 61 pages in length; it was revised twice prior to the publication of the second edition (1974, with many subsequent reprintings). This is a 136 page volume that, naturally, contains much useful information for potential authors. Typical of style guides generally are sections on manuscript organization, writing style, typing and proofing, and precisely detailed editorial guidelines. The subsection dealing with documentation runs a mere 12 pages. Style is consistent with current practice. Every ten years or so, a new edition has appeared, and currently authors use the fifth, which includes a substantial section on electronic formats. It has grown dramatically in size and coverage and runs a generous 439 pages (which is, nevertheless, 517 pages shorter than the *Chicago Manual of Style*). Eighty pages are allocated to the section on documentation, which is replete with countless examples of every conceivable variation. A 14 page appendix offers a summary of legal citation formats as mandated in *The BlueBook*. A sixth edition is in the offing.

The current general system in use in most disciplines in the social sciences and humanities is a weak replacement for the traditional footnote with its array of abbreviated Latin terms that easily and immediately led the reader from one point to another. Indeed, according to Ben Agger, the use of a works-cited list in APA style

> further reduces talk between text and subtext, enhancing the text's seeming validity by removing the subjective hand of the author as a nonidentifying mediator between prose and the world [qtd. in Tribble, *Margins* 163].

And Charles Bazerman claims that the scientific aspirations of psychology are reflected in the prescriptive *Manual*, which "symbolizes and instrumentally realizes the influence and power of the official style" (259). In-text documentation requires that a broad panoply of physical entities be intercalated (parenthetically) into the text. Depending on the system, these may include authors' names, titles, dates, and pages (and sometimes much more information — e.g., interview data — which is not included in the works-cited list at all). It is possible that a substantial percentage of textual space may be allocated to these truly annoying distractions, so much so that one may lose the thread of the argument or discussion. The system also requires constant repetition of these referrals. In MLA, a typical in-text referral might look like this: "(Liu 3)," and there will only be a few of these on any given page. MLA's goals are readability and concision. APA is more interested in precise, immediate, and repetitive accuracy. Thus, an analogue to the MLA version may be a bit more verbose:

> (e.g., Knight, Bernal, Cota, Garza, & Ocampo, 1993; Knight, Bernal, Garza, Cota, & Ocampo 1993; Marshall, 1995; Phinney & Chavera, 1995; Quintana & Vera, 1999; Spencer, 1983; Stevenson, Reed, Bodison, & Bishop, 1997) [Hughes et al. 747].

The third of a page of text on which this is found also contains five additional and similar parenthetical referrals. Bazerman observes that "...the dates and the names of authors now serve as kinds of facts in the argument..." (263) and furthermore, that "[t]he format is not designed for the close consideration of competing ideas and subtle formulations" (274). Are these graphic and distracting abominations really helpful? I do not stand alone in my condemnation. G. W. Bowersock is even nastier:

> For writers who take no thought for the niceties of style, abbreviated citations in parentheses can be implanted into the text at desirable points, thereby compelling the reader who wants to unravel Ungeziefer 1973:375 to consult a bibliographical listing in some other place. This grotesque form of annotation is much favored by those social scientists who imagine that it confers scientific precision on their work, whereas at best it simply keeps the reader from noticing the inadequacies of their prose [54–55].[1]

And APA forgot to demand pagination. (In APA, one *must* cite precise pagination only for direct quotations; otherwise it may be elided, and it usually is. The works-cited list only contains inclusive pagination.) Thus, anyone seeking precise information from one of the above-noted sources on the consequences of certain practices discussed in the article would have to read the entire new document. This is a hardship even for a journal article; when dealing with a large monograph, it is a true horror entailing the expenditure of much time and energy. Most people will give up.[2] If the APA arbiters had considered precedent more seriously, they might have modified their position. David Henige, among others, discusses the accusations that Henry Davis leveled at Gibbon's "inadequate" citations. Here is Davis on Gibbon's lack of pagination:

> He sometimes only mentions the author, perhaps the book; and often leaves the reader the toil of finding out, or rather guessing at the passage [qtd. in Henige, "Being" 103].

One easily gets the idea here that pagination is crucially important, even if this happens to be a distorted picture. Gibbon certainly felt that it was and provided a vindication, adducing extreme numbers: The two chapters under consideration here are referenced in 383 notes containing a total of 800–1,000 supporting quotations. He adds,

> As I had often felt the inconvenience of the loose and general method of quoting which is so falsely imputed to me, I have carefully distinguished the *books*, the *chapters*, the *sections*, the *pages* of the authors to whom I referred ... [qtd. in Henige, "Being" 103].

I am sure that he did. Social scientists do not. (Nor do scientists.) And that is why Henige offers a 20 page diatribe on missing or inadequate pagination. He points out that since the purpose of documentation is to learn more or verify, expunging it is a scholarly disservice, one that causes readers to waste much valuable time searching for a precise location. (Even prestigious publications such as *Nature* and *Science* consistently fail to include the citational data necessary for efficient access.) ("Discouraging" 99–100, 101). (See also Garfield, "When" 453–454 on "pageless documentation.")

Unlike MLA, the APA manual begins its presentation of citation paradigms with journal entries. This is undoubtedly because APA privileges the journal over all other formats. This is the medium of choice in the sciences, where immediacy of communication is crucial; indeed, scientists hardly communicate at all in monographs. Psychologists think that their discipline is similar to physics or biology, so naturally the journal is the more important venue. Refined for more than three quarters of a century, here is how the basic citation appears:

> Mellers, B. A. (2000). Choice and the relative pleasure of consequences. *Psychological Bulletin, 126,* 910–924 [*Publication* 2001, 240].

The designers of these extremely casuistic and demanding systems attempt to cover every conceivable exigency, but the structural logic of this (and other) bibliographic citations is frequently bizarrely incomprehensible. In APA first and middle names are expunged in favor of initials (based on the illogical system in use in the hard sciences); this is a most confusing and annoying means of "helping" the reader track down sources. J. Smith is basically meaningless and useless, especially in the long lists of names included in catalogues and citation indexes. John Smith is not much better, but John Lemaitre Smith or Jasmine X. Smith would help the reader home in on a particular person in a much more efficient fashion. I have chosen an extreme case to make my point, but even less common surnames are hard to identify and trace with only a first initial as a delimiter. The only advantage is the conservation of a bit of space; feminists might claim that it eliminates gender prejudice, but I fail to see how. When a piece has a single author, the surname and initial(s) are inverted for easy alphabetization. APA also inverts the names and initials of second and subsequent authors in multi-authored entries (as if they too were alphabetized). This is illogical, unnecessary, and foolish. The only thing accomplished here is some kind of imaginary hierarchical equalization, but the authors are *not* equal. The first one is always more equal than the others! In such a sequence, an ampersand (unnecessarily preceded by a comma) rather than *and* is used. Since these signs are usually avoided in scholarly writing, they should be abjured in citations as well.

The date follows the name and this is fine. But why not enclose the article title in quotation marks, which would alleviate confusion? Why use lower case except for the initial word (and the first word following an internal colon)? Why is the volume number italicized? These inconsequential eccentricities are annoying and counterintuitive: Even sophisticated scholars often incorrectly capitalize, since the original titles are so demarcated and common usage requires them to do so.

Herewith follow a series of minor quibbles. In the sciences, especially physics, articles sometimes have multiple authors: 10, 50, 200, 700. In psychology, some articles are also multiply-authored, although the numbers cannot compete with the results of work done with accelerators. So, why cite six authors and then cut off the seventh and subsequent people who also contributed? It seems much fairer to either always cite one (or two, since many articles do have just two authors) or cite all, regardless of the total number. Again, this is a quibble, but for the seventh or tenth contributor, it is probably a real emotional and academic hardship. A magazine article is similar to a journal's, but for some inexplicable reason, a newspaper entry requires a visual sign before the page number, thus: "p. A12" or "pp." when there are two or more pages. Many years ago, MLA also required this, but no longer. There appears to be no real necessity for these signs and they should be expunged. When an issue number follows an italicized volume number, its confining parenthesis touches the preceding number because no space is intercalated.

Book citations present many of the same annoyances noted above, as well as some additional problems. Herewith follows the basic entry with two other necessities:

> Mitchell, T. R., & Larson, J. R., Jr. (1987). *People in organizations: An introduction to organizational behavior* (3rd ed). New York: McGraw-Hill [*Publication* 2001, 248].

All major initial letters of periodical titles are capitalized, but this is not the case here. Book titles are similar to the titles of articles. There is no tangible reason for this shoddy treatment, which ironically diminishes the worth of monographic studies. A chapter in a collection presents two features that are superior to MLA (see below): The word *In* precedes the editor(s) and the inclusive pagination precedes the city and publisher. These subtle differences help to eliminate potential confusion. This is what it looks like:

> Bjork, R. A. (1989). Retrieval inhibition as an adaptive mechanism in human memory. In H.L. Roediger III & F. I. M. Craik (Eds.). *Varieties of memory & consciousness* (pp. 309–330). Hillesdale, NJ: Erlbaum [*Publication* 2001, 252].

Note that here, the ampersand connecting the editors is not preceded by a comma, which is ironic, because with alphabetized names, the reversal calls for a comma, so that the additional and unnecessary punctuation is iconically confusing. When identifying audio-visual materials, why are brackets rather than parentheses used?

> Crystal, L. (Executive Producer). (1993, October 11). *The MacNeil/Lehrer news hour* [Television broadcast]. New York and Washington, DC: Public Broadcasting Service [*Publication* 2001, 267].

Material accessed on the Internet is covered in all of its multiplicity. I note the following permutations. An unaltered electronic version of an article from a hard copy publication is treated exactly as its source would be except for a bracketed intercalation reading "[Electronic version]." No other identifying data, such as a URL, are included. In cases where the electronic version is not duplicated in print, then author, date, and titles are followed by the access date and URL, thus: "Retrieved January 12, 2006, from http://ski.fun/rescue.html[.]" Finally, an article located through a subscription service such as EBSCO takes this form:

> Borman, W.C., Hanson, M.A., Oppler, S.H., Pulakos, E.D., & White, L.A. (1993). Role of early supervisory experience in supervisor performance. *Journal of Applied Psychology, 78*, 443–449. Retrieved October 23, 2000, from PsychARTICLES database [*Publication* 2001, 279].

Because most delivery systems, e.g., CD-ROMs, have migrated to the Web, the next edition of the *Manual* will probably include a URL for this type of entry. Much of the rest (and there is a lot more) follows in reasonable and logical fashion.

Less than 30 years ago, when methods were similar to those in place today, Eugene Garfield unmercifully castigated bibliographic applications in the social sciences:

> [T]heir bibliographic standards tend to be archaic and their references are frequently complex, often citing exotic types of nonjournal material.... It is not unusual to find references scattered throughout the text of a social sciences journal.... Footnotes containing multiple references are common; and the format of references, regardless of where they are found, is eclectic.... The impact of these problems on productivity [of producing citation indexes] is great enough to justify a continuing and sizeable effort to educate editors about the reader and the economic advantages to be gained from adopting simpler, more standardized format rules ["Citation" 26].

Some things have changed but there is still room for improvement.

Despite the foregoing criticisms, and the lamentable fact that very few scholars, even those who ostensibly monitor and evaluate theses and dissertations, manage to document their scholarly submissions in precise accordance with APA format, as the editor of an interdisciplinary journal, I request that potential authors avoid referential footnotes, follow APA guidelines, and observe the nuances of the system in their submissions. They often fail to do so. I doubt that more than a handful of the many hundreds of APA documented papers I have read were error free. (Ironically, sometimes graduate students do a better job at this than their mentors.)

Modern Language Association (MLA)

In 1951, William Riley Parker compiled the first MLA style sheet, which was published in an issue of *Publications of the Modern Language Association* (*PMLA*). The portion of this 31 page guide that deals with documentation covers a mere 12 pages and includes all of the necessary citational permutations. It served well. Indeed, almost 50 years ago, I used it (as a reprinted pamphlet) in freshman English in order to write and document a paper on *Billy Budd*, the critical readings[3] for which I did at the New York Public Library, one of the world's great research collections. I correctly constructed the footnotes and bibliography without the help of a software program.

A quarter of a century ago (on May 15, 1982), I wrote a three page unpublished diatribe to the then editor of *PMLA*, the official journal of the Modern Language Association, the arbiter of MLA style. It was at that time that the Association was contemplating a major revision of its documentation system. The author-date method, favored by the American Psychological Association, had wrought its magic, and MLA bureaucrats did not want to be left behind. I suppose that they thought that to fail to change would indicate a lack of foresight, a foolish and stubborn reactionary adherence to a moribund means of citing one's sources. That foot- and endnotes had served well for 400 years did not appease either the progressives (who always want to keep up with the physicists) and those who practice realpolitik, who knew even then that publishers (especially, and ironically, financially-strapped university presses) would no longer support the costly propagation of noted citations, and would stoop so low as to save a few dollars by entirely expunging bibliographies in monographs. That a mere decade later, typesetting became a moot point, since authors were admonished to accompany their hard copy manuscripts with a disk containing the complete text (including the notes in their correct physical locations) in digital form, did not alter matters. Notes were no longer welcome and many publishers simply do not allow their use (though some demand it).

I complimented the Advisory Committee on Documentation Style on a number of alterations, but the brunt of my frustration was aimed at the shift away from notes and toward in-text documentation accompanied by a works-cited list. I fretted,

> It is sad that the MLA has capitulated to the apotheosizers of scientific methodology. The form of documentation that you now advocate has long been favored by those who attempt to lend scientific prestige to non-scientific disciplines. I have railed against this generally ... and specifically in a review of Steven G. Kellman's *Self-Begetting Novel*, published by Columbia ... which I conclude,
>> This volume once again makes it necessary to castigate those responsible for the degeneration of the critical apparatus in scholarly monographs. The tendency to expunge bibliographies is inexplicable. And footnotes are now being constructed in such a cryptic manner that their form rivals the abominations favored by physicists and psychologists. This is lamentable, indeed, especially in university press publications
>
> [Hauptman, "Documentation diatribe"].

The demise of the note is lamentable, but it is a given, so one must work with the current avatars. MLA's system of documentation is certainly preferable to APA's for many reasons. It does not privilege one form of publication over another, nor does it have the useless and annoying features that the latter includes. Errol Friedberg insists that the multiplicity of citation styles in the sciences is "pathetic." This may be less problematic in the humanities and social sciences generally, but major differences do obtain even here. I agree with Friedberg: Consistency across disciplines is a positive characteristic of *Chicago*, APA, and MLA. Stephen K. Donovan's advocacy (contra Friedberg) for stylistic diversity not merely among disciplines but among individual journals is extremely detrimental. (As noted above, this does indeed exist in some scientific disciplines, e.g., biology and paleontology.) His primary objection is that uniformity is boring ("Research" 231). Naturally, his extreme extrapolation, viz., that all journals could eventually be standardized, is a bizarre exaggeration ("Research" 232). Others, such as Janell Rudolph and Deborah Brackstone, call for standardization of citation formats across disciplines, but this is something that is unlikely to ever occur. That MLA is consistent and insistent are excellent features. This helps to control the wandering proclivities of college freshman (who know the system poorly) and renowned scholars (who believe that since they have reached the pinnacle of their disciplines, they may create bibliographical entries as they see fit; this includes the present author, who dislikes, for example, the use of three hyphens followed by a period or comma to indicate a second or subsequent bibliographical entry by the same author, a convention he refuses to use).

As with the other major style guides, the *MLA Handbook for Writers of Research Papers* contains some ancillary material, but a third of its 361 pages is given over to citation practices. In-text documentation is the preferred method and the means of alerting the reader that it is time to check the references recorded in the works-cited list for an attribution. Here the system is streamlined in a most effective manner: A single last name and a required page number (e.g., Freud 24), for all attributions, not just quotations, are the only necessities. (This allows a reader to easily trace the idea or remark back to a *precise* source.) No punctuation intervenes. Only if there is some confusion because of similar names or additional works by the same author, does MLA call for a second descriptor. (Naturally, there are complex variations on this simple case deriving from multiples of authors, texts, and sets.) This system helps to partially alleviate the annoying and sometimes superfluous interruptions that parenthetical referrals create for the reader. It is difficult enough to follow a complex discussion or argument by Heidegger or Lacan (sometimes in German or French) without being diverted by a plethora of parenthetical notations and apparatus (some of which, ironically, exists in order to help through clarification). A worst-case scenario presents a page of humanistic commentary that resembles a chemistry text. Superscript numbers still lead to substantive notes that are collected at the end of the article, chapter, or book. Some authors may (purposely) use the notes to sneak in bibliographical referrals, at times long lists of them, thus, in a sense, defeating the in-text system, which has as its primary goal the diminution or elimination of foot- or endnotes.

The parenthetical reference leads to the list of works cited, what used to be called the bibliography. A simple, paradigmatic book entry is very similar to its early 20th century ancestors:

> Fukuyama, Francis. *The End of History and the Last Man.* New York: Free Press, 1992.

The arbiters who decided upon the current form wisely chose to include full names rather than last names followed by initials; the title is italicized to differentiate it from the surrounding text; the city of publication is followed by the publisher (which is excluded in work sanctioned by the American Historical Association — as can be seen in the *American Historical Review*; this is anomalous, given many analogous styles, and makes locating a specific volume that much more difficult); and the date of publication concludes the entry. The initial inversion is mandatory for alphabetization; the punctuation is reasonable, logical, and confirmed by a century of practice; and the secondary indentation allows for swift scanning of the entire group of listed entries. The only quibble here is that the publisher's name must be abbreviated, which some critics find objectionable. Where there is no confusion, it hardly seems necessary to repeat words that occur frequently such as the final term in Bantam Books, but where decapitation seems to result (McGraw for McGraw-Hill), it is an unpleasant and harmful convention. Ironically, Harvard or Michigan cannot stand for their respective universities' presses since departments and centers at academic institutions also publish material. All in all, though, one could hardly ask for a more satisfying format, given the five elements requiring inclusion. Many variations on this basic paradigm maintain a logical and useful consistency. For example, an edited anthology is presented in the same way, except that "ed." preceded by a comma is inserted after the name. As noted above, the use of hyphens to indicate a second or subsequent entry by the same author is a most peculiar convention, and if its purpose is to iconically indicate that a given author is represented more than once, it is hardly necessary. Scanning the entries will tell the same story. (And why would knowing this be especially useful to a reader? The gross number of entries is indicative of very little that truly matters; it is what is contained in the studies that will be helpful to the inquiring reader.) The multiply-authored book requires a listing of all of the authors, and this is once again accomplished using a logical approach: The first author's names are inverted so that the person can be listed alphabetically, but subsequent authors' names are presented in their normal order, first name first, last name second (cf. APA style for its illogical variation). The only improvement here would be the use of semi-colons between authors; there is always a bit of immediate confusion, since a comma is inserted between the first author's family and given names.

The innumerable variations for multiply-authored books, corporate authorship, government documents, and so on all follow logically and necessarily from these basic paradigmatic structures.

As I read texts written by historians, I cringe when I consult the notes for an attribution and notice the glaring omission of a publisher's name, something that would immediately alert me to the validity of the work. A volume published by Harvard would ostensibly be reliable and valid whereas something that appears under the imprint of a minor or ideologically oriented press would at least give me some pause. Publishers' names are important. Thus, I am stunned that MLA offers the possibility of eliminating them when dealing with books published prior to 1900. Because it becomes more difficult to locate older volumes, the publisher should be a mandatory inclusion.

A work in an anthology concludes with its pagination thus:

> Camille, Michael. "Glossing the Flesh: Scopophilia and the Margins of the Medieval Book." *The Margins of the Text*. Ed. D. C. Greetham. Ann Arbor: University of Michigan, 1997. 245–267.

This leaves the pagination lonely and dangling in space. It would have been preferable (and logical) to place it directly after the chapter's title. The same situation and suggested modification obtain for other variations as well as for periodical articles, to which I now turn. The general paradigm for all such popular publications (magazines and newspapers) resembles the following:

> *Updike, John. "Notes." *The New Yorker* 26 January 1957: 28–29.

(Newspapers may add the edition.) This is reasonable, concise, and consistent for all periodicals. No longer do we need abbreviated and superfluous pagination demarcators (p. or pp.) just for popular material, and the date without volume or issue numbers is all that is required to easily track down the source. The pages continue to dangle. For citations to scholarly materials in journals, the volume number is added:

> Elkins, James. "Critical Response: What Do We Want Photography to Be? A Response to Michael Fried." *Critical Inquiry* 31 (2005): 938–956.

Note that in this entry, the issue number (4) and the quarter (summer) are not included. They are not required in a continuously paginated publication, i.e., one that begins a volume's first issue with page number one, continues with page 250 as the first page of the second issue, and so on through the entire volume. Only journals that do not paginate continuously cite the issue number. Even they, however, do not include the quarter or month. The logic is impeccable: These additional demarcators are unnecessary to locate the material and concision is a worthy objective, one that I applaud. But the omission of one or both of these is detrimental (since they are the keys to a specific issue) and a real hardship, which the editors did not consider: In a library collection (and we continue to use libraries despite the digitization of all of the world's knowledge), when one approaches bound volumes on the shelf, one is met with spines embossed with titles, volume numbers, and dates. If the publication occurs very frequently, it may take many frustrating minutes to locate the precise physical volume in which the April 1952 issue resides. (I have endured this frustration with some frequency.) The inclusion of the issue and quarter or month are useful adjuncts and I recommend them to the arbiters of MLA style. Their use also makes patently clear a distinction between those publications that only include issue numbers, which will be confused with those that employ continuous pagination. As for the rest, it follows reasonably and consistently and I am grateful for this helpful system (although I too bemoan the extirpation of the footnote).

There are many other formats including media (recordings, films, video cassettes, DVDs, CDs, etc.), broadcast programs, performances, computer software, and so on. These all follow in a reasonable fashion, and I have few quarrels here. I do think that citations to audio CDs are too cryptic. The only thing that distinguishes them from books is the lack of a city, and it is perhaps asking too much for a reader to keep this in mind when perusing bibliographies. Here is the basic MLA paradigm:

> Bartoli, Cecilia. *Dreams and Fables.* London, 2001 [Gibaldi 196].

It is quite possible that in addition to recording vast quantities of contemporary classical vocal music, Bartoli also wrote a book. That, naturally, is precisely what a reader who is versed in the historian's format would conclude, as would an ingenuous literary reader who vaguely recalls that books published prior to 1900 do not require publishers. (It so happens that London is the publisher rather than the city, which adds to the confusion.) The abbreviation *CD*, analogous to *LP* or *Rec.*, placed just before the publisher would clarify this ambiguity. Precisely the same thing obtains for films which are privileged over other formats, e.g., DVDs. The former descriptor is not required so that one may not realize that the item falls under this rubric, although confusion here is less likely since the director and actors are often included.

Online citation also calls for some comment. Many types of online sources exist. They are reached in very different ways and so they require very different citation formulae. If a site does not charge and is accessible using a concise Internet address or URL, e.g., <www.boisestate.edu/melville>, then this a gift one should input. If the address is bizarrely long and complex, as is this one for an article from *ABI/Inform*, <http://proquest.umi.com/pqdweb?index=7&did=1143733391&SrchMode=1&sid=2&Fmt=3&VInst=PROD&VType=PQD&RQT=309&VName=PQD&TS=1161118877&clientId=32215>,

then it is foolish to expect that anyone would be willing or able to accurately type it into an address box (although if it is already in digitized form, then it could be copied and pasted in); and it is worth noting that if it derives from a commercial source such as *ABI/Inform* and one does not have privileges to this database, then it will not allow access. Thus, using long addresses in citations is counterproductive. Sometimes, astonishingly, the best way to arrive at a destination is to use a search engine and a precise descriptor; although sites are transitory and migrate or cease to exist while others come online, all of which alters the search results and their sequencing, the chances are often good that in many cases the sought site (and precise item) will come up within the first few screens. Even ostensibly proscribed material, e.g., a journal article on a database, which is unavailable to a nonsubscriber, may have been downloaded onto the Internet (by the author or publisher). At any rate, materials archived on the Internet are extremely transitory, and even those that one might think will be available many years hence may turn out to have disappeared. The best we can do is use common sense when citing electronic sources. MLA's system attempts to do just that. The basic MLA entry for an Internet site is very similar to a citation for a print journal. To this are added the sponsoring organization, the date of access, and the URL thus:

> Zeki, Semir. "Artistic Creativity and the Brain." *Science* 6 July 2001: 51–52. *Science Magazine*. 2002. Amer. Assn. for the Advancement of Science. 24 Sept 2002 <http://www.sciencemag.org/cgi/ content/full/293/ 5527/51> [Gibaldi 212].

I am not certain that the sponsoring organization and the date of access are really necessary features of citations to periodicals on Web sites; one does not include the former nor a date of reading for print material. Well, this is a petty criticism and there may be some negligible reasons for including them. If the URL opens the article, then it is mandatory. If it does not, then it is superfluous, since the point here is not to know the article's Web address but rather to access it. (As it happens, this URL does bring up the full text of Zeki's essay.) Other types of sites and documents follow similar logical formats. For example, articles in periodicals are cited in basically the same way as the aforementioned site. If they derive from a subscription service, e.g., EBSCO or Information Access Corporation, then the full title of the database is placed after the pagination to which, surprisingly, is added the name and location of the subscribing library. This appears to serve no purpose, especially since the material may have been accessed at a distant location by utilizing the library's server via the Internet. Otherwise, it is hard to quibble with MLA's formatting generally. Given the extirpation of the bibliographical note, MLA's system is probably the best one can expect. As the foregoing discussions make clear, it is certainly preferable to APA's.

Among the most difficult citations to create are those that lead to various electronic sources. June Kronholz lays out the difficulties in this "mess," which is compounded by the transitory nature of the media, sites, and content . One of the things that she makes iconically clear in her *Wall Street Journal* piece is that traditional references can be quite concise, whereas Internet citations are often uselessly verbose (A1). Each system has come up with its own sometimes divergent format, but other solutions are possible. Sheila and Richard Beck have recently proposed that a new tag, "biblio," be added to HTML pages. The data included under this rubric would help readers to create a complete bibliographic entry. More importantly, they claim that "Browsers could be programmed to display the bibliography in full and correct form" (par. 10).

Software

As with so many other processes and procedures in the contemporary world, convenience takes precedence over virtually all other considerations. And so it is now possible to avoid constructing the bibliography manually; instead, one can have a software program create the citations in the format of one's choice. The naive might imagine that these programs are easy to use and require little preparation, but nothing could be further from the truth: The *EndNote 6* manual runs on for 523 detailed and confusing pages. It might be easier to simply learn to construct one's own citations in the traditional manner. This is especially the case for references that are not accessible online. Here one must key in the data manually. It is no more time consuming to do this in the correct order rather than arbitrarily. It is true that scanning might alleviate some keyboarding, but I am fairly certain that a bibliographically adept person could create citations from scratch as fast as one of these programs can if scanning time were included. *RefWorks* will even aid in constructing the in-text referrals. True believers point out the advantages, including the fact that these programs simplify matters, save time, discourage plagiary, and, once the citation is created, allow one to change formats with real ease (Kiernan A29). But many older, traditional scholars will never be able to master the intricacies of the software; soon, these skills will be lost and only a small group of cognoscenti will be able to construct entries by hand (in the same way that calculators have delimited people's abilities to do math mentally or even with a pencil); but most important is that the enjoyable and intellectually profitable exercise of creating the bibliography is now allocated to a machine. Thus, the document's author will not be intimately familiar with his or her sources, will not recall precise materials, and will make additional textual and citational blunders that could lead to accusations of dishonesty (from my perspective, these programs will result in inadvertent plagiary and encourage purposeful padding), because the person who simply manipulates bits of data for hundreds or even thousands of sources will not be able to recall any of them. The author who stops to record a citation as he or she composes and then checks and rechecks text, in-text referral, and the bibliographical entry will never forget it, no matter how many citations are involved.

Some of these software packages have been around for quite some time, but it is only fairly recently that *RefWorks* has become available to academic users as a subscription service. It is quite expensive and may not be worth the ongoing investment, if not used by a large percentage of the institution's faculty and students. It is also complex enough to warrant an instruction session, and it has been criticized for not creating perfect citations; e.g., it may make formatting mistakes. Thus, careful checking of each citation with excellent *a priori* knowledge of what the citation should look like is mandatory. *ProCite* and *Stylease* are analogous programs; free software is also available; some aggregated databases provide citation formatting; and other new packages allow for more complex and interrelated work.

Since very few people manage to construct "perfect citations," this probably matters less than the critics think. M. Garrett Bauman sarcastically comments on the preposterous and confusing diversity of some of the documentation systems discussed in this chapter: "I ... was spending hours in class teaching students how to evaluate sources and to reason, when I could have filled the time with date-placement and capitalization issues" (par. 2). Though some people hope for a single system derived from a group of existing methods, Bauman disagrees: "...a unified, simplified format will violate three of academe's most sacred principles: culture, control, and confusion" (par. 3). He goes on to exemplify why the many systems in use will continue to exist independently (and will undoubtedly become ever more complex and esoteric). He writes with a heavy hand in order to amuse, but what he says is incisive and lamentably true.

8

Errors

> *The errors we encounter every day ... lead us to conclude that there is an attitude rampant in academe—an underlying carelessness—that threatens bibliographic control in scholarship.*
> —Janell Rudolph and Deborah Brackstone

Authors make mistakes in documentation, lots of them. Most are inadvertent and are caused by haste, carelessness, sloppy research and recording methods, or a non-clinical form of dyslexia that results in minor transpositions. (When finalizing a text just prior to submission, an author is so familiar with what he or she has written that the tendency is to read blocks of text rather than word by word or letter by letter. Thus, and despite spell-checking programs, alphabetic transpositions remain intact.) Virtually all authors would have avoided or expunged these anomalous or inadvertent errors in research, analysis, and data or text recording, had they had the opportunity. Naturally, some scholars also perpetrate various forms of misconduct. (These purposeful distortions are discussed in chapter 9.) There exist two major classes of documentation errors. The first consists of transcription mistakes: An author cites a source, but misreads or mistranscribes the journal title or the volume number or the date or the page. This occurs so frequently that one wonders whether these academics' graduate school training was deficient. It is also astonishing that anything is traceable. The second class concerns format. Here an author manages to get all of the documentation data correct, but has failed to learn that in MLA, volume numbers follow the title without an interceding comma; in APA, a comma is required; and in scientific publications, the number is frequently bolded. These are petty errors but they require correction, and hundreds of such annoyances in the manuscripts for a single journal issue keep the copy editor busy and frustrated. Mistakes are usually more blatant than misplaced commas and occur with extraordinary frequency. It is most unusual for even a renowned scholar to present a manuscript whose documentation is both free of substantive error and in unequivocal conformance with the required format.

Over a 20 year period during which I have edited collections and various journals, I have worked with only one person whose documentation is *always* impeccable. Some authors, even those whose credentials and publication records would seem to imply an absolute mastery of this simple necessity, are incapable of getting things just right. Indeed, there is a very real possibility that some scholars, no matter what they have managed to achieve in their fields, have a mental block that does not allow them to fully learn how to document, cite, or create a bibliography. Occasionally, even in the face of precise requirements or directions for a solicited article, e.g., "Use APA style" or "Do not use footnotes," authors will combine formats or create their own systems! I once received an important essay that incorporated three different sets of numbered and lettered notes. This was an extremely complex piece of scholarship and there were legitimate reasons for this bizarre structure, but there are other viable solutions. Here is how Stephen Donovan, an editor at a number of scientific journals, puts it:

> Despite the experience they have presumably gained from publishing regularly over an extended period, many established authors submit typescripts for publication that are, frankly, untidy, inaccurate, and not in the correct format, as well as failing to follow the instructions for authors ["How" 239].

Readers who have never edited will be extremely skeptical that this is not hyperbolic ranting. They will be annoyed that editors appear arrogant and treat potential authors, who may hold earned doctorates or medical or law degrees or in some cases all three, like misbehaving children. They will be aghast that in 1944, Anderson and Valentine list six frequent mistakes that appear in psychology manuscripts including "incorrect alphabetization" and non-consecutive reference numbers and then embarrassingly admonish authors by outlining precisely how a full professor at Harvard or Berkeley (as if they were taking a freshman composition course) should proceed:

> Authors are urged to prepare bibliographies with great care. Bibliographic references should first be written on separate cards, a procedure which makes checking new insertions and alphabetizing easier and more accurate. In early copies of the manuscript, spaces between parentheses, as ( ), can be left for inserting references.
> ....
> Since references are useless unless correct, every reference in the final manuscript should be verified against the source with regard to the fol-

lowing details: spelling, journal, date, volume number, page numbers, and punctuation, and, above all, accents [363].

Confirmation

Indeed! In order to confirm that these fumbling scholars' successors are still making the same mistakes, I queried members of the Council of Editors of Learned Journals (CELJ). Some 400 editors of scholarly journals in the humanities and social sciences belong to this organization, and its Listerv offers lively discussions of editing conundrums. Sixty-two editors were kind enough to respond to my brief survey, and the results are consistent with what I have offered above. Some of these people have had countless years of editing experience, so their remarks are based on their work with many thousands of manuscripts. (When one considers that even in the distant past *The Southern Review* received 15,000 manuscripts a year, the numbers can be astronomically high. Some editors may deal with as many as half a million manuscripts during their careers.) In the demographics that follow, numbers do not add up because respondents did not always answer each query. Two had worked as editors for just a few months; many others range from two to 25 years; two had 28 years of experience; one 29; one 30; one 31; one 35; one 38; and one 40. The 62 editors represent a broad array of disciplinary areas including literature, history, philosophy, religion, feminist studies, criminal justice, bibliography, education, and so on. Twenty-nine of them use MLA in their publications; 24 *Chicago*; three APA; and two some other hybrid. I asked whether even excellent scholars document poorly, i.e., whether they make various types of mistakes in their documentation. Fully 54 editors insist that they do and only four indicate that they do not. I next wondered whether submissions contain documentation errors of some kind. Astonishingly, 57 answered affirmatively: five said a few; 16 yes; 13 many; 18 most; five all or almost all; and only one said none. One might suppose that academics, scholars, and researchers, many of whom teach and mentor, would know the basic attributes of the system used in their disciplines, and yet 31 editors noted that they have received papers that confuse systems, i.e., the authors use two systems simultaneously; 29 said that they had not received such a submission. Fifty-two editors silently correct petty errors (in names, for example); only two do not. Finally, I wanted to know whether they or their assistants check citations to verify their accuracy and whether anyone searched out the article or book. Thirty-two check and 29 do not; 25 seek out the work and 19 do not. Sometimes a photocopy of quoted material must accompany submissions, but this is rare, although because of both errors and ethical problems this requirement may increase in the future in all disciplinary areas.

8. Errors 171

The numbers noted above overwhelmingly indicate that authors almost always make errors in their documentation. A few of the respondents offered additional comments. (Since I did not specifically request permission to attribute remarks, I will present these anonymously.) One listed a host of documentation errors he encounters. Another comment helps us to understand the etiology of these many blunders. It is not merely that authors are careless, inept, or unknowledgeable; they sometimes purposely subvert the system: "...one of my authors [said], when I asked her to provide a page number, 'I find page numbers superfluous.'" Two note that senior scholars are more inept than their juniors: "Established scholars are often more careless than neophytes...." And again, "...the more renowned the scholar, the worse the documentation...." One insisted that "...during my tenure as editor [23 years] at most 10% of the submissions I received had correct documentation." And this is confirmed by another person: "Once every year or two an author sends complete documentation along with quotations that are 99 percent accurate." But here is a twist that reflects badly on editors: "...I've seen a ... nursing editor discard papers out-of-hand immediately because the author's margins were too narrow, wrong font size, wrong style (APA), etc...." This is overly harsh, unnecessary, and harmful to both authors and the publication, which may have lost an excellent document. I am certain that this attitude and behavior can be generalized to at least a small percentage of (supercilious) editors.

A colleague of Henk Moed analyzed 22 million references derived from the ISI databases and found almost one million discrepancies that occurred in various data fields such as name, volume number, or year. Some of these are due to author error, others to complexities in foreign names and transliteration. Some are minor variations, but others are major errors (174–176) and will result in difficulties for searchers and skewing when statistical analyses are run.

A quarter of a century ago (before the existence of online sources), Information Access Corporation disseminated its periodical indexes on reels of microform contained within their own high-speed readers. Sometimes these led directly to other devices that allowed one to read microfilm versions of the cited articles. The index was replete with errors. Someone explained to me that the company wanted to get the indexes out very quickly and the haste allowed errors to slip in. There is always a tradeoff: Here an immediate indexing response to publication was certainly beneficial to people searching for current information, but when the citation led to an incorrect location, the result was frustration or anger. If the percentage of false hits was low, then the tradeoff was worthwhile; otherwise, it might have been better to take more time in compiling the monthly indices. Accurate newspaper indexing is particularly difficult. Even when the data are correct, the result for the researcher may be less than perfect. Some papers have different chronological and geographic editions, and these shift articles around. Thus, if one has a page for the eastern version, it may not lead to the correct location in the national edition. Not everyone is familiar with such subtleties (and sometimes the correct page for the held edition is unavailable).

But even the sophisticated will be astounded by what some newspapers do. About ten years ago, I visited my mother. I awoke at six A.M. and retrieved the delivered *New York Times*, in which I discovered an important article. I clipped it. It was so meaningful that my brother, who, like our mother, receives *The Times* at six A.M., also clipped it and subsequently mailed it to me. The articles appeared in the same edition of the same paper on the same day, delivered at the same time in the same city (New York). My relatives' houses are about ten miles apart. The articles were similar in every detail except that, impossibly, the headlines were totally different. I cannot imagine that a relevantly plausible and defensible explanation for this madness exists. Such bizarre editorial practices help to introduce documentation errors into the historical record, which in the future will confuse or even harm. The detrimental aspects of this are magnified now that national newspapers such as *USA Today* or the *Wall Street Journal* are printed at various locations around the country. Do these presses make subtle changes in the text? One would hope that editorial decisions and alterations only occur at the editorial headquarters. An additional complication that results in errors is that many newspapers (and other publications) may alter the online versions of hard copy articles. In cyberspace, there is no archival copy. Rather there are multiple archival copies, some of which may eventually be expunged. A thousand years hence, one will still be able to access the original hard copy versions of *The Tatler* or *Spectator*, though the pages may be brittle and their use heavily proscribed, limited to those who, for some legitimate reason, require the original sheets. (Forty years ago, the British Library allowed scholars to handle the *Lindisfarne Gospels* or the *Beowulf* manuscript, whereas today, a superb facsimile is provided.) It is highly unlikely that periodically published material (journals, newspapers) currently available on the Internet will be accessible in similar format or at all. The delivery systems will be so different that we simply cannot imagine them. A pessimist might conclude that much electronic data and information will be lost to future generations, though 5,000 year old Sumerian tablets and 4,000 year old Egyptian papyri both in pristine condition are currently accessible in collections around the world.

Even outstanding scholars introduce inadvertent errors into their citations (sometimes of their own previous works) through haste, carelessness, or a failure to check and recheck the petty details that comprise a complete reference, especially now that software programs are manipulating citational elements. These mistakes intrude upon the scholarly literature far more frequently than one might imagine. What this means is that citations and bibliographies are often unreliable. Grafton describes Bayle's errors thus:

> [H]e often gave incomplete bibliographical details in his own references. He regularly found himself forced to cite books no longer in his hands from memory or from notes that he could not verify. Worse still, he cited sources that he had not read at all ... [*Footnote* 211–212].

When one scrupulously studies a work's references, errors magically appear, indeed, even in commentaries on citational errors: references are completely lacking; pagination is haphazard or expunged; numerical demarcators (volume, issue, date, pagination) are incorrect; and even terminology is conflated, e.g., the author Ball becomes Bal or the title phrase "brief review" somehow metamorphoses into "brief overview." Consider the bizarre case that this very article by Ball, indicating that citational errors prove that scholars do not read the articles they are citing, and published in *Nature*, perhaps the world's most prestigious scientific journal, contains an identifying inscription at the bottom of the page that informs us that this is the "12 December 20002" issue! If *Nature*'s innumerable copy editors and proof readers can miss such a blatant (though petty) typographical mistake, it is little wonder that such anomalies sneak into the literature.

Almost 20 years ago, Janell Rudolph and Deborah Brackstone published an incisive and helpful essay in which they describe citation error as a ubiquitous and harmful problem. They are pragmatists: As librarians, they have to help patrons locate material and they find this difficult to do because insignificant as well as major mistakes lead them astray. Naturally, they are skeptical concerning oral referrals but, surprisingly, they insist that published bibliographies and especially the data contained in ISI's citation indexes are often inaccurate and thus unreliable; the reason for this is that unlike regular subject indexes, ISI data are gleaned from the references included in journals and monographs; if the authors introduce errors (and they do) then these mistakes are simply carried over into the citation listings. Even today, these may go uncorrected, since not many users will bother to inform ISI that a name, page, or volume number is incorrect (and if they do, the indexers may not believe them and they may not be willing to seek out the cited material and correct the error (although they do make many corrections, 46 percent according to Robert Buchanan [302]), which is impossible in a published hard copy, but easily rectifiable in the electronic versions of the three citation indexes. Janne Kotiaho confirms the ubiquity of citational mistakes:

> Indeed, there is generally an astonishing number of errors in citations.... Price ... analysed all of the citations that he could trace on three highly

cited publications and found that all of the publications were cited incorrectly in more than 200 different ways. Moreover, approximately every sixth citation to these publications was erroneous ... [summarized in Kotiaho 13].

Rudolph and Brackstone discovered a single name, A. T. Beck, listed in the *Social Science Citation Index* "as A. Beck, A. H. Beck, H. T. Beck, T. Beck, T. A. Beck, and A. J. Beck." This is perhaps an extreme (and from some perspectives petty) instance, but it does exemplify how easily errors are propagated. Their analytic diatribe confirms the many statistical citation surveys published during the past century: The percentage of mistakes found range from less than 25 to more than 50. (In the latter case, one of every two citations in the analyzed population contains a mistake!) For example, M. Faith McLellen and her colleagues found that more than half of all citations in the 1988 issues of four anesthesiology journals contained errors (186) and Migiwa Asano and his collaborators discovered that all 1990 issues of the *Canadian Journal of Anaesthesiology* produced citational errors at the rate of 48 percent; after a concerted attempt to improve was made, this dropped to 22 percent in 1994 (371). What is most interesting here is that the editors of the journals in which these two articles appeared felt that they were the single most important pieces in their respective issues, despite the fact that these publications deal with anesthesiology, not citational misconception: Each issue contains an editorial commenting on the problem. Julien Biebuyck advises readers that "[t]he omission of pertinent references or 'citation amnesia' is an important form of bibliographic misbehavior" (1), and David Bevan and Janet Purkis observe that "[t]here is no point, but much frustration, in quoting a reference in which the citation is inaccurate or fictitious." They also mention that because their publication's citational error rate had been so high, the journal now requires a copy of "the first page of each reference" (367). This is an excellent, if annoying, way to help eliminate mistakes, most of which are introduced into the literature through the carelessness of authors, but Beverley Geer points out that some inconsistencies may derive from the clash that exists between disciplinary style regulations and standardized cataloging rules (70–71).

It is not necessary to multiply examples, but it is worth mentioning the incredible Uplavici case, which James Sweetland describes, and which I concisely summarize: Dr. Jaroslav Hlava's 1887 paper was published in a Czech journal; the author's name was omitted in a German abstract, which disseminated the fact that the important paper existed; instead, the abstract was headed by its Czech title, "O Uplavici" ("On Dysentary"), which subsequently was transmuted into an author's name, Dr. O. Uplavici (plus many variants including combinations of Hlava and Uplavici), and was erroneously passed down for 51 years, until the mistake was discovered (293). There is a surprisingly large body of literature on citational errors. A limited number of these articles deal with the problem generally or theoretically but most of them, especially those in biomedical journals, present the dismal results of surveys that consistently find that citational errors are rampant. (See, *inter alios,* Geer; Henige, "Discouraging"; McLellen et al.; Rudolph and Brackstone; and Sweetland, all of whose references lead to additional informative, if repetitive, material.) Theoretically worse than citational errors in journals and monographs are mistaken instructions in style guides:

> Similar problems with miscitations, incorrect abbreviations, and confusing terminology related to government publications have been found in Kate Turabian's manual, *The Chicago Manual of Style,* and the "Bluebook" ... [Stuart M. Basefsky summarized in Sweetland 301].

If citations in hard copy publications have always contained some erroneous data, at least they maintain stability. Unless some Borgesian lunatic undertakes to visit the world's libraries and remove a particular page from every journal issue or book or alter or expunge individual citations, the printed documentation has a high degree of reliability. This is not the case in the electronic environment: Citations and references are often worthless because the addresses (URLs) are incorrect (either because they have changed or because the complex sequences of letters, numbers, and symbols were misrecorded) or the Web sites to which they refer have disappeared. Consider that Carmine Sellitto, writing on this very topic, cites the following ludicrous URL: <http://web.archive.org/web/20030321172332/http://qualitative-research.net/fqs-texte/20030321172331-20030321172303/20030321172331-20030321172303 metcalfe-e.htm>. (This repetitive format is verified because Sellitto offers another extremely similar address.) Is it any wonder that it does not work (at least not for me)? Ironically, Sellitto also manages to introduce two errors into his paper (published in the prestigious *Journal of the American Society for Information Science and Technology*): In two of his sections (results and conclusion), he indicates that 1,043 Web sites are referenced (699, 702), but in the abstract the number is given as 1,068 (695); he also changes the title of Chuck Zerby's study, *The Devil's Details,* to *The Devil's Advocate* (703).

Undergraduates do an especially poor job with Web site choice and citation: For example, of 344 URLs cited in 1996, only one still worked 14 months later (Koehler noted in Davis and Cohen 310) or again, of 72 URLs cited in student papers in 1996, 53 percent were not locatable (Davis and Cohen 312). Michael Bugeja has shown that cited web sources simply disappear. When revising the first draft of a manuscript (for Oxford University Press), some years ago, he discovered that one third of his online citations no longer gave access to the material. He feared that readers could accuse him of fabrication;

he had thought that "linkrot" was exclusively a linking problem, but it obviously occurs within a citational environment as well (see <www.halfnotes.org>) (Nardini, pars. 1, 3). Bugeja and a colleague investigated this phenomenon, and they discovered that of "108 Internet citations" in a group of papers only 55 (51 percent) were operative "when clicking on the link" less than a year later. (The numbers increased slightly when an address was input.) Incredibly, of those that did work, barely more than half led to the material cited in the reference (Bugeja and Dimitrova 81). And Sellitto discovered that of 1,043 Web citations found in 123 conference papers, 45.8 percent could not be located at the indicated URL (702). He wisely insists that

> [a] scholarly list of citations associated with an article should always be accessible, available and, in the electronic environment, retrievable [702].

It is too bad that this is quite frequently not the case.

Many reasons exist for link malfunctions: The address is incorrect, the site or its server is down, the specific location on the site has been excised, or the site no longer exists. Consider that the *Journal of Medical Ethics* provides "[l]inks from references to the full text of more than 340 journals"; thus, an online reader can click on a citation and immediately access the text to which it refers. This is an extraordinary service, one that is certain to become ubiquitous in electronic scholarly publishing, although, naturally, the result is not entirely new. It is merely a matter of convenience: Seventeenth century readers could accomplish the same thing; it just required a great deal of time and energy. But here, as in most recent developments in information technology, the convenience is so dramatic that it brings a qualitative change along with the new access possibilities. For example, a disabled, bed-ridden medical researcher can now quickly and efficiently accomplish everything that a mobile colleague in a library can, but only if the citations are accurate and the links function. (I wonder how completely and carefully the tens of thousands of linked citations in a single volume of any expansive [weekly] medical journal are checked. If, for example, an editor only opens and scrutinizes every tenth citation, contemporary readers may be disappointed to discover that the electronic citations are as unreliable as their hardcopy siblings. Future scholars will undoubtedly have even more problems, as archived publications are weeded, i.e., eliminated.) Obviously, each journal or publisher will have a different policy in place, but since very few editors follow up on every citation noted in a typical article or monograph, merely to see if it really leads where it is supposed to, I am guessing that despite the ease and simplicity of clicking, many of the countless citations to these 340 publications mentioned above are not investigated. (This appears to be the type of task that might be assigned to an intern; but since scholars with medical and research doctorates introduce, on average, an error into 50 percent of their citations, even a responsible college student may not manage to achieve an extremely high rate of accuracy, and this amounts to the same thing: non-existent, random, or inaccurate checking will lead to frustrated readers, few of whom will follow up on a single malfunctioning link (by accessing the hard copy, if it is available), when other electronic sources are immediately at hand. Robert Buchanan indicates that the citational errors created by authors are multiplied by data inputters at ISI and Sci-Finder Scholar (another citation index), who manufacture additional mistakes, though not many (292, 295). WebCite <www.webcitation.org> offers an archiving service for web references.

One of the ways in which *Wikipedia,* the online, multi-authored encyclopedia, forestalls factual errors, astonishingly, is to disallow original research in its posted articles: "Only citable material that has already been published elsewhere is permitted" (Read A33, sidebar). Upon reflection, this is an understandable tactic, since the source material can easily be verified, should someone choose to do so. Apparently, many readers do, because errors are quickly rooted out and removed (Read A31). But surprisingly, articles may be posted without the certifying documentation, and the overseers then request readers other than the author to create the attributions: At the head of "Examples," the second section in the article "Moral panic," one finds the following request: "This article or section does not cite its **references or sources.** You can help Wikipedia by introducing appropriate citations" (highlighting and Roman in original) ("Moral panic"). This notice was posted no later than June 25, 2006; five months later, it was still there. This is a strange way to forward scholarship, but *Wikipedia* is an unusual agglomeration of diversely authored materials. And because all texts are susceptible to ongoing revision, citations can change or disappear. That is why it is suggested that when citing a *Wikipedia* article, one should include not only the date, but also the hour of access; that would allow a reader of the citation to check it even if it has been expunged, because *Wikipedia* articles are accompanied by a history page of all previous versions (Read, A36, sidebar).

With the exception of problems introduced by overzealous copy editors or data-entry clerks, citational errors (including factual mistakes in commentaries) result from authorial lapses. Thus, blaming peer reviewers, editors, and publishers for not catching them is an unacceptable abrogation of responsibility. These people do what they can to root out mistakes, but it is not the job of manuscript reviewers to catch petty errors or even ferret out misconduct, although if they do, that is an excellent bonus. Peer reviewers are asked to evaluate manuscripts in terms of their publishability. Few people would volunteer to participate in this unrewarding procedure if expected to check each of the article's 112 esoteric references. He or she would need a herd of graduate assistants to follow up here. Editors do catch mistakes, but they too have better things to do than search in physical or electronic archives in order to verify hundreds of arcane references to Zulu history. They spend much of their time correcting grammatical and stylistic anomalies, mistakes in citational *format*, and factual errors (such as misspelled names, with which they are intimately familiar, since they are often experts in their fields). Despite the exaggerated use of fact checkers, at *The New Yorker*, for example, the responsibility for accurate references lies in the hands of the author, who should delegate recording or checking only to the most responsible and caring assistants. If these anonymous helpers blunder, the guilt must devolve upon the author's already burdened shoulders. Generally, small, petty, or typographical errors are negligible, although even they may result in unpleasant consequences. Larger or frequent (cumulative) mistakes may be tantamount to misconduct.

9
Misconduct

[C]itations are the reward system of scientific publication.
— Eugene Garfield

Three general classes of authors exist. The first group includes academic, organizational, and independent scholars; the second consists of those who write non-fiction for a lay audience, and includes historians, science writers, and magazine and newspaper reporters; and the third covers authors of creative works such as poetry, drama, popular and serious fiction, and screen plays. Writers from each of these groups have been guilty of misconduct, which derives from any type of fabrication, falsification, or plagiarism. Not all forms of authorial misconduct are relevant to this discussion, but misconduct is often forwarded or affirmed through misleading, deceptive, or false documentation. It is crucial to bear in mind that misconduct is very different from error. In the former case, people purposely attempt to deceive; in the latter, they make inadvertent mistakes, which they would ameliorate given the opportunity. But if errors come in droves, and they derive from unacceptable habits (irresponsible activity, consistently sloppy data collection or recording), then error may metamorphose into misconduct (see Ball). Naturally, biomedical scholars or historians fabricate or plagiarize more frequently than novelists, and they are also more culpable because the harm that may accrue is much greater in the medical field, for example, than it would be in or because of a fictional construct. (This remark, of course, is not meant to be ethically or legally mitigating in any way.) Misconduct of various sorts is epidemic in general (newspaper reporting, for example) and in most academic disciplines, but this chapter is only concerned with unethical activity that is perpetrated though documentation distortion.

When to Cite

Long before the introduction of the World Wide Web, elementary and middle school children were taught that one must allocate credit to authors whose work forms the basis for the compositions, reports, essays, and research papers demanded of students without surcease. This lore (conventions, rules, regulations) is drummed in throughout the course of one's primary, secondary, and tertiary school experiences: Honor those upon whose shoulders one stands, acknowledge debt, apportion credit, attribute sources, avoid plagiarism. Now that plagiary is ubiquitous among students, researchers, and scholars, even in the western world, where it is unequivocally condemned, it is more important than ever to emphasize correct (ethical) habits. And we do, both for those just learning the rules and protocols and for those who are already professional writers. Nevertheless, an astonishing percentage of students and scholars fail to cite their sources in an equitable and accurate manner: Naturally, writers sometimes make mistakes, but what is far worse is that many distort, mislead, or steal. Thus, it appears rather disingenuous for Rob Kling and subsequently Eugene Garfield to wonder when one should cite (Garfield, "When" 449). This is what is taught in class, and the various style manuals (for high school and college students) *do* contain some instruction on this topic. At any rate, a concise practical taxonomy (as opposed to a casuistic listing of every possible contingency and variation) would appear as follows:

- It is *not* necessary to cite, reference, or attribute common knowledge or well-known facts.
- It is *not* necessary to cite what one has known for a long period of time (it is common knowledge to the person, as a specialist or expert, for example).
- It *is* necessary to cite data and information that one learned (anything he or she did not know) during the course of reading or research.
- It *is* necessary to cite other people's original opinions, ideas, or perspectives.

A reference should be constructed in the required cases regardless of whether the source is quoted briefly or at length, is paraphrased (the fact, idea, or opinion is rearticulated so that a new and different syntactic and lexicographic construct emerges), or is completely reconstructed so that the original idea is buried in a new and different context. The only thing that matters is that someone else said something that the citing author did not know: He or she has a human, scholarly, ethical, and legal obligation to apportion credit. It is also ethically incumbent to know when *not* to cite:

- One should not cite unread material (unless it is included in a comprehensive bibliography, and this purpose is made clear).

- One should not cite non-existent material.
- One should not cite constructed references to plagiarized material.
- One should not cite fabricated data.

Students and scholars are human and prone to all of the foibles that seduce the lazy, ambitious, desirous, or greedy. Thus, they all too frequently take short cuts or fabricate situations or results, falsify data or citations, and plagiarize in whole or in part. They construct fictional citations or do not protect their data. A postdoctoral fellow accused Thereza Imanishi-Kari of recording her data so sloppily (altering or fabricating laboratory records) that the validity of their work was affected (Altman and Hernon 149). The *Cell*/Baltimore case, as it is called, had many undesirable concatenating results, despite Imanishi-Kari's exoneration, including an explanation of the paper and the resignation of the Nobelist, David Baltimore, from the presidency of Rockefeller University. This type of careless behavior (Imanishi-Kari claimed that she was *only* guilty of carelessness) is so egregious that it transcends mere error. That is why this case created such an uproar. Nevertheless, governing boards, agencies, and academic committees in the biomedical sciences are so lenient, offering condemnations so infrequently, and doling out *severe* punishment only in the most unusual circumstances and only for officially defined misconduct, which consists of fabrication, falsification, or plagiary, that the miscreants are back in business shortly thereafter, rendering peer-review decisions or publishing new material, all of which may have a potent effect in their fields.

Scientific misconduct is much more widespread than scientists are willing to admit. Because science is indeed self-correcting, it appears to practitioners that fraud, fabrication, and even plagiary are minor anomalies that will be discovered early, during the peer review process, or later on, through replication of the study. Even if this were true, much harm can accrue before the deception is discovered. But it is not: peer review is not designed to ferret out misconduct and often misses it, and most studies are never replicated. Original or cited data and references to other studies are often confirmed or noted in the references, and thus this falls under the rubric of documentation misconduct.

Fabrication

Both Cyril Burt and Zoltan J. Lucas fabricated fictional references to articles that did not exist (Sweetland 299). Burt's deviant behavior here and in the misconstruction of his data had an extremely detrimental effect on twentieth century psychology. Practitioners were deceived concerning the importance of heritability in the development of intelligence and may have caused harm to individuals who were sent in directions that might have been different had Burt never published his misleading studies. (Not everyone is convinced that Burt was a fraud.) Henige recounts the impossible case of Robert Sobel's *For Want of a Nail: If Burgoyne Had Won at Saratoga*, a "counterfactual" study whose extensive apparatus, including 850 notes, "is *entirely fictitious*" ("Being" 123, italics in original). Almost every page is riddled with footnotes, and 16 of its 441 pages are given over to a bibliographic listing of innumerable works, which apparently do not exist. Burt was convinced that genetic predisposition is more influential than the environment and his goal was to forward this agenda, even if dishonestly; he probably believed that he was accomplishing something meaningful and useful. The possibility exists that his fabrications could have gone undetected, since they were based on his own experimental data. Alan Sokal (see below) also had a meaningful purpose, and he did accomplish what he set out to do. But Sobel's work, which must of necessity derive from historical precedent recounted in documents (few people could recall Revolutionary war battles in 1973) is apparently a hoax for its own sake and one quite likely to be quickly unmasked by knowledgeable readers. Though the catalogers at the Library of Congress gave it a legitimate historical classification, the reviewers at both *Choice* (Rev.) and *Time* (Skow) immediately realized that it was a hoax and unmasked it and its apparatus.

Falsification

Both fabrication and falsification are endemic in the hard sciences, especially biomedical research, but instances do turn up in other disciplines. Grafton comments on a number of cases of documentation falsification including that of David Abraham (a fellow Princeton historian), who made many mistakes in his study of the Weimar Republic. Henry Turner accused Abraham of doing what Michael Bellesiles would do many years later, purposely distorting (through misdating, misattribution, and mistranslation) to further an ideological agenda (Grafton, *Footnote* 17). As an aside, it is worth noting that Grafton comes up with a series of ostensibly reasonable defenses for Abraham's actions. Naturally, in cases such as this, there will always be accusers and defenders and both sides may be motivated by matters extraneous to the discovery of truth. But the point I am making here is that the comparatively wealthy and famous often get away with things for which the disempowered may suffer. Much worse is the case of Bellesiles in *Arming America*, because, unlike Abraham who was pursuing a scholarly topic with limited contemporary relevance, Bellesiles's ideological thesis (that colonial Americans were not heavily armed), if true, could have had an impinging effect on the legality of current gun ownership. It is therefore not surprising that his documentation was scrupulously scrutinized. Critics found that it is riddled with purposeful distortions. Clayton Cramer, among others, discovered many discrepancies including misleading quotations and a distorted use of sources. Bellesiles's notes lead to material that not only does not confirm his text, it sometimes indicates precisely the opposite unless it is entirely irrelevant (2). Cramer scrupulously examines the cited works in turn and points out the discrepancies. For example, Bellesiles observes that

> [i]n 1797 Governor James Wood informed the legislature that his government had searched the state to find anyone who could make arms for the militia, without success [qtd. in Cramer 16].

Giles Cromwell, the cited source for this, states that

> ... scattered throughout the mountain and valley regions were many individual rifle makers who advanced their skills by making exceptionally fine rifles [qtd. in Cramer 16].

This is but one of innumerable examples of how the text and its cited sources do not jibe. On the surface the documentation appears to be confirmatory, and unless the sources are examined, Bellesiles's argument appears to be overwhelmingly convincing. (Early on, astonishingly, no one checked the sources. That is why the book garnered the Bancroft Prize, which eventually was revoked, and Bellesiles lost his academic position, so in this case the falsifier did suffer negative repercussions.) The documentation does not support the thesis; the evidence is ignored or distorted and the truth is falsified (3–7): "The sources that Bellesiles cites for his claim of distrusted, disarmed colonists *never* support it, and usually contradict it..." (7), or "What is again interesting is how Bellesiles' sources differ from Bellesiles' representation of them" (12). (See also Ron Robin, who discusses Bellesiles's non-existent probate records, which play a major role in his study [68–70].)

Although some thinkers may vacillate when it comes to legitimate useful deception in research (as opposed to self-serving and harmful misconduct), most scholars are either strongly opposed to or pragmatically in favor of twisting the truth in order to accomplish something beneficial. (Governmental agencies, organizations such as the APA, university administrations, and institutional review boards are all unequivocally against deception, although permission may occasionally be granted for innocuous experiments as long as a subject suffers no negative consequences; but this is a debatable point, since participants in experiments must sign a legally binding informed consent waiver, which in this case would be misleading, and anyone who is fooled in this manner will feel tricked.) The difference between typical misconduct and this type of deception is that in the former case, it only succeeds if the deception remains undiscovered, whereas when Stanley Milgrim deceived experimental subjects in order to discover whether they would obey orders or William Epstein deceives peer reviewers or editors in order to evaluate the merits of a profession, the value of their discoveries only emerges when the deception is revealed. This is unequivocally the case with Alan Sokal, who perpetrated a beneficial hoax, for which he nevertheless was understandably castigated, especially by those he fooled and their intellectual supporters. This tale has been retold many times, not least, by Sokal himself. What is important in this context is that the many notes he provided to his bizarre text are accurate citations to the statements of the postmodern critics of science, whose remarks he cobbled together into an ostensible critique of gravity:

> As deliberately parodic as Sokal's pronouncements were, they seemed nowhere near as silly as the bits he quoted from post-modernist icons like Jacques Derrida, Jacques Lacan and Luce Irigaray and from their numerous American interpreters, who showed up in a cataract of footnotes [Holt].

The notes are neither falsified nor fabricated, but the documentation's objective is to trick the reader. The entire article devolves into gibberish because the quoted statements are based on the misunderstandings, misconstructions, and agenda-ridden nonsense of people who have little scientific training and appropriate complex concepts that they do not understand and then misapply them in a non-scientific context in order to criticize the scientific enterprise. (This is at least analogous to, though more serious than, the misappropriation of entropy or the Uncertainty Principle, two favorite scientific concepts of modern novelists.)

Plagiarism

Plagiarism is an ongoing epidemic in all disciplinary areas: Ostensible or verified cases of historical (Stephen Oates, Stephen E. Ambrose, Doris Kearns Goodwin), literary (Susan Sontag, Kaavya Viswanathan, Ian MacEwen), scientific (See LaFollette, *Stealing*, and Price for many examples), and student plagiary (70 percent of all students cheat) are of concern here because the theft of another's words or ideas always entails either expunging or occasionally fabricating documentation. Eugene Garfield refers to this as "citation amnesia," when the transgression is a minor oversight and "bibliographic plagiarism" when it is intentional ("From" 503). Marcel LaFollette emphasizes the structural aspect: "The term plagiarism applies beyond the misappropriation of body text, to speeches and to the text of footnotes and citations" (*Stealing* 49). The literature on plagiary is enormous and continues to increase.

(See Judy Anderson's annotated bibliography, now almost ten years old.) This section is not a survey or overview of the topic. Rather, it presents a small culling in order to exemplify the role of documentation, and the excuses that are tendered when the problem comes to light. First, though, I must observe that it would be kind of scholars to offer some benefit of doubt here, for it is indeed possible that Susan Sontag, for example, meant no harm, did not consider her few unattributed quotations or paraphrases (12 cases ranging from a sentence to eight lines of poetry for a total of ca. three out of 387 pages [Carvajal, "So" B9]) to constitute a breach of ethics, and honestly believed the nonsense that she articulated when accused of theft. This is possible because she was not a serial plagiarist, did not really need these few items in her enormous novel, was intimately familiar with the conventions of attribution (since she was a scholar), and must have realized that she could get "caught." And it is also possible that historians and scientists really are disorganized; keep messy records; mix up or lose cards, slips of paper, or computer files; and employ inept assistants who confuse or destroy materials, attributions, and citations. (Thus, it is little wonder that history can be confused and distorted and that ostensible evidentiary data can be of little value and prove absolutely nothing, despite the purported value of the discovery, drug, or procedure.) This mitigation having been offered, one may still stand aghast at what transpires.

In 2000, Sontag published *In America*, a novel based on the life of a Polish-American actress. Although she acknowledges that she did make use of unnamed source material, Sontag does not attribute quotations or paraphrases. When confronted, she claimed that historical fiction does not require footnoting and said, furthermore, "There's a larger argument to be made that all of literature is a series of references and allusions" (Carvajal, "So" B9). Indeed, and I presented it earlier in this study, but it is no excuse for theft. Sontag continued to defend herself using bizarre logic, but she was not very convincing. She should have either attributed or admitted to an error in judgment and documented the material on an errata slip and, subsequently, in a second edition. But very few plagiarists admit that they have transgressed. Shortly thereafter, the situation was precisely mirrored in Ian McEwan's *Atonement*. Once again, the author acknowledges the use of a source, but he too fails to document some paraphrases and quotations. Despite obvious textual similarities, McEwan denies that he copied material (Cowell). These minor instances of negligent attribution, which can have devastating concatenating effects on an author's career, could easily be obviated by the use of quotation marks and a simple comprehensive attribution. Both of these instances are different from the Stephen Oates affair: Here, the author, an historian rather than a novelist, was accused of including many unattributed passages in his biography of

Lincoln, and then subsequently in many of his earlier works. Ron Robin offers a perceptive overview of this case (as well as others). He points out that Oates was producing hybrid scholarship, which confused imaginative musings with factual history (41). The finding of the American Historical Association was, to some extent, exculpatory; its wording makes clear that documentation plays a pivotal role. There was

> "no evidence that Stephen Oates committed plagiarism as it is conventionally understood," although there was "evidence in Mr. Oates' work of too great and too continuous dependence, even with attribution, on the structure, distinctive language, and rhetorical strategies of other scholars and sources" [qtd. in Ron Robin 44].

Undocumented material that closely mirrored other authors' locutions are what originally attracted attention, but even attributed passages were apparently too close to their sources to offer fair credit.

Plagiary can be a complex business. Garfield summarizes Loren Eiseley's accusation that Darwin fails to fully credit the work of Edward Blyth, as well as Stephen Jay Gould's disagreement with this evaluation ("From" 504–505). Benson Tong apportions credit to Judy Tzu-Chun Wu by frequently citing her dissertation in a chapter he contributed to a collection, but it is merely "a condensed version of her" work and "...the most damning evidence could be found in the footnotes." Most of Tong's references precisely replicate Wu's (Bartlett and Smallwood, "Four" A10), something that would be impossible if Tong had done his own research rather than merely plagiarizing Wu's study. Alan Price recounts the 19 cases of scientific plagiary that the Office of Research Integrity adjudicated between 1992 and 2005. (See the two "Plagiarism" issues of the *Journal of Information Ethics* inspired by the Oates brouhaha; Mallon for additional cases of literary plagiary; and <www.plagiary.org> for contextual material and scholarly investigations.) As is so usual in cases of this nature, the well-placed and powerful suffer few negative consequences for their egregious behavior (because their prestige carries them through[1] or their resources allow them to fight back), whereas the young college student (who also should know better) is not allowed to graduate or has her book recalled and pulped.

Detecting and Preventing Prevarication

Most purposeful bibliographic distortion occurs because an author fails to include the requisite sources, falsifies them, or pads a bibliography with inappropriate, unread, or nonexistent material. There was a time when descriptive bibliographies served a crucial intellectual purpose. More than mere listings, these citations traced the intellectual history of the author or the precise structure of the scrupulously described book. In order to make certain that thieves would not plagiarize, authors would purposely insert ghosts, fictional citations, that led nowhere. Anyone foolishly copying one of these had obviously never looked at the non-existent item. Richard Hamilton has shown that Max Weber's notes in *The Protestant Ethic and the Spirit of Capitalism,* one of the twentieth century's seminal studies, do not indicate what Weber claims or they lead to dead ends. This type of intellectual misconception or deception can only be detected if someone is willing to carefully trace a work's citation chain backwards until the contentions are either confirmed or denied. After the Internet began to provide researchers (of all ages and abilities) with an abundant source of material that could easily be purchased or plagiarized, developers created software programs that can detect plagiarized passages. These are used by academics to verify that papers are the legitimate work of the submitting student. (It is a shame that instructors must waste their time on such drivel, because human beings cannot be trusted to do their jobs fairly and honestly.)

Because so many cases of misconduct, especially in biomedicine, have recently come to light, journals (especially medical publications) now insist on full disclosure. Thus a short article may conclude with columns listing hundreds of people and organizations under headings such "author contributions," "financial disclosures," "funding/support," "acknowledgment," and "previous presentations." How a brief account of a clinical trial or research program could possibly be indebted to such an extraordinary array of supporters is a real mystery. Despite all of this, though, those who prefer dissimulation to honesty and hard work will continue to prevaricate their way to the top of their professions.

Repercussions

There are no repercussions for citational misconduct. Well, that is an exaggeration, but for the well-placed, it happens to be fairly accurate. Whenever famous authors are accused of misconduct, others weigh in against them. But simultaneously, a host of countering peers arises. The motivation for this varies, but the bottom line is that even when a star is unequivocally culpable, voices are raised in his or her defense. When McEwan, who is a highly regarded novelist, was accused (for the second time) of plagiary, the uproar was overwhelming: Margaret Atwood, Kazuo Ishiguro, John Updike, Martin Amis, and, impossibly, Thomas Pynchon all sent letters of support. Apparently, they were not embarrassed to defend his right to plagiarize in terms of their own putative transgressions (Lyall B1). Even the editors of *The New York*

Times ("At") and *The Wall Street Journal* ("Novelty") came to his defense. McEwan undoubtedly will suffer no ill consequences, no law suits, and no contractual abrogations. This situation is mirrored in the Oates case: Many accused; many defended (including such notable scholars as Hans L. Trefousse and Richard N. Current). Although it was a long and unpleasant affair (especially for the protagonist, who undoubtedly suffered from the unrelenting stress), nothing untoward resulted. Is it really necessary to point out what happened to Kaavya Viswanathan, a young, unknown college student? She too plagiarized; she too had lots of excuses, but her peers were too busy plagiarizing their own research papers to speak up and her living literary idols (whoever they may be) ignored her. Her book was recalled and she lost her contract with Little, Brown; she is lucky that Harvard did not sanction her in some way. Where was Eugene Volokh, a UCLA law professor, when someone really needed him? He concludes a *Wall Street Journal* opinion piece on McEwan by informing us that

> ... not all use of another's words requires detailed acknowledgment. Words represent facts; and facts, once revealed, are there to be used, including in novelists' unfootnoted prose.

There, encapsulated in two brief sentences, is the difference between the legal and ethical points of view. (James Frey was roundly castigated for a deception that did not rely on documentation, but it is worth noting that his second appearance on Oprah Winfrey's show only increased book sales.) Even lesser-known researchers who are found guilty of scientific misconduct are slapped on the wrist, though an occasional egregious academic perpetrator is forced to resign or is fired. Most continue to deny that they did anything wrong. The most amazing recent case concerns a graduate student who accused his mentor of stealing his work; the mentor continues to insist that he had a right to use it (Bartlett and Smallwood, "Mentor" A14–15). And to be fair, even the well-placed occasionally lose a job or a Pulitzer Prize or go to prison, but these people are guilty of extreme transgressions such as fabricating stories for *The New York Times*. "Appendix A" in Ellen Altman and Peter Hernon's *Research Misconduct* contains a detailed listing of scientists who falsified, fabricated, or plagiarized. Punishments are often lenient: retractions or corrections are published; researchers may not apply for grants or serve on panels or committees; those fired are reinstated.

10
Citation Indexing and Analysis

> *[The] bibliometric unity of science is the direct result of the connectedness of the citation network.*
> — H. Small
>
> *The benefits of using impact factors as a means of scholarly evaluation appear to be few.*
> — Brian D. Cameron

In the past, citations served many allied purposes: They acknowledged, attributed, traced, and validated. They still do these useful tasks, but they are also collected, stored, collated, and manipulated on computer systems so that the influence (importance) of an author or work or journal can ostensibly be ascertained. For many years, the Institute for Scientific Information's three citation indexes were the only way to efficiently track citation usage; now Elsevier's *Scopus* offers similar possibilities. In 1964, Eugene Garfield implemented the idea for a commercial citation index for the hard sciences. This was later expanded first to the social sciences and finally to the arts and humanities, so that today, three indexes to almost 9,000 publications give access to virtually all disciplinary areas, and are searchable online via the *Web of Science*, a product of the Institute for Scientific Information (ISI), which also includes *Journal Citation Reports*, the source of various quantitative measures. Originally, the idea was to allow a researcher to easily ascertain who has cited a particular work in order to track the influence of previous papers and authors, and concomitantly to search the citations within a given paper or monograph. But as the indexes developed, they turned out to have additional practical applications. For example, they can be used to search a subject in the same way that one uses a traditional tool such as *Art Index;* they can access statistics for all scholars at a particular institution or geographical location; they are useful for tracing the development of ideas; and they can help to predict future trends. They are an extraordinary contribution to scholarship and an extremely beneficial reference tool, but sometimes the extrapolations and conclusions drawn from their data are misleading or harmful.

Indexing and Analysis

Long before Garfield founded the citation indexes, and when this type of work had to be done manually, scholars analyzed various constructs in terms of agglomerated references. In an award-winning article, Brian Cameron discusses the development of journal ranking (he also includes a history of ISI and a critique of the applications of the bibliometric data it produces based, in part, on a broad array of previously published commentaries). He cites a ranking study published as early as 1927 (107). Forty years later, Edwin B. Parker and his colleagues attempted to correlate bibliographic citations with scientific communication. Despite their numerous data arrays, I am not certain that they offer any meaningful or useful conclusions. In 1975, Charles Avery Bolles summarized the applications of citation analysis to informational usage (8–10). There is no doubt that a statistical analysis of a large group of citations will yield some valid generalizations for the population. But just how meaningful or useful these are is highly debatable. As Bolles notes, based on his ca. 15,000 citations drawn from *American Quarterly,* English language monographs are cited most frequently (170). But what if he had discovered that German language journals were the predominant form? Just because it is possible to draw correlations does not mean that one should do so, and if one does, the result may be meaningless or even harmful. It is now possible to correlate vast quantities of data using computer programs and new statistical tools. Many germane correlations are brought forth, but this does not mean that their application is beneficial.

In 1979, Garfield published *Citation Indexing,* a seminal study in which he laid out and explained the principles involved. Nothing has changed since then except that the applications and analyses have become ever more complex and esoteric (as can be seen in the titles of typical articles published in *Scientometrics*), the wide-spread application and misuse of axiological indices (such as the impact factor) have, to some extent, supplanted the original use of these tools, and the importance and wide usage of the former enterprise have been called into question, though to little avail. More than a quarter of a century later, Henk Moed published the second major monographic treatment of the subject. In *Citation Analysis in Research Evaluation,* he summarizes and discusses the enormous and diverse body of literature that has developed. Moed has a large investment in citation analysis (this work is based in part on 27 of his authored or coauthored publications), but he is not a close-minded advocate for quantitative measures. He presents a fair and balanced overview, and details the various perspectives offered by sometimes dissenting scholars. For example, though he indicates that ISI coverage (inclusion of publications) is excellent in some areas (physics, chemistry) and good in others (engineering, mathematics), he admits that it is only moderate in most of the social sciences and humanities (sociology, anthropology) (3). Inadequate coverage may result in skewed or misleading correlations and indices such as the impact factor. Or he insists that rankings (which are so important to authors, journals, departments, and countries) are not necessarily accurate: "...scholarly quality is not as straightforwardly measured and ranked as performance is in many other societal domains" (7). And finally, he does not believe that purely quantitative measures should be used in order to make hiring, promotion, or tenure decisions (29). As he notes, "This book illustrates that citation analysis is much more than merely counting absolute numbers of publications and citations" (32). He offers tenable solutions to the many technical problems that result in inaccurate statistics (48).

Counts and correlations result in authors, pairs of authors, specific works, or ideas being culled and noted for their citation frequencies, which ostensibly indicates something of value, e.g., they are cited more frequently and, therefore, they are more influential: "The 'importance' of an idea is measured by the number of citations received by the document(s) in which it is embodied" (Borgman 19). This may be a valid conclusion in some cases, but not as a matter of course, e.g., a tract on creation science may be cited frequently in the serious scholarly literature, but its author should not be lauded (allowing that creation science is nonsense; naturally, if one is a creationist, the opposite point of view obtains). Practical extrapolations derived from this process are often an abuse of data analysis. An egregious example occurs in the academic environment when committees or provosts base retention, tenure, or promotion decisions partially or exclusively on citation analysis. Quantitative measures of scholarly production can be so misleading that some years ago, Harvard limited the number of publications a person could submit in order to achieve academic rank.

Analytic Problems

Even defenders admit that "[b]ibliometric methods are misapplied when their measurement limitations are ignored." Quantitative analysis reflects neither quality nor eminence (Paisley 287), which are not necessary concomitants of citation counts or correlations. Upon superficial consideration the basic assumptions that undergird citation analyses and allow its results to be applied in practical situations do appear to be logical constructs, but Linda Smith questions and criticizes many of them (86–89). Sydney J. Pierce, echoing Smith, does as well. For example, that citations exist implies use, merit, "similarity of content," and equality. But it is possible for an author to simply pad a bibliography, not include seminal sources, and list inappropriate material (48–49). If any of these obtain, then the value of the citation is markedly diminished, the extrapolated conclusions of the analysis are partially or completely invalid, and their application yields a distorted or false picture, one that can cause harm. Smith additionally observes that problems arise because of multiple authors, name duplication, self-citation, varying citation rates in different fields, errors, and so on (91–93). A most interesting if peripheral observation is that those authors who may be extremely influential at one point sometimes quickly lose relevance just a few years later. After the Second World War, few philosophers were as important as Jean-Paul Sartre (and his existentialism); today, he is hardly noticed. Sometime thereafter, along came a triad of French thinkers (who changed the face of scholarship in the humanities and social sciences). The reputations of Lacan, Foucault, and Derrida are now much diminished. Indeed, Foucault (who, naturally, has his defenders) has been shown to have purposely distorted historical fact. The rewards heaped upon these men based on citation analysis (probably none) may have been undeserved. Here is how Anne Stevens puts this in a rebuttal to a critique:

> As we discuss in our article [see Stevens and Williams], number of citations does not equal importance. Some ideas have been so absorbed into the discourse that they no longer require footnoting, while other figures enjoy brief periods of trendiness, where they are more cited than actively engaged with.

To be fair to Garfield and his original impetus, which was citation indexing and then analysis in the hard sciences, scholars in these areas do continue to cite researchers and papers whose ideas have been "absorbed," either because they are still truly influential or because the citer gains prestige by mentioning a hundred-year-old Einstein paper.

Almost 30 years ago, this is how Garfield explained the new axiological applications:

> Although it was developed primarily for bibliographic purposes, and in spite of its recognized utility as a search tool, the most important application of citation indexing may prove to be nonbibliographic. ... [T]he SCI data base is being used to do such things as evaluate the research role

of individual journals, scientists, organizations, and communities; ... [and] measure the impact of current research ... [*Citation* 62].

One index of quantitative value is co-citation, "...the number of documents that have referenced a given pair of documents" (Garfield, *Citation* 99). Upon superficial reflection this result appears to be a quasi-mystical number, and the process ludicrously expandable: If a pair of texts is indicative of importance, then a trio would be superior and a quartet even better, and if the cited materials are what are termed "citation classics" then the results are truly impressive indeed, and so on. Perhaps it is at least partially for such reasons that quantitative measures of scholarly work are being called into question, at least by some critics. Even Garfield admits that "...the nature of the quality that citation rates measure is elusive...," and he goes on to discuss some of the problems (*Citation* 63), many of which are now cited by critics of another measure, the purely quantitative impact factor (IF), the ostensible indicator of true scholarly merit and value, which has become "the number that's devouring science" (Monastersky A12). The IF is derived by dividing the number of citations garnered in a two year period by a journal by the number of articles published in that periodical. A high IF lends credibility to a publication, which seduces scholars into submitting articles, which, if they in turn receive many citations, confirm the journal's reputation. The authors reap various rewards for their frequently cited discoveries. The impact factor is used by librarians as a criterion in collection development and by academic administrators to evaluate faculty. It is also used to preen: In 2005, it was ascertained that Canadian astronomers' papers (for a ten year period) were cited more than those of any other country. (Their impact factor was 15.91, whereas the IF for American astronomers was a mere 15.18.) "We're getting better, and it shows," said one proud scientist, who "hoped to use the new rankings to shore up support..." (Overbye D1). Is this subtle distinction of any real scholarly or national importance?

In *Citation Indexing* (244–249) and subsequently in innumerable briefer publications (e.g., "Journal"), Garfield anticipates, discusses, and sometimes defends against much of the (recent) critical commentary aimed at the impact factor. As early as 1984, Blaise Cronin concisely summarized the many problems associated with citational quantification, ascribing the criticisms to specific authors (*Citation* 27–28). Two medical scholars, Sidney Bloch and Garry Walter, present a well-thought-out critique of the IF (and by implication of citation analysis generally). They criticize all of its logically deficient characteristics and call for a change. The IF confuses quantity with quality, delimits the time during which the article's influence can be felt, is manipulated (through editorial or self-citation), and is misapplied (564, 565). In a sidebar included in Per Seglen's argument against the use of the IF for evaluating research, the author lists 21 problems associated with the IF's application, among which are the following: the journal's IF is not a surrogate for the individual articles; authors do not exclusively rely on the IF when deciding to submit to a specific publication; books are excluded from citation counts; American journals predominate; and "[s]mall research fields tend to lack journals with high impact" (499). Other negative aspects include the limited number of publications analyzed and the many mistakes that sneak into citation indices, and Cameron adds the rather arbitrary two year time frame, the sub-discipline and the number of publications it produces, and journal size (109, 111). Finally, and most telling, scholars cite for many and diverse reasons and the substantive content of the article is not necessarily one of them: Mikhail Simkin and Viwani Roychowdhury show that authors cite, although they have failed to read the work. They explain that if an author reads an article, he or she is unlikely to carry over a citational error contained in the literature. Logically, he or she will correct it, when re-citing the piece. But these errors are propagated, and Simkin and Roychowdhury indicate, amazingly, "that four out of five authors had not done their homework." They base their conclusion on a survey of 4,300 citations to an important paper on condensed matter: The "mis-citations of it were often identical to each other." And "[t]he most common misprint appeared 78 times" (summarized in Ball). The mere fact that something is noted or referenced is of very little consequence. To be truly meaningful, one would have to know why it is included and not merely that it is.

A number of points require more detailed explication. The basic parameters that control the material included in the citation indexes, as well as the structure and content of the sources themselves, influence the bibliometric measures, including the IF, that ISI produces. For example, the indexes cover some 9,000 journals, which represents but a minuscule percentage of the half million serials published throughout the world. The language of choice, naturally, is English, which means that Farsi, Kazakh, Mongolian, or Yoruba but even Portuguese or Dutch publications will be slighted. (This is a manifestation of the same attitude that privileges western scholarship over third-world work and which keeps much of this material out of the citation indexes. See Gibbs for an excellent critique.) The type of material published precisely controls the number of citations accorded by future researchers. Opinion pieces, general remarks, and letters are unlikely to elicit citations, so they may be delimited; original (and ground-breaking) research will stimulate other scholars to follow a similar path or attempt to replicate the study, which will yield a plethora of citations. And those publications that emphasize or exclusively publish review articles receive a disproportionate number of citations, because it is more efficient for a scholar to read and cite a single overview of ten or more publications rather than scurry from one source to another (even in cyberspace). Cameron points out that based on the IF, "...60 percent of the top 25 [biomedical] journals are review journals" (111). (It is a point worth noting that review articles may be extensively documented, e.g., almost seven pages of a 23 page overview of postoperative nausea are allocated to 262 endnotes [Watcha and White]). When considering the IFs of hundreds of similar publications, no one will take into account the fact that those with higher scores are larger or more influential or concentrate on reviews. The only thing that matters is that one journal has an IF of 15.2 whereas its competitor's is only 3.67.

The sources from which the ISI data are derived and the data themselves can be manipulated so that authors, journals, and publishers unfairly benefit. Self-citation, superfluous bibliographic inclusions, editorial solicitations, and other misleading or unethical practices may appear to be of negligible value in altering the IF, but the agglomerated numbers can quickly multiply to effect a major change. If an editor requests that authors add three additional (superfluous) citations to their works referencing articles published in the accepting journal, and it publishes 100 articles a year, this increases the gross citational count by 300 completely irrelevant references (if the potential authors cooperate). Depending on the overall statistics involved, the IF's increase could be dramatic. In a notorious but representative case, the editor of *Leukemia* included the following request in a letter to researchers who had submitted papers: "...We kindly ask you to add references of articles published in *Leukemia* to your present article...." This was described as "an appalling lapse of editorial judgment" (Richard Smith), but apparently castigation of this nature has had little effect, since in 2006, an editor of the *American Journal of Respiratory and Critical Care Medicine* solicited analogous citations from an article's author: A decade after the *Leukemia* incident, Dr. John B. West was equally "appalled" (Begley B1). Paul Wouters and Repke de Vries observe that hyperlinks that are included within references and citations are often included by the paper's author, but at times the publisher adds others that lead directly to it own database (1258). This may prove beneficial for the reader, but it is also manipulative and increases the linked journal's IF. Cameron observes that when *The Lancet* started to include citations to its research pieces in short editorial columns, its IF increased by ca. 35 percent (118); this is an extraordinary change for such a minor alteration. Author and editor self-citation may appear to be a small problem in this context, but it obviously increases the gross number of references and thus skews the IF, even if at times only slightly. Ken Hyland points out that studies indicate that self-citations comprise 10 to 20 percent of all references (252). And Weiner observes that

Garfield's "self-citation rate" is 79 percent (summarized in Cronin, *Citation* 32). In Garfield's defense, it should be mentioned that for decades, he has produced a brief essay for each week's *Current Contents* and these may refer back to previous discussions. Noting the earlier work alerts the reader to the interconnectedness of what he offers; failure to cite the previous columns (or his other publications) would cause critics to complain that he is merely repeating himself. Ironically, authors who act ethically and refuse to cite their own (sometimes only tangentially relevant) previous works may be accused of self-plagiarism.

Perhaps the most egregious misuse and abuse of citation counts and the IF occur in academia. It is impossible in most cases to arrive at a fair and judicious judgment when quantitative measures of publication are used to evaluate a scholar's merit in retention, promotion, and tenure decisions. Gross numbers of publications or citations to a scholar's works mean very little. Many authors turn out lots of rubbish — useless, repetitive, ghost-written by graduate or research assistants (who usually are not credited, although their "help" may be acknowledged), or plagiarized. Academics employ many tricks to increase their publications. For example, scientists may split the results of an experiment into three or four parts and publish three or four short papers. Naturally, the same literature review, methodology, statistical analysis, and general conclusions obtain. This is considered unethical, if done for the exclusive purpose of padding one's bibliography. Professors may suggest that a graduate student's paper or short thesis is publishable; after working to improve it, the empowered person may suggest that his or her name be affixed as a second author. This may also occur when a graduate student works closely with a researcher in a laboratory environment. (I presume that this does not occur very often at the doctoral level, and when a dissertation is published, the director's [extensive] help is merely acknowledged.) These tricks unfairly add to one's publications and thus may increase one's citation counts. Quantitative measures have a place in professional evaluation, but there is no substitute for true qualitative assessment of the individual publications. That is why committed and judicious departments require a scholar from another institution to read the actual documents and evaluate the candidate's scholarship. In some cases, the committee may request a recommendation of some kind. This is obviously an extremely logistically complicated, demanding, and time-consuming process, the necessity for which, dependence on purely quantitative measures obviates. But efficiency and convenience may yield misleading or harmful results. In the academy, failure to advance or loss of one's job can change one's life. It is not an exaggeration to insist that because it can take a year or more to locate a new position, evaluative dependence on citation indices can have a dramatic, sometimes negative impact on a person's career, forcing one to seek work outside of academia. In more cases than the uninformed could possibly imagine, a negative retention, promotion, or tenure decision leads directly to depression, sickness, or death.[1] Quantitative indicators should be applied judiciously.

Eun-Ja Shin analyzed the effect that publication in different media have on the IF and found that for psychology journals, in some cases, a shift from hard copy to both paper and electronic formats increased the IF on average by an astonishing 37 percent (527, 529). This makes sense though, since electronic publication broadens access, which in turn increases a journal's readership, and thus allows for additional citings. Unlike the illegitimate adjustments that editors make in order to manipulate the IF, this increase is merely a peripheral effect of electronic delivery, though a beneficial one for the involved journals.

Mike Hapgood and Russ Evans take a different tack: They do not call for the amelioration or elimination of applicable citation indices, in particular, the impact factor. Rather, they insist that since the IF is subject to statistical noise, which alters its validity and significance, it should be analyzed with statistical rigor, which is currently not done. Even more disheartening is Michael Jensen's prediction that as more material becomes available on the Web, and users attempt to locate it, we will confront a "Google access citation effect." Material retrievable via the Internet, especially if it is not proscribed by commercial fees that act as a deterrent, may result in a false measure of scholarly influence and importance. Webometrics is now a legitimate branch of research, and evaluative applications of quantified Web citations are probably already a *fait accompli*. A special issue of the *Journal of the American Society for Information Science and Technology* is given over to this general topic (Thelwall and Vaughan), and Mike Thelwall and his colleagues offer a summary of the current state of the art in a long and detailed overview published in 2004. Wouters and de Vries's survey of 38 journals produced in five fields in 1995, 1998, and 2000 shows that citations, references, and hyperlinks are differently motivated and play different roles, and that the latter often lack stability (1253, 1251, 1258, 1252). Not surprisingly, they conclude that traditional citation patterns continue to obtain, but hyperlinked references are generally increasing (1256).

Despite the onslaught of legitimate criticism, bibliometrics and citatology (citationology) are now an extremely influential part of the scholarly process. They are discussed and applied in articles published in two highly specialized journals, *Scientometrics* and *Cybermetrics: International Journal of Scientometrics, Informetrics and Bibliometrics;* additionally, apposite material appears in the publications of many disciplines including the sciences, medicine, and information studies. "...[I]mpact factors have assumed so much

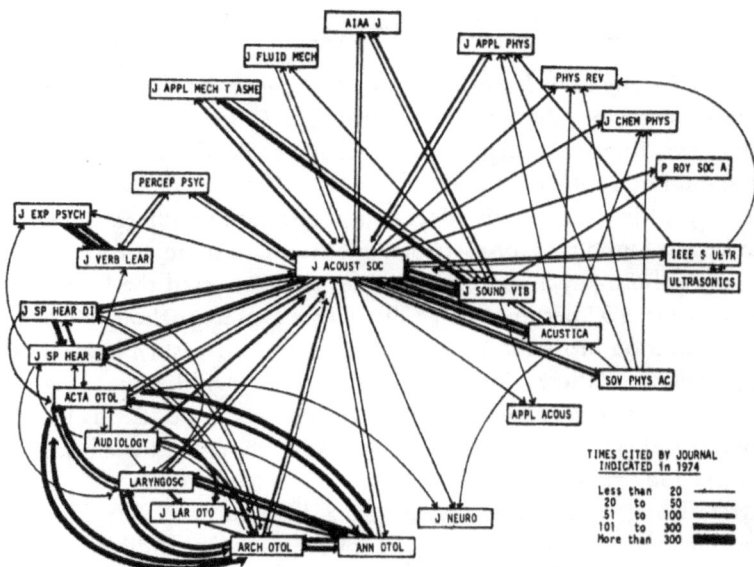

Figure 9.6 JCR 1974 acoustic journal citation connections

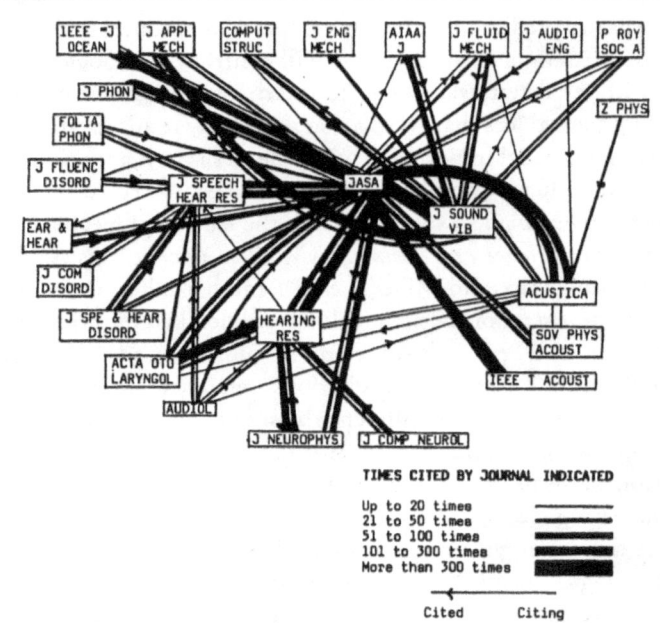

Figure 9.7 JCR 1987 acoustic journal citation connections

Map of citational interconnections. Tony Cawkell in *The Web of Knowledge* published by Information Today. Used by permission of ASIS&T.

power ... that they are starting to control the scientific enterprise...": In Spain and China, rewards and cash bonuses respectively are offered for publishing in high IF journals; rather than pursuing their own real interests, scientists now generally accommodate the research demands of high IF journals in order to insure publication; editors actually consider submissions in terms of their potential influence on their IFs (Monastersky A12, A14, A16); and academic departments as well as countries are ranked by the IF (Cameron 114). In a letter to the editor, Loet Leydesdorff suggests that "a discipline specific impact factor might be more useful." He also alerts readers to his Web site <users.fmg.uva.nl/lleydesdorff/jcr04>, where one can find the basic material necessary to construct graphic "maps of the citation neighborhoods of all the journals..." (A55). Such graphic representations have been used for years to visually map citational interconnections. Tony Cawkell discusses these and presents a diversity of visual examples, which have become more sophisticated but also more complex.

Bibliometric, scientometric, and cybermetric analyses merely yield quantified data that have no intrinsic axiological significance. The evaluative implications of the data are based on *a priori* epistemological suppositions that may or may not be valid, e.g., that more is better: A larger number of bad articles is thus superior to a smaller number of good ones, or 75 citations to a specific paper are automatically superior to 15. This is nonsense for the many reasons discussed above. Extrapolated axiological assessments based entirely on quantifiable measures can be extremely misleading. As a helpful example, take the presumption that the per capita income (PCI) in America is greater than its analogue in Fiji. This may be true (though an average means that some Americans have very high PCIs, while others are much lower than some Fijians'), but the implications that are immediately deduced from this are all based on sociological suppositions that may be false: Earning more is better; a Fijian cannot purchase as many basic necessities as his or her American counterpart; extensive purchasing is a positive activity; owning material possessions results in happiness; and so on. Strong correlations between bibliometric measures and positive accomplishments (winning a Nobel Prize, for example), are good indicators that in that specific case the quantified citations do indicate a positive evaluation, but unique cases are not extrapolatable to every assistant professor who hopes to achieve tenure. Quantified bibliometric data should never automatically be correlated with qualitative work.

11
Conclusion

Documentation is a study and critique of the apparatus that traditionally validates and enhances scholarly (and, infrequently, creative) works. It has been limited to the text and its parentheses, marginalia, notes, and bibliographic listings. But there is much more to be found in what Gérard Genette calls paratext. Indeed, during a long and arduous climb, a friend, who happens to be a classics scholar, suggested that I discuss both *para* and *paragraph*. Georg Stanitzek, summarizing Genette, adds "the author's name, title..., preface, dedication, epigraphs, illustrations, book design..., interviews, commentaries" and observes that no text can exist without paratext though the reverse is possible (30). David Henige offers a 26 page essay ("Being, II") on these secondary characteristics of annotation including indexing, which I do not discuss. (But Henige is correct: Indexing falls within a broad definition of documentation or annotation, since it is peripheral to the text but gives access to it and, in a long and complex work, makes connections that otherwise might be impossible for the reader to see ["Being, II" 81–82]. It can thus be precisely analogous to a noted commentary, but in a most unusual form.) Additionally, typography, graphic layout, paper, binding, and all of the other attributes of a publication may also come into play here. Indeed, some claim that the very form of the material can reflect its meaning.

In iconic imagery, form controls, defines, and is analogous to or in extreme cases concomitant with meaning. Thus, the physical depiction (the form) of a wealthy citizen in a Van Dyke portrait represents the person. The formal elements comprise and therefore, in a sense, are the image; an alteration in the configuration of the individual, component parts, shapes, colors, and textures would yield something quite different. Some commentators on bibliographical matters indicate that this also obtains in a typographical environment. But it would be difficult or impossible to provide empirical evidence for this contention. There is no doubt that a page differs in both physical and intellectual impact depending on its configuration, and the differences between an unmediated page and one that leads to endnotes or is replete with either footnotes or marginalia carries readers through the text in different ways. But the formal qualities, the physicality of the imaged page, are just not diverse enough to truly alter meaning, though they may influence its physical access and mental reception, impact, and influence. D. F. McKenzie, in discussing bibliography, observes that "forms effect meaning" (13). Well, naturally this is true in descriptive bibliography, where the precise image of a title page is reproduced symbolically using specific signs and conventions, so that a sophisticated bibliographer can create a mental image of the page, *see* the page in its description. One could also make the case that within historical bibliography, the form of the book and its innumerable constituent parts would allow one to claim that form and meaning are closely related. It is more difficult to insist upon this in analytical, textual, and especially enumerative bibliography, under whose encompassing heading I would include much that is discussed in this study. And yet McKenzie tries:

> ... I must now turn to consider the special case of printed texts. In doing so, the particular inquiry I wish to pursue is whether or not the material forms of books, the non-verbal elements of the typographic notations within them, the very disposition of space itself, have an expressive function in conveying meaning, and whether or not it is, properly, a bibliographical task to discuss it [17].

He goes on to cite six scholars, including Erwin Panofksy and Nicolas Barker, who have defended "the symbolic function of typographic signs as an interpretative system" (17) in order to show that "forms effect sense" (18). I would like to be convinced and make the case as well, but I cannot in good conscience do so, when one considers that the example that McKenzie so fully and forcefully proffers does not really indicate that emendation in form alters meaning: Mispunctuation, decapitalization, and word transmutations are not merely formal (graphic) changes (as alterations in typeface, point size, leading, or margin allocation would be). The noted emendations do not fall within a merely indexical class of signs, but rather are a set of conventions whose use carries, implies, or indicates precise meanings. Missing commas, for example, can completely alter the meaning of a phrase, clause, or sentence. As we know, "Eats shoots and leaves" is not quite the same thing as "Eats, shoots and leaves." *Wrote* is not *wrought:* This is a major semantic alteration, and has little to do with form. McKenzie's discussion is hardly convincing, let alone a telling proof that form elicits meaning.

Robert J. Connors makes a slightly different case: He claims that the form that the documentation takes effects epistemic value. Notes allow one to trace attributions, but they are less intrusive and less insistent than in-text citations, especially in those cases in which innumerable sources are listed in a single parenthetical insert; here the citations (often included in the required literature review) lend historical credence and authority to the writer's later assertions. The author-date method privileges the date (the historical precedent) over the author, thus altering the source's impact on and value to the reader ("Rhetoric II" 238), since the date of publication is ostensibly more important than the author. This is convincing, but seems to be of marginal importance. Even if everything that Connors contends is true, does it have any real effect on readers and the way they go about incorporating knowledge or tracing sources?

Since the formal influence of documentation structure is a crucial point in this study, it will be useful to look at this from a slightly different perspective. The guiding tenet of modernist architecture is that "form follows function." Frank Lloyd Wright's entire oeuvre, both the large buildings and private homes, attests to this simple yet incisive apothegm. (Naturally, this changed when postmodern theory invaded schools of architectural design. Now Frank Gehry produces buildings in which form and function move in antithetical directions.) The contention that the form of the documentation influences its function (here, its meaning) is perhaps too extreme; Slights holds only that marginal annotation controls the reader (whereas the direct influence of notes diminishes as they move farther from their texts). Other scholars insist that the close proximity of footnotes to their texts affects the reader and effects a meaning differently than the notes would if they were banished to the end of the chapter or work or even to a separate volume. Although I understand and even sympathize with this, I cannot endorse it. I insist that if a reader is led to an annotation of some kind (even a parenthetical bibliographic attribution that goes on for many lines and confuses the sentence's meaning), he or she will follow up, often immediately, if it appears that there is something of importance to be gleaned. The semantic impact of an annotation remains the same regardless of whether one glances at a marginal note as one reads the text or consults the same comment, even, annoyingly, in a separate volume or, barbarically, on a Web site, after one completes the article or chapter, although the real effect on the reader, admittedly, could be quite different. More important is the probability that as the annotation diverges physically from its progenitor, so will the likelihood of a reader consulting it diminish. And this would be of great moment to G. Nigel Gilbert, because he orients citation in terms of persuasion: Referring bibliographically to an authoritative work is an attempt to convince the reader that something is the case.

So, the physicality of the page affects the impression that it has on the reader, but the purely formalistic features are not concomitant with meaning. A simple change in a formal feature does not alter the text's implication in any meaningful way. Even a shift from a highly marginated page to one that presents the same material in displaced endnotes will only change the means of accessing the information. It will not alter the semantic meaning of the identical text and its transported marginalia, whose information is now accessible in the endnotes (despite the discussion in chapter 4). Semantic meaning is massaged, but it remains constant regardless of its medium, format, or form, although the impression it gives and its intellectual import may vary, if only slightly. An identical text read in a brightly illuminated publication such as *Wired,* in a sedate university press monograph, on a popular, graphically active Web site, or on a serious aggregator's database all yield the same information (though what the reader takes away may vary, but for sociological reasons not pertinent to these remarks).

Documentation, in all of its many permutations, is the life blood of scholarship. Though some systems and forms are preferable to others, though some scholars defend footnotes, for example, over all other possibilities, and though some applications and conventions are truly barbaric, the only thing that matters is that scholars honestly, precisely, and fully inform readers that an idea or quotation derives from another's hard work. This allows authors to acknowledge their sources, ascribe credit, offer implicit thanks, provide a trail, and defend against potential accusations of citational fabrication, falsification, or plagiary. Documentation, additionally, provides readers with a diversity of tangential remarks that may come to displace the text in relevance, importance, and interest. This is its glory. It is lamentable that we currently inhabit a pragmatic era in which costs and profits take precedence over scholarly necessity and its concomitant apparatus. Things will probably get worse before they improve.

Notes

Chapter 1: Purpose

1. Francis Burkle-Young and Saundra Rose Maley create a brief taxonomy of specific types of information that footnotes can present; these include bibliographical, biographical, geographical, descriptive, tangential, definitional, relational, and translational material (passim). Eugene Garfield lists 15 reasons to cite, but these are extremely delimited, e.g., he distinguishes between honoring pioneers and honoring peers; many of the others fall under the general rubric of commentary ("When," 451–452). In *The Citation Process,* Blaise Cronin includes Weinstocks's 15 reasons to cite, which resemble Garfield's taxonomy (30). And Carolyn Frost creates a concise catalogue of citation functions in literary research; she distinguishes between primary and secondary sources and subtle subclasses such as approval or disapproval of an opinion or a fact, but she does not take commentary, translation, or other necessities into account (405–409).

2. Tim Carvell satirizes this in "A Million Little Corrections," a concise op-ed page essay: "The portions of my book dealing with Depression-era Ireland are, I have been reliably informed, copied verbatim from Frank McCourt's *Angela's Ashes.* I can only conclude that I accidentally confused my manuscript with my notes for my memoir in which I copied large portions of other writers' works, just to see how they were structured. In hindsight, the fact that I was born 40 years after the Depression should have been a tip-off."

3. Many years ago, a reference librarian at a major research institution told me of a student who had requested help: He wanted to learn how to construct fictitious citations to an encyclopedia article that he had plagiarized. The librarian claimed that she was professionally obligated to render assistance despite the warning contained in the university's handbook that plagiary is unacceptable and is grounds for punitive action.

Chapter 3: Commentary

1. Burton is one of only a handful of non–Moslems to visit Medina and Mecca, return, and present a detailed description of matters complete with drawings and diagrams; had he been discovered, he would have been killed.

2. During half a century of scholarly pursuits, I have been privileged to physically encounter and occasionally interact personally with some outstanding and kind authors and scholars including Ai, Mary Catherine Bateson, Bruno Bettelheim, Michel Butor, Umberto Eco, Erich Fromm, Carlos Fuentes, Stephen Greenblatt, Steven Jay Gould, Barbara Johnson, Galway Kinnell, Oliver Sacks, Samuel Schoenbaum, Stephen Spender, Gloria Steinem, and Robert Penn Warren. I have found, lamentably, that some of these well-known people, especially Europeans, not only lack respect for Americans but are quite willing to share their displeasure in a public forum. More than forty years ago, I attended

a lecture presented by Erich Fromm at an excellent New York City college. The audience consisted of perhaps a thousand students and faculty members. Toward the end of his talk, Fromm thanked us for attending by suggesting that we follow up on what he had said, "if you can read." Bruno Bettelheim and Gloria Steinem were equally offensive to the audience's collective intellect. No one dared to challenge these self-aggrandizing people.

Nabokov follows in this tradition:

> Among some fifty college students whom I once happened to ask (in planned illustration of the incredible ignorance concerning natural objects that characterizes young Americans of today) the name of the tree, an American Elm, that they could see through the classroom windows, none was able to identify it ... [II, part 2, 9].

His intellectual superciliousness and concomitant arrogance can be gauged by his remark in the foreword to the commentary that four metrical translations are "unfortunately available to students" (II, part 1, 3); he is congenitally incapable of imagining that although they may not live up to his high, though peculiar, standards, and with whatever anomalies, hazards, or mistranslations they may contain, it is nevertheless possible that they are preferable in a host of ways to his. He continues, "Even worse are two rhymed versions, which, like grotesque satellites, accompanied the appearance of the first edition of this work..." (II, 4). Walter Arndt's is characterized as "a paraphrase, in burlesque English, with preposterous mistranslations..." (II, part 1, 4).

Chapter 4: Marginalia

1. According to Lawrence Lipking, Poe theorized that marginal notes were nonsensically unpredictable, whereas Valéry held that they contain the "essential logic ... of all reading" and the mind. They both seem to believe that the note requires deciphering (611, 610). The present text does not offer a comprehensive theory of marginalia, though some remarks toward that end can be found below.

2. Slights offers a partial list that differs from mine; it includes amplification, annotation, appropriation, correction, emphasis, evaluation, exhortation, explication, justification, organization, parody, preemption, rhetorical gloss, simplification, and translation (*Managing* 25–26).

3. The primary bibliographies for both of Jackson's studies are invaluable sources of books containing hand-written marginalia. The annotator's name, when known, is listed.

Chapter 5: Footnotes

1. This is a most peculiar title. Since it is in German, one might reasonably assume that the article is as well, but it is not. This English-language piece has a German title because it is more impressive. Nimis also drops the last part of the philologist's name, which usually appears as Wilamowitz-Moellendorff.

2. Despite the ostensible changes in scholarly conventions and the alterations brought about by economic pressures within publishing, even at the most prestigious university presses, some authors still manage to convince their publishers to produce extraordinarily complex volumes. In 1996, the Free Press brought out Robert Strassler's *Landmark Thucydides*, a 706 page edition of the Greek historian's work on the Peloponnesian War. In 2007, Pantheon produced Strassler's 953 page edition of Herodotus's *Histories*. The latter work contains two prefaces, an introduction, outline, key, glossary, source list, bibliography, extensive index, appendices labeled A through U, other items, and countless maps and illustrations. Every page of text contains footnotes as well as marginal text and, infrequently, marginal illustrations. The Thucydides is similar.

Chapter 7: The Major Systems

1. Bowersock is correct and witty as well. Ungeziefer, his cited author, is the German word for (noxious) insect. What he may not have realized is that it is the very term that Franz Kafka uses to describe Gregor Samsa, the protagonist of *Die Verwandlung* (*The Metamorphosis*), who awakes one morning to discover that he has been transformed into an "*ungeheueren Ungeziefer*" ("a monstrous insect"). As for the pretensions of non-scientists, I have ranted against these in "Titans

Clashing: The Art of the Science and the Science of Art," a detailed disquisition that apparently has had little effect, since social scientists continue to emulate chemists and physicists, deluding themselves into believing that quantitative analyses of human beings are possible and that they will yield practicably useful results.

2. In working on this study, I came across a reference to a hypercritical comment (a direct quotation) on APA style. I wanted to locate the source (despite the lack of pagination) to see if there was anything additional that I could use. I found the enormous volume, skimmed the pages, read the table of contents, and consulted the index — all to no avail. It would have taken a week of committed reading (of a monograph of little interest or use) for me to locate the comment. I put the book back on the shelf. Attributions require pagination!

3. The professor for this course was the well-known poet Robert Kelly. He informed the class that plagiary was unacceptable; one way in which he intended to avert this possibility was to ask the students to orally identify the color of the bindings of the various monographs cited in the paper's bibliography. He never followed through on this threat, at least not in my case.

Chapter 9: Misconduct

1. In late 2006, Bob Dylan released a new CD. Listeners discovered that he had appropriated lines from the poetry of Henry Timrod without any mention or attribution (Vega). This is analogous to the unethical plagiaries of authors, but it also falls into the class of musical quotation discussed in the first chapter, though the snippets here are words rather than melodies. Suzanne Vega concludes her brief piece thus:

> But I am trying to imagine a Bob Dylan album with footnotes, asterisks, ibid.'s and nifty little anecdotes about the origins of each song. It's not going to happen. He's never pretended to be an academic, or even a nice guy. He is more likely to present himself as, well, a thief.

I suspect that this controversy produced no consequences other than a surge in sales.

Chapter 10: Citation Indexing and Analysis

1. The skeptical will scoff, but they are wrong. As a grievance officer (and chair of the committee) with many years of service at an institution with almost 800 full-time faculty members as well as a host of adjunct instructors, I am privy to occurrences that elude the typical academic. Those people who were not retained or who were denied promotion or tenure sometimes got ill; occasionally, they became so sick that they were incapable of carrying out their duties and were forced to resign. Much worse is the outcome in the following case: My own father was unjustly denied promotion to full professor (of physics) after many years of superb service and unflinchingly high standards in a world of nepotistic appointments, illiteracy and innumeracy, and grade inflation. He sank into a severe depression (which necessitated electroshock therapy) from which he never fully recovered. Despite his ultimate promotion, his health degenerated and he died from no attributable medical cause; his parents, who were born in the nineteenth century, lived longer than he did.

Bibliography

One of the goals of this study is to collect the apposite material on the broad subject of documentation and include it in a comprehensive bibliography. (Except for those works used as illustrative examples, I have partially or fully read everything noted below.) Even though a few of these works are not mentioned in the text, because they are not relevant to the specific discussion, they do offer insights into the history and application of documentation, and so they are cited. This will save readers much frustration. Even the two pointed monographic studies of the footnote (see Grafton and Zerby) require hours of scanning of footnoted pages to cull out the germane material (since many irrelevant studies are included), because their respective publishers failed to include bibliographies.

Those citations marked with an asterisk deal precisely with documentation issues.

Abraham, David. *Collapse of the Weimar Republic: Political Economy and Crisis.* Princeton, NJ: Princeton University Press, 1981.
"An Account of the Invention of Grinding Optick." *Philosophical Transactions* 33 (1668): 631–633.
An Admonition to the Parliament. N.p.: 1572.
Agin, Dan. *Junk Science.* New York: St. Martin's, 2006.
*Altman, Ellen, and Peter Hernon, eds. "Appendix A: Some Publicly-Discussed Cases Involving Scientific Misconduct and the Research Literature." In *Research Misconduct: Issues, Implications, and Strategies.* Greenwich, CT: Ablex, 1997. 135 157.
*Anderson, John E., and Willard L. Valentine. "The Preparation of Articles for Publication in the Journals of The American Psychological Association." *Psychological Bulletin* 41.6 (June 1944): 345–376.
*Anderson, Judy. *Plagiarism, Copyright Violation, and Other Thefts of Intellectual Property: An Annotated Bibliography with a Lengthy Introduction.* Jefferson, NC: McFarland, 1998.
Aquinas, St. Thomas. *Commentary on Saint Paul's Epistle to the Ephesians.* Trans. and intro. Matthew L. Lamb, O.C.S.O. Albany, NY: Magi Books, 1966.

Aquinas, St. Thomas. *Summa Theologiae*. Tr. Thomas Gilby. Vol. I. New York: McGraw-Hill, 1964.
Arias, Arturo. "Authoring Ethnicized Subjects: Rigoberto Menchú and the Performative Production of the Subaltern Self." *PMLA* 116 (Jan. 2001): 75–88.
Aristotle. *Historia Animalium*. Tr. A. L. Peck. I. (The Loeb Classical Library.) Cambridge: Harvard University Press, 1965.
Aristotle. *Meteorologica*. Tr. H. D. P. Lee. (The Loeb Classical Library.) Cambridge: Harvard University Press, 1962.
*Asano, Migiwa, et al. "Improvement of the Accuracy of References in the *Canadian Journal of Anaesthesia*." *Canadian Journal of Anaesthesia* 42.5, part I (May 1995): 370–372.
*"At the End of the Book." Editorial. *The New York Times* 7 Dec. 2006: A34.
Auerbach, Erich. *Mimesis: The Representation of Reality in Western Literature*. Trans. Willard Trask. Garden City, NY: Anchor, 1957.
Austin, Arthur D. "Footnotes as Product Differentiation." *Vanderbilt Law Review* 40 (1987): 1130ff. 8 Nov. 2006. <web.lexis-nexis.com>.
[Bacon, Francis.] *The Works of Francis Bacon*. Ed. [James] Spedding, [Robert Leslie] Ellis, and [Douglas Denon] Heath. Vol. I. Boston: Houghton, Mifflin, n.d.
*Baldi, Stéphane. "Normative Versus Social Constructivist Processes in the Allocation of Citations: A Network-Analytic Model." *American Sociological Review* 63.6 (Dec. 1998): 829–846.
Ball, Philip. "Paper Trail Reveals References Go Unread by Citing Authors." *Nature* 420 (12 Dec. 2002): 594.
Bamford, James. "Where Spying Starts and Stops: Tracking an Embattled C.I.A. and a President at War." Review. *The New York Times* 9 January 2006: B6.
*Barney, Stephen A., ed. *Annotation and Its Texts*. New York: Oxford University Press, 1991.
*Baron, Sabrina Alcorn, comp., ed. *The Reader Revealed*. Washington, DC: Folger, 2001.
*Bartlett, Thomas, and Scott Smallwood. "Four Academic Plagiarists You've Never Heard Of: How Many More Are Out There?" *The Chronicle of Higher Education* 17 Dec. 2004: A8–A12.
Bartlett, Thomas, and Scott Smallwood. "Mentor vs. Protégé." *The Chronicle of Higher Education* 17 Dec. 2004: A14–A15.
Barzun, Jacques. "The Artist as Prophet and Jester." *The American Scholar* 69.1 (Winter 2000): 15–33.
*Bauman, M. Garrett. "The Devilments of Style." *The Chronicle of Higher Education* 9 Nov. 2001: B5. 2 Nov. 2006. <chronicle.com/weekly/v48/i11/11b00501.htm>.
Bayle, Pierre. *Dictionaire Historique et Critique*. 5th ed. Vol. I. Amsterdam: La Compagnie des Libraries, 1734.
Bayle, [Pierre]. *A General Dictionary Historical and Critical*. Vol. I. London: n.p., 1734.
[Bayle, Pierre]. *Selections from Bayle's Dictionary*. Ed. and introd. E. A. Beller and M. duP. Lee, Jr. Princeton, NJ: Princeton University Press, 1952.
*Bazerman, Charles. *Shaping Written Knowledge: The Genre and Activity of the Experimental Article in Science*. Madison: University of Wisconsin Press, 1988.
*Beck, Sheila, and Richard Beck. "Web Citation: A Proposal for Standardized Specification. *Online* July/Aug. 2006: 31–34. *Academic Search Premier*. EBSCO. 27 Sept. 2006. <web.ebscohost.com>.
*Beehler, Rodger. "In Editing a Good Novel, The Best Footnote Is Zero." *The Chronicle of Higher Education* 9 Mar. 2001: B14–B15. 18 Nov. 2006. <web.ebscohost.com>.
*Begley, Sharon. "Science Journals Artfully Try to Boost Their Rankings." *The Wall Street Journal* 5 June 2006: B1, B8.
Behrendt, John C. *The Ninth Circle: A Memoir of Life and Death in Antarctica, 1960–1962*. Albuquerque: University of New Mexico Press, 2005.

Bellesiles, Michael A. *The Arming of America: The Origins of a National Gun Culture.* New York: Knopf, 2000.
*Benstock, Shari. "At the Margin of Discourse: Footnotes in the Fictional Text." *PMLA* 98.2 (March 1983): 204–225.
Beowulf. (Manuscript — Cotton Vitellius A.xv — held by the British Library.)
*Bevan, David R., and Janet M. Purkis. Editorial. "Citation Errors Can Be Reduced." *Canadian Journal of Anaesthesia* 42.5, part I (May 1995): 367–369.
The Bible of the Poor *[Biblia Pauperum].* Trans. and comment. Albert C. Labriola and John W. Smeltz. Pittsburgh: Duquesne University Press, 1990.
*Biebuyck, Julien F. Editorial. "Concerning the Ethics and Accuracy of Scientific Citations." *The Journal of Anesthesiology* 77.1 (July 1992): 1–2.
*Bloch, Sidney, and Garry Walter. "The Impact Factor: Time for Change." *Australian and New Zealand Journal of Psychiatry* 35 (2001): 563–568.
Blum, Ann Shelby. *Picturing Nature: American Nineteenth-Century Zoological Illustration.* Princeton, NJ: Princeton University Press, 1993.
Boethius, Anicius Manlius Severinus. *The Consolation of Philosophy.* Trans. I.T.; ed. and intro. William Anderson. Carbondale: Southern Illinois University Press, 1963.
*Bolles, Charles Avery. "Characteristics of the Literature of American Studies as Indicated by Bibliographic Citations." Diss. University of Minnesota, 1975.
Boltanski, Luc, and Laurent Thévenot. Trans. Catherine Porter. *On Justification: Economies of Worth.* Princeton, NJ: Princeton University Press, 2006.
The Book of Kells: Reproductions from the Manuscript in Trinity College, Dublin. With a Study of the Manuscript by Françoise Henry. New York: Knopf, 1974.
Book of Mac Regol. (Manuscript — Auct.D.II.19 — held by the Bodleian Library, Oxford Univ.)
*Borgman, Christine L. "Editor's Introduction." *Scholarly Communication and Bibliometrics.* Ed. Christine L. Borgman. Newbury, Park, CA: Sage, 1990. 10–27.
*Bosman, Julie. "Loved His New Novel, and What a Bibliography." *The New York Times* 5 December 2006: B1, B8.
*Bowersock, G. W. "The Art of the Footnote." *The American Scholar* 53 (Winter 1983-1984): 54–62.
*Braun, Tibor, ed. "Theories of Citation?" *Scientometrics* 43.1 (Sept 1998). 3–148 (14 articles). 3 Jan. 2007. <springerlink.metapress.com>.
Braziel, Jana Evans. "Défilée's Diasporic Daughters: Revolutionary Narratives of *Ayiti* (Haiti), *Nanchon* (Nation), and *Dyaspora* (Diaspora) in Edwidge Danticat's *Krik? Krak!*" *Studies in the Literary Imagination* 37.2 (Fall 2004): 77–96.
*"Breaking Bread: Horowitz vs. Bérubé." *The Chronicle of Higher Education* 8 Dec. 2006: A8–A11.
Bredeson, Dale, et al. "Cell Death in the Nervous System." *Nature* 443 (19 Oct. 2006): 796–802.
*Breyer, Stephen. "Opinion on Footnotes." *ABA Journal* 81.10 (Oct. 1995): 39. 27 Sept. 2006. <web.ebscohost.com>.
Brown, James Robert. "Proofs and Pictures." *British Journal for the Philosophy of Science* 48.2 (June 1997): 161–180.
Buchanan, Elizabeth. Personal communication. 19 Oct. 2006.
*Buchanan, Robert A. "Accuracy of Cited References: The Role of Citation Databases." *College and Research Libraries* 67.4 (July 2006): 292–303.
*Bugeja, Michael, and Daniela V. Dimitrova. "Exploring the Half-Life of Internet Footnotes." *Iowa Journal of Communication* 37.1 (Spring 2005): 77–86.
*Burkle-Young, Francis A., and Saundra Rose Maley. *The Art of the Footnote.* Lanham, MD: University Press of America, 1996.

Burton, Sir Richard F. *Personal Narrative of a Pilgrimage to Al-Medinah and Meccah*. Vols. I, II. New York: Dover, 1893, 1964.
Byrd, Richard E. *Alone*. New York: Putnam's, 1938.
*Cameron, Brian D. "Trends in the Usage of ISI Bibliometric Data: Uses, Abuses, and Implications." *Portal: Libraries and the Academy* 5.1 (Jan. 2005): 105–125. 18 Nov. 2006. <muse.jhu.edu/journals/portal_libraries_and_the_academy/v005/5.1cameron.html>.
*Camille, Michael. "Glossing the Flesh: Scopophilia and the Margins of the Medieval Book." *The Margins of the Text*. Ed. D. C. Greetham. Ann Arbor: University of Michigan, 1997. 245–267.
*Camille, Michael. *Image on the Edge: The Margins of Medieval Art*. Cambridge: Harvard University Press, 1992.
*Carlson, Scott. "Here Today, Gone Tomorrow: Studying How Online Footnotes Vanish." *The Chronicle of Higher Education* 30 April 2004: 33.
*Carvajal, Doreen. "The Book's in Print, but Its Bibliography Lives in Cyberspace." *The New York Times* 29 May 2000: A1, A12.
*Carvajal, Doreen. "So Whose Words Are They, Anyway?" *The New York Times* 27 May 2000: B9, B11.
*Carvell, Tim. "A Million Little Corrections." *The New York Times* 11 January 2006: A29.
*Cawkell, Tony. "Visualizing Citation Connections." *The Web of Knowledge: A Festschrift for Eugene Garfield*. Ed. Blaise Cronin and Helen Barsky Atkins. Medford, NJ: Information Today, 2000. 177–194.
**The Chicago Manual of Style*. 15th ed. Chicago: University of Chicago Press, 2003.
Coetzee, J. M. *Diary of Bad Year*. New York: Viking, 2007.
Cohen, Benjamin R. "The Element of the Table: Visual Discourse and the Preperiodic Representation of Chemical Classification." *Configurations* 12.1 (Winter 2004): 41–75.
Coke, Edward. *The First Part of the Institutes of the Laws of England or A Commentary upon Littleton*. Ed. Francis Hargrave. London: Printed by G. Kearsly..., 1775.
Coleridge, Samuel Taylor. "The Rime of the Ancient Mariner." In *Immortal Poems of the English Language*. Ed. Oscar Williams. New York: Washington Square Press, 1962. 269–288.
*Connors, Robert J. "The Rhetoric of Citation Systems Part I: The Development of Annotation Structures from the Renaissance to 1900." *Rhetoric Review* 17.1 (Fall 1998): 6–48.
*Connors, Robert J. "The Rhetoric of Citation Systems Part II: Competing Epistemic Values in Citation." *Rhetoric Review* 17.2 (Spring 1999): 219–245.
Copernicus, Nicolaus. *On the Revolutions*. Ed. Jerzy Dobrzycki; trans. and comment. Edward Rosen. Baltimore: Johns Hopkins University Press, 1978.
Cory, Catherine et al., eds. *Christian Theological Traditions*. Upper Saddle River, NJ: Prentice Hall, 2003.
*Cosgrove, Peter. W. "Undermining the Text: Edward Gibbon, Alexander Pope, and the Anti-Authenticating Footnote." In *Annotation and Its Texts*, ed. Stephen A. Barney. New York: Oxford University Press, 1991.
*Cowell, Alan. "Eyebrows Are Raised over Passages in a Best Seller." *The New York Times* 28 Nov. 2006: B1, B8.
Cowley, Abraham. *Poems: Miscellanies, The Mistress, Pindarique Odes, Davideis, Verses Written on Several Occasions*. Ed. A. R. Waller. Cambridge: Cambridge, 1668, 1905.
Cox, Michael. *The Meaning of Night: A Confession*. New York: Norton, 2006.
*Cramer, Clayton E. "Why Footnotes Matter: Checking *Arming America's* Claims." *Plagiary: Cross Disciplinary Studies in Plagiarism, Fabrication, and Falsification* 1.11 (2006): 1–31. November 2006. <www.plagiary.org>.
*Cronin, Blaise. *The Citation Process: The Role and Significance of Citations in Scientific Communication*. London: Taylor Graham, 1984.

*Cronin, Blaise. *The Scholar's Courtesy: The Role of Acknowledgement in the Primary Communication Process*. London: Taylor Graham, 1995.
*Cronin, Blaise, and Helen Barsky Atkins. *The Web of Knowledge: A Festschrift for Eugene Garfield*. Medford, NJ: Information Today, 2000.
Curtius, Ernst Robert. *European Literature and the Latin Middle Ages*. Trans. Willard R. Trask. Princeton, NJ: Princeton University Press, 1990.
Darwin, Charles. *The Descent of Man and Selection in Relation to Sex*. Vol. II. New York: D. Appleton, 1874.
Darwin, Charles. *On the Origin of Species*. Intro. Ernst Mayr. Facsimile rpt. of the 1859 ed. Cambridge: Harvard University Press, 1964.
Darwin, Charles. *The Voyage of the Beagle*. Garden City, NY: Doubleday, 1962.
*Davis, Philip M., and Suzanne A. Cohen. "The Effect of the Web on Undergraduate Citation Behavior, 1996–1999." *Journal of the American Society for Information Science and Technology* 52.4 (2001): 309–312.
Dee, John. *General and Rare Memorials*. London: John Day, 1577. (Copy held by the Huntington Library.)
de Guzman, Maria Rosario T., et al. "Gender and Age Differences...." *Sex Roles* 51.3/4 (August 2004): 217–225.
Derrida, Jacques. *Glas*. Trans. John P. Leavy, Jr., and Richard Rand. Lincoln: University of Nebraska Press, 1986.
Derrida, Jacques. "Living On/Border Lines." Trans. James Hulbert. In *Deconstruction and Criticism*. New York: Seabury, 1979. 75–176.
*Derrida, Jacques. "This Is Not an Oral Footnote." *Annotation and Its Texts*. Ed. Stephen A. Barney. New York: Oxford University Press, 1991. 192–205.
Derrida, Jacques. "Tympan." In *Margins of Philosophy*. Trans. and notes Alan Bass. Chicago: University of Chicago Press, 1982. X–xxix.
Diderot, Denis. *A Diderot Pictorial Encyclopedia of Trades and Industry*. Ed. and intro. Charles Coulston Gillispie. Vol. I. New York: Dover, 1959.
"Dissertatio de Praecedentia Regum Galliae...." Review. *Le Journal des Sçavans* I (1665): 5–7.
Donovan, Stephen K. "How to Alienate Your Editor: A Practical Guide for Established Authors." *Journal of Scholarly Publishing* 36.4 (July 2005): 238–242.
*Donovan, Stephen K. "Research Journals: Toward Uniformity or Retaining Diversity?" *Journal of Scholarly Publishing* 37.3 (April 2006): 230–235.
Dove, Mary, ed. *Gloss Ordinaria, Pars 22, in Canticum Canticorum*. Corpus Christianorum Continuatio Mediaevalis CLXX. Turnholti: Brepols, 1997.
Dunn, Mark. *Ibid: A Life: A Novel in Footnotes*. San Francisco: MacAdam/Cage, 2004.
Ebbell, B. *The Papyrus Ebers....* Copenhagen: Levin and Munksgaard, 1937.
*Editors: *Columbia Law Review*, et al., comps. *The BlueBook: A Uniform System of Citation*. 18th ed. Cambridge: Harvard Law Review Association, 2005.
Edney, Matthew. Personal communication. 25 Oct. 2006.
Eliot, T. S. "The Waste Land." In *The Complete Poems and Plays: 1909–1950*. New York: Harcourt, Brace and World, 1962.
Eliot, T. S. *The Waste Land: A Facsimile and Transcript of the Original Drafts Including the Annotations of Ezra Pound*. Ed. and intro. Valerie Eliot. New York: Harcourt Brace Jovanovich, 1971.
Elkins, James. "Critical Response: What Do We Want Photography to Be? A Response to Michael Fried." *Critical Inquiry* 31.4 (Summer 2005): 938–956.
Epstein, William M. "The Lighter Side of Deception Research in the Social Sciences: Social Work as Comedy." *Journal of Information Ethics* 15.1 (Spring 2006): 11–26.
Euclid. *The Thirteen Books of Euclid's Elements*. Trans., intro., and comment. Thomas L. Heath. 2nd ed. 3 vols. New York: Dover, 1956.

Facts and Observations Relating to the Temple Church, and the Monuments Contained in it. London, 1811. (Copy held by the British Library.)

Forbes, Elliot, rev., ed. *Thayer's Life of Beethoven.* 2 vols. Princeton, NJ: Princeton University Press, 1964.

Freehof, Solomon B. *The Responsa Literature.* Philadelphia: The Jewish Publication Society of America, 1959.

*Friedberg, Errol C. "Call for a Cull of Pointlessly Different Reference Styles." *Nature* 437 (27 October 2005): 1232.

*Frost, Carolyn O. "The Use of Citations in Literary Research: A Preliminary Classification of Citation Functions." *Library Quarterly* 49.4 (Oct. 1979): 399–414.

Fukuyama, Francis. *The End of History and the Last Man.* New York: Free Press, 1992.

Fulda, Joseph S. "Citation Ethics: Practical Ethics on How and When to Cite Sources in Articles." *Journal of Information Ethics* 17.1 (Spring 2008): 54–67.

Galen. *On the Usefulness of the Parts of the Body.* Intro. and trans. Margaret Tallmadge May. Vol. I. Ithaca: Cornell, 1968.

Gallacher, Ian. "Cite Unseen..." *Albany Law Review* 70 (Mar. 2007): 491–536.

Gardner, Martin, ed., intro. *The Annotated Ancient Mariner by Samuel Taylor Coleridge.* New York: Bramhall House, 1965.

*Garfield, Eugene. *Citation Indexing—Its Theory and Application in Science, Technology, and Humanities.* New York: Wiley, 1979.

*Garfield, Eugene. "From Citation Amnesia to Bibliographic Plagiarism." *Essays of an Information Scientist.* Vol. 4, 1979–1980. Philadelphia: ISI, 1981. 503–507.

*Garfield, Eugene. "Journal Impact Factor: A Brief Review." *CMAJ: Canadian Medical Association Journal* 161.8 (19 Oct. 1999): 979–980.

*Garfield, Eugene. "When to Cite." *Library Quarterly* 66.4 (October 1996): 449–458.

*Garfield, Eugene, and I. H. Sher. "New Factors in the Evaluation of Scientific Literature through Citation Indexing." *American Documentation* 14 (1963): 195–201.

*Garfield, Eugene, et al. *The Use of Citation Data in Writing the History of Science.* Philadelphia: Institute for Scientific Information, 1964.

*Geer, Beverley. "Unusual Citings: Journal Citation Integrity and the Public Services Librarian." *RQ* 35.1 (Fall 1995): 67–73.

*Gibaldi, Joseph. *MLA Handbook for Writers of Research Papers.* 6th ed. New York: Modern Language Association, 2003.

Gibbon, Edward. *The History of the Decline and Fall of the Roman Empire.* Notes Dean Milman, M. Guizot, and William Smith. 6 vols. New York: Harper, n.d.

Gibbs, W. Wayt. "Lost Science in the Third World." *Scientific American* Aug. 1995: 92–99.

*Gilbert, G. Nigel. "Referencing as Persuasion." *Social Studies of Science* 7.1 (February 1977): 113–122. 28 Nov. 2006. <www.jstor.org/journals/03063127.html>.

*Goldbort, Robert. *Writing for Science.* New Haven: Yale University Press, 2006.

*Grafton, Anthony. *Defenders of the Text: The Traditions of Scholarship in an Age of Science, 1450–1800.* Cambridge: Harvard University Press, 1991.

*Grafton, Anthony. *The Footnote: A Curious History.* Cambridge: Harvard, 1997.

Greenhouse, Linda. "Roberts Dissent Reveals Strain Beneath Court's Placid Surface." *The New York Times* 23 March 2006: A1, A18.

*Greetham, D. C., ed. *The Margins of the Text.* Ann Arbor: University of Michigan, 1997.

Gregory, Frank. "The EU's Response to 9/11...." *Terrorism and Political Violence* 17.1/2 (Winter 2005): 105–123.

Grey, Robin, ed. *Melville and Milton: An Edition and Analysis of Melville's Annotations on Milton.* Pittsburgh: Duquesne, 2004.

Grudin, Robert. *Book: A Novel.* New York: Random House, 1992.

Gruener, Gustav. "The *Nibelungenlied* and *Sage* in Modern Poetry." *Publications of the Modern Language Association of America* XI (New Series, IV) (1896): 220–257.
Hall, Bert S. "The Didactic and the Elegant: Some Thoughts on Scientific and Technological Illustrations in the Middle Ages and Renaissance." *Picturing Knowledge: Historical and Philosophical Problems Concerning the Use of Art in Science*. Ed. Brian S. Baigrie. Toronto: University of Toronto Press, 1996. 3–39.
*Hamilton, A. C. "The Philosophy of the Footnote." *Editing Poetry from Spenser to Dryden*. Ed. A. H. De Quehen. New York: Garland, 1981. 127–163.
*Hamilton, Richard F. *The Social Misconstruction of Reality: Validity and Verification in the Scholarly Community*. New Haven: Yale University Press, 1996.
*Hapgood, Mike, and Russ Evans. "Impact Factors — Signal or Noise?" *A and G: Astronomy and Geophysics* 46 (April 2005): 2.15. 27 Sept. 2006. <www.blackwell-synergy.com/links/doi/10.1111/j.1468-4004.2005.46215.x/>.
*Hauptman, Robert. "Documentation Diatribe." Unpublished letter to the editor of *PMLA*. 15 May 1982.
*Hauptman, Robert. *Ethics and Librarianship*. Jefferson, NC: McFarland, 2002.
Hauptman, Robert. "Titans Clashing: The Art of Science and the Science of Art." *Journal of Thought* 15.4 (Winter 1980): 53–64.
*Hauptman, Robert. "Whatever Happened to Bibliographies? *The Chronicle of Higher Education* 12 February, 1999: B10.
Havens, George R. *Voltaire's Marginalia on the Pages of Rousseau: A Comparative Study of Ideas*. Columbus: Ohio State University, 1933.
*Henige, David. "Being Fair to the Hounds: The Function and Practice of Annotation." *History in Africa* 28 (2001): 95–127.
*Henige, David. "Being Fair to the Hounds: The Function and Practice of Annotation, II." *History in Africa* 29 (2002): 63–88.
*Henige, David. "Discouraging Verification: Citation Practices across the Disciplines." *Journal of Scholarly Publishing* 37.2 (Jan. 2006): 99–118.
Herodotus. *Herodotus Books I and II*. Tr. A. D. Godley. Vol. I. (The Loeb Classical Library.) Cambridge: Harvard University Press, 1960.
Herodotus. *The Landmark Herodotus: The Histories*. Ed. Robert B. Strassler. Trans. Andrea C. Purvis. New York: Pantheon, 2007.
*Heron-Allen, Edward. "Footnotes." *Notes and Queries* 179.17 (26 Oct. 1940): 300–301.
*Hilbert, Betsy. "Elegy for Excursus: The Descent of the Footnote." *College English* 51.4 (April 1989): 400–404.
*Hill, W. Speed. "Commentary upon Commentary upon Commentary: Three Historicisms Annotating Richard Hooker." *The Margins of the Text*. Ed. D. C. Greetham. Ann Arbor: University of Michigan Press, 1997. 323–352.
*Himmelfarb, Gertrude. "Where Have All the Footnotes Gone?" *On Looking into the Abyss: Untimely Thoughts on Culture and Society*. New York: Knopf, 1994. 122–130.
Hippocrates. Volume VII. [Epidemics.] Ed. and trans. Wesley D. Smith. (The Loeb Classical Library.) Cambridge: Harvard University Press, 1994.
Hodgson, Godfrey. *A Grand and Godly Adventure*. New York: Public Affairs, 2006.
Hodgson, John. *A History of Northumberland*. Part II, vol. I. Newcastle-upon-Tyne: N.p., 1827.
The Holie Bible: Conteynyng the Olde Testament and the New. [London: Printed by Richard Lugge, 1568.]
Holt, Jim. "Is Paris Kidding? *Fashionable Nonsense*." Review. *The New York Times Book Review* 15 Nov. 1998: 8.
*Honan, William L. "Footnotes Offering Fewer Insights.'" *The New York Times* 14 Aug. 1996: B9.

Hooker, Richard. *Lawes of Ecclesiasticall Politie*. Book V. London: Printed by John Windet, 1597.
The Hours of Catherine of Cleves. Facsimile. Intro., commentaries John Plummer. New York: George Braziller, n.d. [1966?].
*Howard, Jennifer. "Call Me Digital." *The Chronicle of Higher Education* 17 February 2006: A14–A16, A18–A19.
*Howard, Jennifer. "Scholarship on the Edge." *The Chronicle of Higher Education* 21 October 2005: A14–A16, A18.
Hughes, Diane, et al. "Parents' Ethnic-Racial Socialization Practices: A Review of Research and Directions for Future Study." *Developmental Psychology* 42.5 (2006): 747–770.
*Hyland, Ken. "Self-Citation and Self-Reference: Credibility and Promotion in Academic Publication." *Journal of the American Society for Information Science and Technology* 54.3 (1 Feb. 2003): 251–259.
"Instructions in Regard to Preparation of Manuscript." *Psychological Bulletin* 26 (1929): 57–63.
"Introduzione." *Giornale de Letterati d'Italia* I (1710): 13–67.
*Jackson, H. J. *Marginalia: Readers Writing in Books*. New Haven: Yale University Press, 2001.
*Jackson, H. J. *Romantic Readers: The Evidence of Marginalia*. New Haven: Yale University Press, 2005.
Jacobs, Louis. *Jewish Ethics, Philosophy and Mysticism*. New York: Behrman House, 1969.
*Jensen, Michael. "Presses Have Little to Fear from Google." *The Chronicle of Higher Education* 8 July 2005: B16.
Jonckheere, Frans, ed. *Le Papyrus Médical Chester Beatty*. Bruxelles: Fondation Égyptologique Reine Élisabeth, 1947.
Josephus. *The Jewish War, Books I–III*. Tr. H. St. J. Thackeray. Vol. II. (The Loeb Classical Library.) Cambridge: Harvard University Press, 1967.
Joyce, James. *A Shorter Finnegans Wake*. Ed. Anthony Burgess. New York: Viking, 1966.
Joyce, James. *Ulysses*. New York: The Modern Library, 1942.
Kafka, Franz. "Die Verwandlung." *Das Urteil und Andere Erzählungen*. Frankfurt am Main: Fischer, 1962. 23–105.
Kanogo, Tabitha. *African Womanhood in Colonial Kenya, 1900–50*. Oxford: James Curry (et al.), 2005.
*Kaplan, Norman. "The Norms of Citation Behavior: Prolegomena to the Footnote." *American Documentation* 16.3 (July 1965): 179–184.
Karamustafa, Ahmet T. "Introduction to Islamic Maps." *The History of Cartography: Cartography in the Traditional Islamic and South Asian Societies*. Ed. J. B. Harley and David Woodward. Vol. II, book 1. Chicago: University of Chicago Press, 1992. 3–11.
Kavan, Anna. *Ice*. London: Peter Owen, 1967.
Kelley, Kitty. *The Royals*. New York: Warner Books, 1997.
*Kelly, Kevin. "Scan This Book!" *The New York Times Magazine* 14 May 2006: 43–49, 64, 71.
Kemp, Martin. *Seen/Unseen: Art, Science, and Intuition from Leonardo to the Hubble Telescope*. Oxford: Oxford University Press, 2006.
*Kenner, Hugh. *Flaubert, Joyce and Beckett: The Stoic Comedians*. Boston: Beacon, 1962.
*Kiernan, Vincent. "Toss Out the Index Cards." *The Chronicle of Higher Education* 9 June 2006: A29, A30.
*Kochen, Manfred. "How Well Do We Acknowledge Intellectual Debts?" *Journal of Documentation* 43.1 (March 1987): 54–64.
Kornhauser, David. *Japan: Geographical Background to Urban-Industrial Development*. 2nd ed. London: Longman, 1985.
Koster, R. M. *The Dissertation*. New York: Harper's Magazine Press, 1975.
*Kotiaho, Janne S. "Ethical Considerations in Citing Scientific Literature and Using Cita-

tion Analysis in Evaluation of Research Performance." *Journal of Information Ethics* 11.2 (Fall 2002): 10–16.
Kramer, Samuel Noah. *From the Tablets of Sumer.* Indian Hills, CO: The Falcon's Wing Press, 1956.
*Kronholz, June. "Bibliography Mess: The Internet Wreaks Havoc with the Form." *The Wall Street Journal* 2 May 2002: A1, A6.
Krutch, Joseph Wood. *The Modern Temper: A Study and a Confession.* New York: Harcourt, 1956.
Kusukawa, Sachiko. "Leonhart Fuchs on the Importance of Pictures." *Journal of the History of Ideas* 58.3 (July 1997): 403–427.
*LaFollette, Marcel C. "Avoiding Plagiarism: Some Thoughts on Use, Attribution, and Acknowledgment." *Journal of Information Ethics* 3.2 (Fall 1994): 25–35.
*LaFollette, Marcel C. *Stealing into Print: Fraud, Plagiarism, and Misconduct in Scientific Publishing.* Berkeley: University of California, 1992.
Latour, Bruno. "Drawing Things Together." *Representation in Scientific Practice.* Ed. Michael Lynch and Steve Woolgar. Cambridge: MIT Press, 1990. 19–68.
*Leydesdorff, Loet. Letter. "The 'Abuse' of Journals' Impact Factors." *The Chronicle of Higher Education* 18 Nov. 2005: A55.
*Leydesdorff, Loet. "Theories of Citation?" *Scientometrics* 43.1 (Sept. 1998): 5–25. 3 Jan. 2007. <springerlink.metapress.com>.
Lindisfarne Gospels. (Manuscript — Cotton Nero D.IV — held by the British Library.)
*Lipking, Lawrence. "The Marginal Gloss." *Critical Inquiry* 3.4 (Summer 1997): 609–655.
*Lipson, Charles. *Cite Right: A Quick Guide to Citation Styles....* Chicago: University of Chicago Press, 2006.
Liptak, Adam. "When Rendering Decisions, Judges Are Finding Law Reviews Irrelevant." *The New York Times* 19 Mar. 2007: A8.
Llull, Ramon. *Selected Works of Ramon Llull (1232–1316).* Ed. and trans. Anthony Bonner. Vol. I. Princeton, NJ: Princeton University Press, 1985.
[Locke, John.] *The Works of John Locke.* Ed. J. A. St. John. Vol. II. 1877. Rpt. Freeport, NY: Books for Libraries Press, 1969.
Love, Harold. *Attributing Authorship: An Introduction.* Cambridge: Cambridge University Press, 2002.
Lucretius. *On the Nature of the Universe.* Tr. Ronald Latham. Baltimore: Penguin, 1957.
*Lyall, Sarah. "Novelists Defend One of Their Own Against a Plagiarism Charge in Britain." *The New York Times* 7 Dec. 2006: B1, B9.
Machiavelli. *The Art of War.* Trans. Peter Whitehorne (1560). *The Prince.* Trans. Edward Dacres (1640). Intro. Henry Cust. Vol. I. 1905. New York: AMS, 1967.
*Magruder, Kerry. E-mail to the author. 3 January 2006.
*Mallon, Thomas. *Stolen Words.* New York: Ticknor and Fields, 1989.
*Margolis, J. "Citation Indexing and Evaluation of Scientific Papers." *Science* 155 (1967): 1213–1219.
Marks in Books. Cambridge: Houghton Library, Harvard, 1985.
*Marsh, Emily E., and Marilyn Domas White. "A Taxonomy of Relationships between Images and Text." *Journal of Documentation* 59.6 (2003): 647–672.
Mayer, Arno J. *Why Did the Heavens Not Darken?: The "Final Solution" in History.* New York: Pantheon, 1988.
Mayhew, Robert, ed. *Ayn Rand's Marginalia.* New Milford, CT: Second Renaissance Books, 1995.
*McEathron, Scott. Personal communication. 25 Oct. 2006.
McEwan, Ian. *Atonement: A Novel.* New York: N. A. Talese, 2002.
*McFarland, Thomas. "Who Was Benjamin Whichcote? or, The Myth of Annotation."

Annotation and Its Texts. Ed. Stephen A. Barney. New York: Oxford University Press, 1991. 152–177.
McHugh, Roland. *Annotations to* Finnegans Wake. Baltimore: Johns Hopkins University Press, 1980.
*McKenzie, D. F. *Bibliography and the Sociology of Texts.* Cambridge: Cambridge University Press, 1999.
*McLellen, M. Faith, L. Douglas Case, and Molly C. Barnett. "Trust but Verify: The Accuracy of References in Four Anesthesia Journals." *Anesthesiology* 77.1 (July 1992): 185–188.
Melograni, Piero. *Wolfgang Amadeus Mozart: A Biography.* Tr. Lydia G. Cochrane. Chicago: University of Chicago Press, 2007.
*Merton, Robert K. *On the Shoulders of Giants.* New York: Free Press, 1965.
*Mikva, Abner J. "Goodbye to Footnotes." *University of Colorado Law Review* 56.4 (Summer 1985): 647–653.
Milgrim, Stanley. *Obedience to Authority: An Experimental View.* New York: Harper, 1962.
*Moed, Henk F. *Citation Analysis in Research Evaluation.* Dordrecht: Springer, 2005.
*Monastersky, Richard. "The Number That's Devouring Science." *The Chronicle of Higher Education* 14 Oct. 2005: A12–A14, A16–A17.
Monmonier, Mark S. *How to Lie with Maps.* Chicago: University of Chicago Press, 1996.
"Moral Panic." *Wikipedia.* 29 November 2006. <en.wikipedia.org/wiki/Moral_panic>.
Nabokov, Vladimir, ed., trans., intro., and comment. *Eugene Onegin* by Aleksandr Pushkin. 2 vols. 1964. Princeton, NJ: Princeton University Press, 1990.
*Nabokov, Vladimir. *Pale Fire.* New York: Putnam's, 1962.
*Nardini, Bob. "Invisible Links." *Academia: An Online Magazine and Resource for Academic Librarians* July 2005: 11 pars. 19 Oct. 2006. <www.ybp.com/acad/features/0705_bugeja.html>.
*Newman, Andrew Adam. "How Should a Book Sound? And What About Footnotes?" *The New York Times* 20 January 2006: B31, B35.
*Nicolaisen, Jeppe. "Citation Analysis." In *Annual Review of Information Science and Technology 41 2007.* Ed. Blaise Cronin. Medford, NJ: Information Today, 2007. 609–641.
*Nimis, Steve. "Fussnoten: Das Fundament der Wissenschaft." *Arethusa* 17.2 (Fall 1984): 105–134.
Norgay, Jamling Tenzing with Broughton Coburn. *Touching My Father's Soul: A Sherpa's Journey to the Top of Everest.* New York: HarperSanFrancisco, 2001.
*"The Novelty Factor." Editorial. *The Wall Street Journal* 8 Dec. 2006: W15.
The Nuremberg Chronicle. A Facsimile of Hartmann Schedel's Buch der Chroniken, *1493.* New York: Landmark, 1979.
*Overbye, Dennis. "Canada Looks Up, Way Up." *The New York Times* 24 May, 2005: D1.
Ong, Walter J. *Orality and Literacy: The Technologizing of the Word.* New York: Methuen, 1982.
*Paisley, William. "The Future of Bibliometrics." In *Scholarly Communication and Bibliometrics.* Ed. Christine L. Borgman. Newbury Park, CA: Sage, 1990. 281–299.
*Palmeri, Frank. "The Satiric Footnotes of Swift and Gibbon." *The Eighteenth Century* 31.3 (1990): 245–262.
*Parker, Edwin B., et al. *Bibliographic Citations as Unobtrusive Measures of Scientific Communication.* [Palo Alto:] Institute for Communication Research, Stanford University, 1967.
*Parker, William Riley, comp. "The MLA Style Sheet." *Publications of the Modern Language Association (PMLA)* 66.3 (April 1951): 1–31.
Perini, Laura. "The Truth in Pictures." *Philosophy of Science* 72.1 (Jan. 2005): 262–285.
Pessl, Marisha. *Special Topics in Calamity Physics.* New York: Viking, 2006.

Pether, Penelope. "Inequitable Injunctions: The Scandal of Private Judging in the U.S. Courts." *Stanford Law Review* 56.4 (May 2004): 1435–1579.
*Pierce, Sydney J. "Disciplinary Work and Interdisciplinary Areas: Sociology and Bibliometrics." *Scholarly Communication and Bibliometrics*. Ed. Christine L. Borgman. Newbury Park, CA: Sage, 1990. 46–58.
*Pinck, Dan. "Let Me Count the Ways." *The American Scholar* 69.2 (Spring 2000): 101–104.
*"Plagiarism, Part I." *Journal of Information Ethics* 3.1 (Spring 1994): 8–88 (eleven articles).
*"Plagiarism, Part II." *Journal of Information Ethics* 3.2 (Fall 1994): 8–63 (six articles).
Pliny. *Natural History*. Tr. W. H. S. Jones. Vol. VI. (The Loeb Classical Library.) Cambridge: Harvard University Press, 1961.
Plutarch. *Plutarch's Lives: Pericles and Fabius Maximus, Nicias and Crassus*. Tr. Bernadotte Perrin. Vol. III. (The Loeb Classical Library.) Cambridge: Harvard University Press, 1958.
Poe, Edgar Allan. *The Complete Works of Edgar Allen Poe*. Ed. James A. Harrison. Vol. XVI. 1902. New York: AMS, 1965.
*Pollak, Oliver B. "The Decline and Fall of Bottom Notes, *op. cit., loc. cit.*, and a Century of the *Chicago Manual of Style*." *Journal of Scholarly Publishing* 38.1 (Oct. 2006): 14–30.
*Pollard, Alfred W. "Margins." *Dolphin* 1 (1933): 67–80.
Pope, Alexander. *The Dunciad*. Ed. James Sutherland. 3rd ed. Vol. V of *The Poems of Alexander Pope*. London: Methuen and New Haven: Yale, 1943, 1963.
Pope, Alexander, trans. *The Iliad of Homer: Books X–XXIV*. Ed. Maynard Mack et al. Vol. VIII of *The Poems of Alexander Pope*. London: Methuen and New Haven: Yale, 1967.
Pope, Walter. "Extract of a Letter." *Philosophical Transactions* 1.1 (1665): 21–26.
Posner, Richard A. "Goodby to the Bluebook." *University of Chicago Law Review* 53 (1986): 1343–1368.
*Price, Alan R. "Cases of Plagiarism Handled by the United States Office of Research Integrity 1992–2005." *Plagiary: Cross Disciplinary Studies in Plagiarism, Fabrication, and Falsification* 1.1 (2006): 1-1 1. November 2006. <www.plagiary.org>.
Proclus. *A Commentary on the First Book of Euclid's Elements*. Trans. and intro. Glenn R. Morrow. Princeton, NJ: Princeton University Press, 1970.
Publication Manual of the American Psychological Association. 2nd ed. Washington, DC: American Psychological Association, 1974, 1981.
Publication Manual of the American Psychological Association. 5th ed. Washington, DC: American Psychological Association, 2001.
*Rabener, Gottlieb Wilhelm. *Hinkmars von Repkow. Noten Ohne Text*. 1743. *Satiren*. Vol. II. Frankfurt, n.p., 1759. 107–168.
Randall, Lilian M. C. *Images in the Margins of Gothic Manuscripts*. Berkeley: University of California Press, 1966.
Ranke, Leopold von. *A History of England Principally in the Seventeenth Century*. Vols. V, VI. Rpt. New York: AMS Press, 1966.
Rawicz, Slavomir. *The Long Walk: A Gamble for Life*. New York: Harper, 1956.
Read, Brock. "Can Wikipedia Ever Make the Grade? *The Chronicle of Higher Education* 27 Oct. 2006: A31–A36.
"References." *American Speech* 75.3 (Fall 2000): 304–311; 75.4 (Winter 2000): 422–429.
Reid, P. R. *Escape from Colditz: The Two Classic Escape Stories—The Colditz Story, Men of Colditz—in One Volume*. Philadelphia: J. P. Lippincott, 1973.
Rev. of *For Want of a Nail: If Burgoyne Had Won at Saratoga*, by Robert Sobel. *Choice* 10.7 (Sept. 1973): 1069–1070.
Reyes, Rogelio. Letter. *The Chronicle of Higher Education* 2 September, 2005: B17.

Reymond, E. A. E., ed. *A Medical Book from Crocodilopolis*. Wien: Verlag Bruder Hollinek, 1976.
Ridgway, John L. *Scientific Illustration*. Np: Stanford University Press, 1938.
*Riess, Peter. *Towards a Theory of the Footnote*. Berlin: Walter de Gruyter, [1983?].
Roberts, K. B., and J. D. W. Tomlinson. *The Fabric of the Body: European Traditions of Anatomical Illustration*. Oxford: Oxford University Press, 1992.
Robin, Harry. *The Scientific Image: From Cave to Computer*. New York: Abrams, 1992.
*Robin, Ron. *Scandals and Scoundrels: Seven Cases That Shook the Academy*. Berkeley: University of California Press, 2004.
*Rudolph, Janell, and Deborah Brackstone. "Too Many Scholars Ignore the Basic Rules of Documentation." *The Chronicle of Higher Education* 11 April 1990: A56.
Rudwick, Martin J. S. "The Emergence of a Visual Language for Geological Science 1760–1840." *History of Science* 14.3 (no. 25) (Sept. 1976): 149–195.
*Schneider, Steven P. "Crossing Borders with Poetry and Art." *The Chronicle of Higher Education* 24 March 2006: B9.
*Schott, Ben. "Confessions of a Book Abuser." *The New York Times Book Review* 4 Mar. 2007: 31.
Sciabarra, Chris Matthew. Personal communication. 22 Sept. 2006.
Scientific Style and Format: The CSE Manual for Authors, Editors, and Publishers. 7th ed. Reston, VA: Council of Science Editors et al., 2006.
*Seglen, Per O. "Why the Impact Factor of Journals Should Not Be Used for Evaluating Research." *BMJ* 314.7079 (15 Feb. 1997): 498–502.
Seligmann, Linda J. *Peruvian Street Lives: Culture, Power, and Economy among Market Woman of Cuzco*. Urbana: University of Illinois Press, 2004.
*Sellitto, Carmine. "The Impact of Impermanent Web-Located Citations: A Study of 123 Scholarly Conference Publications." *Journal of the American Society for Information Science and Technology* 56.7 (May 2005): 695–703.
*Shin, Eun-Ja. "Do Impact Factors Change with a Change of Medium? A Comparison of Impact Factors When Publication Is by Paper and Through Parallel Publishing." *Journal of Information Science* 29.6 (2003): 527–533.
Simpson, Joe. *Touching the Void*. New York: HarperPerennial, 1998.
Skow, John. "Parlor Games." Rev. of *For Want of a Nail: If Burgoyne Had Won at Saratoga*, by Robert Sobel. *Time* 9 April 1973: 103.
*Slights, William W. E. "The Cosmopolitics of Reading: Navigating the Margins of John Dee's *General and Rare Memorials*." *The Margins of the Text*. Ed. D. C. Greetham. Ann Arbor: University of Michigan Press, 1997. 199–227.
*Slights, William W. E. *Managing Readers: Printed Marginalia in English Renaissance Books*. Ann Arbor: University of Michigan Press, 2001.
*Small, H. Letter. "Citations and Consilience in Science." *Scientometrics* 43.1 (Sept. 1998): 143–148. 5 Jan. 2007. <springerlink.metapress.com>.
*Small, Henry G. "Cited Documents as Concept Symbols." *Social Studies of Science* 8.3 (Aug. 1978): 327–340.
Smiles, Sam. *Eye Witness: Artists and Visual Documentation in Britain, 1770–1830*. Aldershot, Hants, England: Ashgate, 2000.
Smith, James Edward. *Flora Britannica*. 2 vols. London, 1800–1804. (Copy held by the Linnean Society.)
*Smith, Linda. "Citation Analysis." *Library Trends* 30.1 (Summer 1981): 83–106.
*Smith Richard. "Journal Accused of Manipulating Impact Factor." *BMJ* 314.7079 (15 Feb. 1997): 463.
Sobel, Robert. *For Want of a Nail: If Burgoyne Had Won at Saratoga*. New York: Macmillan, 1973.

Sokal, Alan, and Jean Bricmont. *Fashionable Nonsense: Postmodern Philosopher's Abuse of Science.* New York: Picador USA, 1998.
Sontag, Susan. *In America: A Novel.* New York: Farrar, Straus and Giroux, 2000.
*Stanitzek, Georg. "Texts and Paratexts in Media." Tr. Ellen Klein. *Critical Inquiry* 32.1 (Autumn 2005): 27–42.
*Stevens, Anne H. Letter. "Citing Theorists." *Chronicle of Higher Education* 14 July 2006: B13.
*Stevens, Anne H., and Jay Williams. "The Footnote, in Theory." *Critical Inquiry* 32.2 (Winter 2006): 208–225.
*Sullivan, Frank. "A Garland of Ibids." *A Subtreasury of American Humor.* Ed. E. B. White and Katharine S. White. New York: Coward-McCann, 1941. 263–266.
*Sweetland, James H. "Errors in Bibliographic Citations: A Continuing Problem." *The Library Quarterly* 59.4 (Oct. 1989): 291–304.
Swift, Jonathan. *Gulliver's Travels, A Tale of a Tub, The Battle of the Books, etc.* London: Oxford University Press, 1956.
Switalski, B. W. *Des Chalcidius Kommentar zu Plato's Timaeus: Eine Historish-Kritische Untersuchung. Beiträge zur Geschichte der Philosophie des Mittlealters.* Ed. Clemens Baeumker and Georg Freih. von Hertling. Band III, Heft VI (paginated separately). Münster: Aschendorffschen Buchhandlung, 1902. 1–113.
Szasz, Thomas. "'Knowing What Ain't So': R. D. Laing and Thomas Szasz." *Psychoanalytic Review* 91.3 (June 2004): 331–346.
Szasz, Thomas S. "Psychoanalysis and the Autonomic Nervous System." *The Psychoanalytic Review* XXXIX.2 (April 1952): 115–151.
Tacitus. *The Histories.* Tr. Clifford H. Moore. Vol. I. (The Loeb Classical Library.) Cambridge: Harvard University Press, 1962.
Takeyh, Ray. *Hidden Iran.* New York: Henry Holt, 2006.
The Talmud. The Steinsaltz edition. Tractate Bava Mezia. Vol. I, part I. Comment. Adin Steinsaltz. New York: Random House. 1989.
Tancin, Charlotte. Personal communication. 12 Dec. 2006.
*Thelwall, Mike, and Liwen Vaughan, eds. "Webometrics." *Journal of the American Society for Information Science and Technology* 55.14 (Dec. 2004): 1213–1303 (nine articles).
*Thelwall, Mike, Liwen Vaughan, and Lennart Björneborn. "Webometrics." *Annual Review of Information Science and Technology 39 2005.* Ed. Blaise Cronin. Medford, NJ: Information Today, 2004. 81–135.
*Thomas, Rosalind. *Oral Tradition and Written Records in Classical Athens.* Cambridge: Cambridge University Press, 1990.
Thompson, Ann. "Feminist Theory and the Editing of Shakespeare: *The Taming of the Shrew* Revisited." *The Margins of the Text.* Ed. D. C. Greetham. Ann Arbor: University of Michigan Press, 1997. 83–103.
Thucydides. *The Landmark Thucydides: A Complete Guide to the Peloponnesian War.* Ed. Robert B. Strassler. Trans. Richard Crawley. New York: Free Press, 1996.
Topper, David. "Towards an Epistemology of Scientific Illustration." *Picturing Knowledge: Historical and Philosophical Problems Concerning the Use of Art in Science.* Ed. Brian S. Baigrie. Toronto: University of Toronto Press, 1996. 215–249.
*Tribble, Evelyn B. "'Like a Looking-Glas in the Frame': From the Marginal Note to the Footnote." *The Margins of the Text.* Ed. D. C. Greetham. Ann Arbor: University of Michigan Press, 1997. 229–244.
*Tribble, Evelyn B. *Margins and Marginality: The Printed Page in Early Modern England.* Charlottesville: University Press of Virginia, 1993.
*Tribble, Evelyn B. "The Peopled Page: Polemic, Confutation, and Foxe's *Book of Mar-*

tyrs." *The Iconic Page in Manuscript, Print, and Digital Culture.* Ed. George Bornstein and Theresa Tinkle. Ann Arbor: University of Michigan Press, 1998. 109–122.

Tufte, Edward R. *Beautiful Evidence.* Cheshire, CT: Graphics Press, 2006.

Tufte, Edward R. *The Visual Display of Quantitative Information.* Cheshire, CT: Graphics Press, 1983.

*Updike, John. "Notes." *The New Yorker* 26 January 1957: 28–29. <users.fmg.uva.nl/lley desdorff/jcr04>.

van Rahden, Till. "Jews and the Ambivalence of Civil Society...." *The Journal of Modern History* 77.4 (Dec. 2005): 1024–1047.

Vasari, Georgio. *Le Vite: Le Vite de' Più Eccellenti Pittori Scultori e Architettori.* Ed. Rosanna Bettarini and Paola Barocchi. Vol. IV. Firenze: Studio per Edizioni Scelte, 1976.

*Vaughan, Liwen, and Debora Shaw. "Bibliographic and Web Citations: What Is the Difference?" *Journal of the American Society for Information Science and Technology* 54.14 (December 2003): 1313–1322.

*Volokh, Eugene. "Plagiarism and 'Atonement.'" *The Wall Street Journal* 12 Dec. 2006: A18.

Vega, Suzanne. "The Ballad of Henry Timrod." *The New York Times* 17 Sept. 2006: WK15.

Wang, Weiping, et al. "Three-Dimensional Calculation...." *Applied Optics* 44.34 (December 1, 2005): 7442–7450.

Warren, Rosanna. "Odyssey." *American Poetry Review* 35.6 (Nov./Dec. 2006): 47–48.

Watcha, Mehernoor F., and Paul F. White. "Postoperative Nausea and Vomiting." *Anesthesiology* 77.1 (July 1992): 162–184.

Watson, James D., and Francis H. C. Crick. "A Structure for Deoxyribose Nucleic Acid." *Nature* 171.4356 (25 April 1953): 737–738.

Weber, Max. *The Protestant Ethic and the Spirit of Capitalism.* Trans. Talcott Parsons. Los Angeles: Roxbury, 1996.

Whitaker, Robert. *The Mapmaker's Wife: A True Tale of Love, Murder, and Survival in the Amazon.* New York: Basic Books, 2004.

*White, Howard D., Barry Wellman, and Nancy Nazer. "Does Citation Reflect Social Structure? Longitudinal Evidence from the 'Globenet' Interdisciplinary Research Group." *Journal of the American Society for Information Science and Technology* 55.2 (15 Jan. 2004): 111–126.

Wilson, Edmund. "The Strange Case of Pushkin and Nabokov." *The New York Review of Books* 4.12 (15 July 1965): 3–6.

*Wouters, Paul, and Repke de Vries. "Formally Citing the Web." *Journal of the American Society for Information Science and Technology* 55.14 (Dec. 2004): 1250–1260.

<www.boisestate.edu/melville>.

*<www.chicagomanualofstyle.org>.

*<www.halfnotes.org>.

<www.oup-usa.org/sc/0195128427/>.

*<www.plagiary.org>.

*<www.webcitation.org>.

*Zerby, Chuck. *The Devil's Details: A History of Footnotes.* Montpelier, VT: Invisible Cities Press, 2002.

*Zuger, Abigail. "Dropping Detachment and Reconnecting to Patients." Rev. of *The Lonely Patient*, by Michael Stein. *The New York Times* 27 Mar. 2007: D5.

Index

Numbers in ***bold italics*** indicate pages with illustrations.

Abraham, David 182
Acknowledgment 8–9, 14
An Admonition to the Parliament 94
Aesop 18
Agger, Ben 154
Agin, Dan 126
Altman, Ellen, et al. 181, 188
Ambrose 21
American Historical Association: plagiarism 186; style 162, 163
American Psychological Association: *Publication Manual* 149, 154; style 33, 34, 115, 125, 127, 154–159
Anaxagoras 19
Anaximenes 18
Anderson, John E., et al. 154, 169
Anderson, Judy 185
Anselm of Canterbury 21
Aquinas, St. Thomas 14, 21, 39, 41–42
Arias, Arturo 126
Aristotle 14–15, 17, 18, 19, 21, 31
Arming America 182
Arndt, Walter 206
Asano, Migiwa 174
Attribution 9–10, 16; elimination 16, 19, 20, 21, 29, 30; general 17
Auerbach, Erich 10, 125
Augustine 21, 102
Austin, Arthur 123
Authors 33

Bach, Johann Sebastian 8
Bacon, Francis 30, 31
Baldi, Stéphane 118
Ball, Philip 173, 179, 194

Baltimore, David 181
Bamford, James 16
Bancroft Prize 183
Baron, Sabrina Alcorn 94
Bartlett, Thomas, et al. 186, 188
Barzun, Jacques 100
Bauer, Felice 79
Bauman, M. Garrett 167
Bayle, Pierre 7, 44–45, ***45–48***, 49, 54, 113, 145, 173
Bazerman, Charles 119, 155
Beck, Sheila, et al. 166
Beehler, Rodger 61
Beethoven, Ludwig van 8, 55–56
Begley, Sharon 195
Behrendt, John C. 145
Beller, E.A., et al. 44
Bellesiles, Michael 182, 182–183
Beowulf 20
Bettarini, Rosanna, and Paola Barocchi 42
Bevan, David, et al. 174
Bible 16, 22, 43, 94, 143; pauper 103, ***104–105, 106–107, 131***
Bibliography: construction 34, 166–167; descriptive 186–187, 201; error 154, 167, 173; fictitious entries 182; ghost 187; importance 125; instruction 169–170; missing 30, 112, 124–127, 160, 177; novels 127; software 166–167; subsequent entries 161, 162
Biebuyck, Julien 174
Blake, William 142
Bloch, Sidney, and Garry Walter 193
The BlueBook 152, 153, 154
Blum, Shelby 129
Boethius 21, 22, 23, 24

223

Bolles, Charles Avery 190
Boltanski, Luc, et al. 77
The Book of Durrow 20
The Book of Kells 20, 79, 102
Book of Mac Regol 81
Booth, Stephen 117
Borgman, Christine L. 191
Bosman, Julie 127
Bowersock, G.W. 121, 155, 206
Brahe, Tycho 11
Breuning, Stephen 12
Breyer, Stephen 122
Brooks, Van Wyck 123
Brown, James Robert 131
Buchanan, Elizabeth 79, **80**
Buchanan, Robert 173, 177
Bugeja, Michael, et al. 175–176
Burkle-Young, Francis, et al. 112, 205
Burt, Cyril 181–182
Burton, Sir Richard F. 54, 205
Byrd, Richard 52
Byron, George Gordon Lord 8

Caeser 20
Calligraphy: Chinese 61, 80
Cameron, Brian D. 189, 190, 194, 195, 199
Camille, Michael 101, 102, 103, 110
Carvajal, Doreen 124, 125, 130, 185
Carvell, Tim 205
CASSI 34, 151
Cato 19, 20
Cawkell, Tony 198, 199
Chalcidius 38
Chicago Manual of Style 114, 121–122, 125, 149, 150; extraneous material 148; style 150–151
Cicero 20, 21
Citation 184; academic decisions 191, 196–197, 207; analytic problems 191–199; co-citation 193; electronic 166, 175; error 194; ethics 195, 196; failure 175–176; functional 118, 205; graphic map 199; harm 190, 192, 196; hyperlink 176; impact factor 190, 191, 193–194, 195, 196, 197; index 189; indexing and anlaysis 190–191; interconnections *198*; legal 152–154; nationality 119; neutral format 154; normative 118; review article 194–195; scientific 151–152, 160; self-citation 195–196; social pressure 120; standardization 161; symbolic 119; survey 174; third world scholarship 194; tracking 189; Webometrics 197
Citation Analysis in Research Evaluation 191
Citation Indexing 190, 193
Clarke, Mary Cowden 122
Coetzee, J.M. 70
Cohen, Benjamin 129

Coke, Edward 39
Coleridge, Samuel Taylor **97**, **98**, 99
Commentary 12–13, 14, 15; intercalated 55–56; legal 36–38; length 36, 60, 81; location 36; overdone 120
Common knowledge 10
Connors, Robert J. 112, 149, 201
Consolation of Philosophy 22
Copernicus, Nicolaus 15, 21–22, 29, 42, 134–135, **136–137**
Cosgrove, P.W. 51
Council of Editors of Learned Journals 170
Council of Science Editors: manual 149; style 149
Cowell, Alan 185
Cowley, Abraham 42, 61
Cox, Michael 67
Cramer, Clayton 183
Crick, Francis 10
Cronin, Blaise 117, 193, 196, 205
Curtius, Ernst Robert 13, 49
Cybermetrics... 197
Cyrus 16

Dacres, Edward 24
Dante 10, 61, 66, 143
Dark Ages 20
Darwin, Charles 10, 30, 54, 186
Daumier, Honoré 143
da Vinci, Leonardo 130, **131**, 142, 143
Davis, Henry 156
Davis, Philip M., et al. 175
de Bury, Richard 103
Deception 183, 184; beneficial 183–184
Dedication 9
Dee, John **96**, 96
de Gruyter, Walter 116
Democritus 19
Derrida, Jacques 13, 77, 100–101, 115
Descartes, René 11
The Descent of Man 30
The Devil's Details 22
Dickens, Charles 61
Diderot, Denis 138, **139**, **140**
Dioscorides 19
Disparaging 205–206
Divine Comedy 8
Documentation 203; abbreviation 151, 153; abjured 112, 114, 115–116, 122; antiquity 14–20; biological 146; complex **96**, 97–98, 100–101, 159, 167; consistent 161; demographics 149; Enlightenment to present 24–34; fictional 66, 67, **67**, **68**, **69**, 69, 70, 182; inconsistent 31, 56; literary 61; middle ages 20–21; perversity 152–153; Renaissance 21–24; skewed 31; spoof 56–57; trick 184; unreliable 32, 116, 173

Don Juan 8
Donovan, Stephen K. 161, 169
Doré, Gustave 99
Dove, Mary 81
The Dunciad 50–51, 56
Dunn, Mark 67
Dylan, Bob 206

Ebbell, B. 16
Edgerton, Samuel Y., Jr. 128
Edison, Thomas Alva 10
Editors (*BlueBook*) 152, 153
Editors: student 153
Edney, Matthew H. 146
Einstein, Albert 10, 11
Eiseley, Loren 186
Ekphrasis 143
Eliot, T.S. 8, 61, 90–91, **92–93**
Eliot, Vivian 91
Ellman, Richard 91, 94
Empedocles 18
Endnotes 33, 43, 61, 74, 114, 161, 203
Epstein, William 184
Errors: classes 168; confirmation 170ff; extreme 179; inevitable 169; responsibility 177–178; survey 170, 175
Ethics 118, 180–181, 188, 195
Euclid 10, 132, **132-133**
Eugene Onegin 57–60
Eumenides 8
Excursus (digression) 13, 49

Faulkner, William 70
Faust 8
Finnegans Wake 61, **62, 63**, 63–64, **64, 65–66**, 66, 115
Footnote 22, 30, 49, 50, 54, 67, 70, 202; advantage 32, 154; anti-religious 7; confusing 44, 61, **62**, 63, 115; contrarians 121–123; current usage 114, 115; early 26, **27, 28**, 79; excellence 51; first 22, **23**; law 11, 36, 114, 122, 152–154; length 52, 100, 113–114; multiplied 37–38, 122–123; not needed 7, 115; pagination 156, 206; parallel account 7; parody 123; protection 7; satire 49, 51, **68–69**; secondary meaning 7; signs 122; symbols 31; technology 123–124; theory 116–121; unimportant 121
Forbes, Elliott 55–56
Form: epsitemic value 201–202; function 202; meaning 200–201, 202–203
Foucault, Michel 192
Freehof, Solomon B. 39
Frey, James 188
Friedberg, Errol 160, 161
Frost, Carolyn 205
Fukuyama, Francis 32

Galen 17, 20
Galileo 10, 21, 78, **78**
Gallacher, Ian 153
Gardner, Martin 99
Garfield, Eugene 156, 159, 179, 180, 184, 186, 189, 190, 192–193, 196, 205
Geer, Beverley 174, 175
Gehry, Frank 202
Genette, Gérard 200
Gesner, Conrad 128
Gibaldi, Joseph 164, 165
Gibbon, Edward 10, 49, 51–52, 113, 117, 145, 156
Gibbs, W. Wayt 194
Gilbert, G. Nigel 202
Gilby, Thomas 21
Giornale de Letterati d'Italia 26
Glass, Phillip 8
Gloss 80–81
Glossa Ordinaria 81, **82, 83**, 94
Goethe, Johann Wolfgang von 8
Goldbort, Robert 130, 149
Grafton, Anthony 5, 7, 11, 20, 26, 66, 94, 113, 125, 173, 182
Greenhouse, Linda 7
Gregory the Great 21
Grey, Robin 88
Grudin, Robert 70
Gruener, Gustav 31, 54

Hall, Bert 128
Hamilton, A.C. 117
Hamilton, Richard 32, 187
Hamlet 50
Hamlet 8
Hapgood, Mike, et al. 197
Hargrave, Francis 84, **85–86**
Harvard University Press 125
Harvey, Gabriel 84
Hauptman, Robert 125, 160
Havens, George R. 84
Heidegger, Martin 100
Heliocentrism 15, 21
Henige, David 114, 117, 126, 129, 156, 175, 182, 200
Herodotus 14, 16–17, 19
Heron-Allen, Edward 121
Hilbert, Betsy 113
Hildebrandslied 20
Hill, W. Speed 96, 117
Himmelfarb, Gertrude 114
Hippocrates 17, 18, 20
History: scientizing 26, 29
Hlava, Jaroslav 174
Hoax 182, 184
Hodgson, Godfrey 126
Hodgson, John 52, **53**

Hollingshead's *Chronicles* 10
Holt, Jim 184
Homer 18, 19
Hooker, Richard **95**, 96
The Hours of Catherine of Cleves **102**
Howard, Jennifer 79, 87
Hume, David 51
Hyland, Ken 195
Hypertext 71, 114

The Iliad 49
Illustration: anatomical 142, ***142–143***; distort 146; as documentation 128ff; integrated ***131***; maps 144–147; marginal ***132, 136–137***; photographs 143; pop-up ***133***, 134; skepticism 131, 141
Imanishi-Kari, Thereza 181
Index 74, 200
Information Access Corporation 171
Information loss 172
Institute for Scientific Information 171, 173, 177, 189, 191, 194, 195
In-text source 112, 120, 125, 155, 161; abomination 155, 160, 161; early ***25***, ***26***; pagination 155–156, 206
I.T. 22, 24

Jackson, H.J. 79, 84, 105, 206
Jacobs, Dennis G. 153
Jacobs, Louis 56
James, Henry 88, ***90***, 90
James, William 10
Jensen, Michael 197
Jerome 21
Jonckheere, Frans 16
Jones, W.H.S. 19, 20
Jonson, Ben 71
Josephus 19
Journal Citation Reports 189
Journal of Medical Ethics 176
Joyce, James 10, 58, 61, ***62***, ***63***, ***64***, ***65***, ***66***, 90, 91, 94
Jung, Carl 8

Kafka, Franz 79
Kanago, Tabitha 143
Kant, Immanuel 11, 100
Kaplan, Norman 7, 119
Kaplan, Robert 124
Karamustafa, Ahmet 145
Kavan, Anna 71
Kekulé, August 141, ***141***
Kelley, Kitty 9
Kelly, Kevin 123
Kelly, Robert 206
Kemp, Martin 130
Kenner, Hugh 91, 124, 128

Kepler, Johannes 11
Kiernan, Vincent 166
Kling, Rob 180
Knight, David 129
Kochen, Manfred 118
Kornhouser, David 145
Koster, R.M. 66–67
Kotiaho, Janne 173
Kramer, Samuel Noah 16
Kronholz, June 166
Krutch, Joseph Wood 125

LaFollette, Marcel C. 184
Lamb, Charles 99
Latour, Bruno 129
Law reviews 153
Lee, H.D.P. 17
Legal Writing Directors' Manual 153
Leiris, Michel 100
Leonardo da Vinci *see* da Vinci, Leonardo
Leydesdorff, Loet 117, 199
Lindisfarne Gospels 20, 79, 80
Lipking, Lawrence 74, 77, 99, 113, 206
Lipson, Charles 149
Liptak, Adam 153
Livy 20
Llull, Ramon 134, ***134–135***
Locke, John 31
Lucas, Zoltan J. 181
Lucretius 19
Lyall, Sarah 187

Machiavelli 24
Magruder, Kerry 134
Mallon, Thomas 186
Mann, Thomas 8
Manutius, Aldus 132
Maps 144–147
Marginalia 22, 24, 44, ***68–69***; audience 94; controlling 109; defacing 79; extensive 84, 88, 91; hand-written 77ff; images 101ff, ***103***, ***108***; orality 111; printed 94ff; refusal 84; secondary meaning 101–102; sexual 102; social outsiders 110; stabilizing 110; superfluous ***75–76***, 77; theory 109ff
Marlowe, Christopher 8
The Maroon Book 153
Márquez, Gabriel García 71
Marsh, Emily, et al. 147
Mayer, Arno 114
McEathron, Scott 144
McEwan, Ian 185, 187
McFarland, Thomas 7
McGarrell, James 143
McHugh, Roland 64
McKenzie, D.F. 144, 201
McLellen, M. Faith 174, 175

A Medical Book from Crocidilopolis 16
Medical texts 16
Melograni, Piero 126
Melville, Herman 86, *87*, *88*, 88, *89*
Memoir 52
Michelangelo 143
Middle ages: barbarism 20
Mikva, Abner 122
Milgram, Stanley 15, 184
Misconduct 12; deception 183–184; detecting and preventing 186–187; fabrication 179, 181–182; falsification 179, 181, 182–184; plagiarism 179, 180, 181, 184–186, 205, 206–207; repercussions 187–188; software 187; when to cite 180–181
MIT Press 124
Moed, Henk 120–121, 171, 190–191
Modern Language Association: *Handbook* 148; style 24, 33, 115, 125, 127, 155, 159–166
Monastersky, Richard 193, 199
Monmonier, Mark 146
Montgomery, Scott L. 130
Morrow, Glenn R. 38

Nabokov, Vladimir 31, 49, 51, 57–60, 61, 66, 206
Nardini, Bob 176
Newman, Andrew Adam 124
Newton, Sir Isaac 16, 135, *138*, 138
Nicolaisen, Jeppe 117–118
Nimis, Steve 113, 206
Norgay, Jamling Tenzing 9
Notes: author's literary 43; extirpation 165; inaccurate 187
Novum Organon 30
The Nuremberg Chronicle 103

Oates, Stephen 185–186, 188
The Odyssey 49
Ogilby, John 97
On the Origin of Species 29
On the Revolutions 21, 42, 134, *136–137*
Ong, Walter J. 111
Othello 50
Overbye, Dennis 193
Oxford University Press 124

Paisley, William 192
Palimpsest 35
Palmeri, Frank 52, 117
The Papyrus Ebers 16
Le Papyrus Médical Chester Beatty 16
Parallel texts 42–43, 52, *53*, 70
Paratext 200
Parker, Edwin B. 190
Parker, William Riley 159

Peer review 181
Perini, Laura 131
Perkins, Maxwell 74
Perrin, Bernadotte 18
Pessl, Marisha 67
Pether, Penelope 37
Petrarch 24, 66
Philosophical Transactions 24
Pierce, Sydney J. 192
Planck, Max 11
Plato 18
Pliny 19, 20
Plutarch 18
Poe, Edgar Allan 110, 206
Pollak, Oliver B. 112
Pollard, Alfred 82
Pompeii 18
Pope, Alexander 42, 49–51, 54, 56 60, 61, 99
Pope, Walter 24
Pound, Ezra 90–91, 94
Price, Alan R. 184, 186
The Prince 24
Proclus 38
Protection 12
Ptolemy 11, 15
Publications: discrepancies 72
Publishers: alterations 74; costs 32, 74, 77, 110, 112, 125, 160, 203, 206
Pushkin, Alexander 8, 31, 57
Pythagoras 10

Qatsi Trilogy 9

Rabener, Gottlieb Wilhelm 67, *67*
Rand, Ayn 84, 94
Ranke, Leopold von 26, 29, 113
Rashi 14, 36, 38
Ratdolt, Erhard 132
Rawicz, Slavomir 52
Read, Brock 177
Reagan, Nancy 9
"References" 126
Reggio, Godfrey 9
Reid, P.R. 52
Responsa 39
Reyes, Rogelio 122
Reymond, E.A.E. 16
Ridgway, John L. 130
Riess, Peter 116
Risen, James 16
Roberts, K.B., et al. 142
Robin, Harry 138, 141
Robin, Ron 183, 186
Rosen, Edward 42
Rousseau, Jean Jacques 84
The Royals 9

Rubens, Peter Paul 128
Rudolph, Janell, et al. 161, 168, 173, 174, 175
Rudwick, Martin 128
Rutgers University Press 125
The Rutland Psalter **102**

St. John, J.A. 31
Sartre, Jean-Paul 192
Schneider, Steven P. 143
Schott, Ben, 79
Sciabarra, Chris Matthew 84
Science 184
Scientometrics 197
Scopus 189
Seglen, Per 194
Sejanus **72–73**
Seligmann, Linda 143
Sellitto, Carmine 175, 176
Seneca 20
Shakespeare, William 10, 49
Shin, Eun-Ja 197
Shostakovich, Dmitri 8
Simkin, Mikhail, et al. 194
Simpson, Joe 52
Skinner, B.F. 10
Skow, John 182
Slights, William 44, 71, 97, 109, 110, 111, 202, 206
Small, Henry 119, 189
Smiles, Sam 131
Smith, James Edward 108
Smith, Linda 192
Smith, Richard 195
Sobel, Robert 182
Sokal, Alan 182, 184
Sontag, Susan 185
Spinoza, Bernard 134
Stanitzek, Georg 200
Steichen, Edward 128
Stein, Michael 126
Stevens, Anne, et al. 114, 192
Strassler, Robert 206
Style guide error 175
Sullivan, Frank 123
Sumeria 16
Summa Theologiae 21
Sweetland, James 174, 175, 181
Swift, Joanathan 49, 61, 66, 117
Switalski, B.W. 38
Szasz, Thomas 34

Tacitus 19, 20
Takeyh, Ray 125
Talmud 14, 36, 38–39, **40, 41**, 109
Tancin, Charlotte 129
Tennyson, Alfred Lord 90
Terracentrism 15, 22

Thackery, H. St. J. 19
Thelwall, Mike, et al. 197
Thomas, Dylan 58
Thomas, Rosalind 17
Thompson, Ann 122
Thucydides 17, 18
Titles 34
Titus 19
Tolstoy, Leo 74
Tong, Benson 186
Topper, David 129
Torah 14, 36, 109
Touching My Father's Soul **9**
Towards a Theory of the Footnote 116
Tracing 10–11
Tribble, Evelyn 81, 94, 97, 110, 112, 121, 154
Tufte, Edward 129, 130
Turner, Henry 182

Ulysses 91
University of Chicago Press 126
University of Oklahoma 78
University of Tulsa 71, 91
Updike, John 123
Uplavici case 174

Validation 11, 14, 15; hierarchy of 18
van Rahden, Till 33, 60
Vasari, Georgio 42
Vega, Suzanne 207
Venerable Bede 21
Vespasian 19
Virgil 24
Viswanathan, Kaavya 188
Vitruvius 20
Volokh, Eugene 188
Voltaire 84

Wallace, David Foster 124
Warren, Rosanna 143
The Waste Land 90–91, **92–93**
Watcha, Mehernoor, et al. 195
Watson, James, et al. 10, 120
Web of Science 189
Weber, Max 32, 187
Wellington's Victory 8
Welty, Eudora 10
West (publisher) 154
West, John B. 195
Whitaker, Robert 145
White, Howard D., et al. 120
Wikipedia 177
Wilamowitz, Ulrich von 113
Wilson, Edmund 10, 58
Wilson, Edward O. 15
Wolfe, Thomas 74
Works cited list: capitalization 158; confu-

sion 164; disadvantage 154; error 159; initials 156–157, 162; Internet sources 158–159, 164–165; missing data 163–164; multiple authors 157; pagination 163
Wouters, Paul, et al. 121, 195, 197
Wright, Frank Lloyd 202

Xenophon 16

Zerby, Chuck 22, 26, 29, 37, 44, 51, 52, 61, 67, 113, 127, 175
Zuger, Abigail 126

www.ingramcontent.com/pod-product-compliance
Lightning Source LLC
Chambersburg PA
CBHW032049300426
44116CB00007B/663